Reforming Urban Labor

Reforming Urban Labor

Routes to the City, Roots in the Country

Janet L. Polasky

Cornell University Press
ITHACA AND LONDON

First published 2010 by Cornell University Press

Printed in the United States of America

Library of Congress Cataloging-in-Publication Data

Polasky, Janet L.
Reforming urban labor : routes to the city, roots in the country / Janet L. Polasky.
p. cm.
Includes bibliographical references and index.
ISBN 978-0-8014-4794-5 (cloth : alk. paper)
1. Urban policy—Belgium—Brussels—History—19th century. 2. Urban policy—England—London—History—19th century. 3. Labor policy—Belgium—Brussels—History—19th century. 4. Labor policy—England—London—History—19th century. 5. Working class—Belgium—Brussels—History—19th century. 6. Working class—England—London—History—19th century. 7. Brussels (Belgium)—Social conditions—19th century. 8. London (England)—Social conditions—19th century. I. Title.
HN510.B7P65 2010
307.2'409421—dc22 2010022633

Cornell University Press strives to use environmentally responsible suppliers and materials to the fullest extent possible in the publishing of its books. Such materials include vegetable-based, low-VOC inks and acid-free papers that are recycled, totally chlorine-free, or partly composed of nonwood fibers. For further information, visit our website at www.cornellpress.cornell.edu.

Cloth printing 10 9 8 7 6 5 4 3 2 1

for William Lyons

Contents

Preface and Acknowledgments

This book began more than twenty years ago as a challenge in a comparative revolutions course that Laurel Ulrich and I team-taught at the University of New Hampshire. If we required students to write comparative papers for the seminar, we decided that we would, too. The students' papers are long since graded, and Laurel's book about women on both sides of the Atlantic who were not well-behaved is long since published. My comparative project has spanned two sabbaticals and a research leave. A Fulbright Fellowship to Belgium in the fall of 1996 and Senior Faculty Fellowship from the University of New Hampshire in the spring of 1997 allowed me to launch my research, and a University of New Hampshire Faculty Scholars Award in the spring of 2001 provided the means to begin writing it. I revised it on sabbatical in The Hague in the spring of 2003. I have been updating and revising ever since, most recently with the generous support of the Flemish Royal Academy of Belgium at the Flemish Academic Centre for Science and the Arts in the heart of Brussels.

Comparative history requires simultaneous immersion in two separate historiographies and travel between two geographically distinct sets of archives. The practical challenges are often as daunting as the theoretical ones. As I flew, ferried, hovercrafted, and, finally, took the Eurostar back and forth across the Channel, I kept in mind the very different questions Belgian and British historians of transportation and housing ask of their documents. My heartfelt thanks to the accommodating archivists at the Archives Générales du Royaume/Algemeen Rijksarchief, the Bibliotheek Universiteit Gent, the British Library, the British Library of Political & Economic Science at the London School of Economics and Political Science, the Enfield Archives, the Fondérie in Brussels, the Greater London Record Office, the Guildhall Library, the Katholieke Universiteit Leuven libraries, the Katholiek Documentatie en Onderzoekscentrum, Leicester University, the London

Transport Museum, the Musée Royal de Mariemont, the Musée de la Vie Wallonne, the Public Record Office, the Société Nationale des Chemins de Fer Belge/Nationale Maatschapij der Belgische Spoorwegen Archives/Archief, the library at the Société de Logement de la Région de Bruxelles-Capitale/Brusselse Gewestelijke Huisvestingsmaatschappij, and the Université de Liège Bibliothèque. Colleagues who welcomed my questions and lent significant assistance along the way include the late Theodore Barker, Martin Dauntin, Bruno de Meulder, Laura Frader, Nancy Green, Eliane Gubin, Ginette Kurgan, Michel Laffut, Alexander Murphy, Suzy Pasleau, Jean Puissant, Yves Quairiaux, Marcel Smets, Sven Steffens, the late Jean Stengers, Patricia van den Eeckhout, Herman Van der Wee, Leen van Molle, Laura Vaughan, Greta Verburght, Rosemary Wakeman, and Els Witte. I am grateful to Nicky Gavron, deputy mayor of London, and Tony Cumberbrich for discussing planning with me at City Hall. Stefan Cornelis, president of the SLRB/BGH in Brussels, took time to meet with me; Maud Verlinden provided expert assistance in the library; and Pol Zimmer has supplied additional materials on Brussels housing.

William Nelson produced the maps of London railways and London housing projects. Andrew Bedell, a multitalented history student, designed the maps of population density. Robert Hallett of the United States Department of Transportation produced the GIS maps of commuters, claiming throughout that he found the work really interesting. Dan Berry, an always-willing history major, turned my stack of Xeroxed industrial census pages into Excel spread sheets. He also produced the first set of transparency slides from photographs and illustrations. Jeroen Nils and Deborah Needleman tracked down "Tim" (Louis Mittelberg), whose work is featured on the cover; Mike Ross in UNH photographic services captured my 1970s poster; and the Artists Rights Society made reproduction possible as the cover of my book. Jan Roegiers assisted in locating the archival sources of a number of the Belgian images. I am grateful to Fabienne De Sadeleer of La Fonderie, Howard Doble of the London Metropolitan Archives, and Gwénael Guégen of the City Archives of Brussels, for giving me permission to reproduce images from their collections. Jeanne Mitchell and Susan Kilday, in the History Department at the University of New Hampshire, helped me more than they know; and Dee Ann Dixon and Stormy Gleason rescued me from innumerable computer glitches.

My colleagues at the University of New Hampshire have listened to and read drafts of this manuscript; in particular, I have called on Jeff Bolster, Jeff Diefendorf, Jan Golinski, Nicky Gullace, Bill Harris, Aline Kuntz, Julia Rodriguez, and Laurel Ulrich for help. Jeannette Hopkins helped me to find my argument and then to slash excess verbiage from my manuscript. My mother, as always, has been my trusted reader of multiple drafts. My son, David, volunteered to compile the index, so he too read the entire book. At Cornell University Press I am grateful to the director, John Ackerman, for his support of this project over the years in helping to turn the poster over my desk of the rooted peasant into a book, to Michael Morris for his efficient and encouraging e-mails and phone conversations through the editorial process, to Candace Akins and Cathi Reinfelder for their meticulous copy editing, and to Susan Barnett for her work.

I have presented seminars and participated in panels on urban reform, labor relations, comparative history, railways and time, and charity at the International Planning History Society in London and Letchworth; the Society for Netherlandic History in New York; the American Historical Association in Chicago; the Interdisciplinary Conference of Netherlandic Studies, Berkeley; La Fondérie in Brussels; the Western Society for French History in Boston; the Interdisciplinary Conference on Netherlandic Studies, University of Wisconsin, Madison; the Center for the Humanities at the University of New Hampshire; the Berkshire Conference of Women's Historians at the University of North Carolina in Chapel Hill; Carleton College; the Katholieke Universiteit Leuven; the Seminar on Metropolitan History, the Institute of Historical Research at Senate House in London; French Historical Studies in Atlanta; and New York University.

Friends and colleagues in Britain and Belgium continue to make research a pleasure. I am grateful to Jan Roegiers, Hedwig Schwalle, Rob Brusten, Jeroen Nils, Anton Barten, and Herman and Monique Van der Wee for offering me housing and wonderfully delicious and collegial dinners in their Leuven household. Around the corner, I have found warm hospitality with Els Roekens, Eric Min, and their children. And across the street, my friend of forty years, Rita Schepers, offers a sociological perspective and lodging. In Brussels, my fellow Fellows at the Flemish Academic Centre for Science and the Arts, VLAC, made residence in one of the neighborhoods I study a sociable interlude over two productive springs. Marc De Mey, Inez Dua, Kris Brosse, Celine Van Lierde, and Niceas Schamp provided me with a wonderful working space for the last six months of revisions at the Flemish Royal Academy, De Koninklijke Vlaamse Academie van België voor Wetenschappen en Kunsten, in the center of Brussels. I enjoyed my weekly conversations and tea with the late Adrienne Stengers and my outings and dinners with Els Witte. Over dinner with Jean Puissant and Eliane Gubin, I mentioned that while I knew the housing units from books, I had seen only the ones easily accessible on trams and buses around Brussels. The next Friday, Jean retrieved me from the Academy and we spent four hours exploring the faubourgs of Brussels. I was privileged to have such a knowledgeable and engaged guide. He has also read the entire manuscript and saved me from errors. In London, my friend Madeleine Donohue trekked around the city with me to visit the sites of London County Council housing. She took notes as I took pictures while residents peered nervously from their windows. Gillian Howard crossed the Channel to trek around housing sites in Schaerbeek/Schaarbeek.

As is often the case for an author, my family has lived this book. I walked with my son, David, now a law student, then a seventh grader, through the Logis housing complex on the edge of Brussels on his way to the less than welcoming Athenée Royale de Watermael-Boitsfort. I also offered him a week escape from school as my research assistant in London where he scoured microfilmed newspapers in Enfield for reports of riots. In 2008, he shared meals and conversations in Brussels as I rewrote the last chapter and he worked as a paralegal. The staff and families at the Brussels English Primary School where my daughter, Marta, was a third grader were more accommodating of the American animal-lover who dropped into their lovely school on the edge of the forest for a semester, as were the teachers in The Hague, where Marta, then a high school freshman, rode through the forests and along the dunes with friends from around the world, trolls balanced on the back of their bikes. She now helps me with computer issues. This book has been a long time in the making.

My husband, William Lyons, a transportation planner with the United States Department of Transportation, has good-naturedly tolerated my incursion into his territory. He has read grant proposals and chapters and patiently put up with my obsessive dedication to researching and writing this book. All the while, he was solving real-life transportation problems, converting rails to trails, counting bus miles, and curbing global warming. Recently, he was glancing at a Xeroxed journal article on my desk. One of the quotes looked familiar to him; it turned out that he had written it. This book is dedicated to him.

Reforming Urban Labor

Introduction

"From the point of morality, do we even need to compare the city to the countryside?" the principal Belgian inspector of agriculture, Paul De Vuyst, asked his countrymen in 1911. Peasants in the countryside thrived, nourished by "clean air, moralizing work, watchfulness and the encouragement of the family," while industrial workers in the city succumbed to "filthy air, disastrous promiscuity, and were overcome by loneliness in a world filled with indifferent strangers, wicked examples and, at each step, the dangerous lure of unhealthy temptations!"[1] In the first two industrial countries in Europe, Britain and Belgium, factories were drawing masses of laborers off the farms to work in the burgeoning cities. De Vuyst worried about the laborers' families forced to shelter in the notorious rookeries and shadowy impasses or dead-end alleys of the urban centers, where epidemics and debauchery were spawned and criminal conspiracies and rebellions were bred. When the middle class retreated at the end of their own work day to the bucolic greenery of the suburbs and the countryside, they abandoned the city's crowded streets to the newly recruited industrial labor force.

Reforming Urban Labor is a history of the social engineering that sought to mold the home environment of the working classes in Britain and Belgium as the site of nascent citizenship. The urban labor force that had migrated to the industrial city sheltered nightly by the tens of thousands in what Belgian reformer Joseph Dauby described as "narrow, dark streets, almost always damp and muddy, lined with houses or more often slums giving off repugnant odors."[2] Amidst the stately monuments and wide avenues,

1. Paul De Vuyst, *Le rôle social de la fermière* (Brussels: Albert Dewit, 1907), 14–15.
2. Joseph Dauby, *La question ouvrière en Belgique: Causes de nos crises ouvrières; remèdes possibles* (Brussels: Librairie de A.-N. Lebègue et Cie., 1871), 10.

the ever-multiplying multitude of laborers bedded down on "heaps of dirty rags, shavings or straw," huddled together in filth. "Who can wonder that every evil flourishes in such hotbeds of vice and disease?" the Congregational minister Andrew Mearns asked. "Immorality is but the natural outcome of conditions like these."[3] Reformers in the capitals of London and Brussels sought to reassert control over the densely packed, chaotic cities as they civilized and domesticated the most respectable of the urban workers. Cities stifled family life, the reformers had observed, but they believed families flourished in rural gardens. The respectable workers, like the middle classes, were to find refuge in cozy cottages in the midst of a century of dramatic social and technological upheaval.

The industrial revolution originated in Britain, but by the early nineteenth century, Belgium, with its coal and textiles, had emerged as the industrial leader on the Continent. Just a decade or two after the laborers, the "hands" of Charles Dickens's *Hard Times,* fueled the first industrial revolution in Britain, mine owners and textile manufacturers harnessed their labor power to propel the industrialization of Belgium. Industrial production depended on a concentrated labor force, but the crowding of workers and their families into tenements and hovels in the capital cities threatened to overwhelm the civilization that they were laboring to build. The Belgians, like the British two decades earlier, Socialist Emile Vandervelde explained, found themselves in the middle of the nineteenth century in a conflict "between the interests of industrial, scientific production that requires the coming together of a large number of men in the cities, and the interests of public health that protests against such an agglomeration."[4] How could the Belgians and the British manage the labor force that drove the industrial revolution and now threatened to overwhelm the cities?

Contemporary Belgian economic historians, citing the new role of technology in the economy, the accumulation and centralization of capital, the development of credit and high finance, the availability of a reserve army of labor, and the links established between the economy and political leadership, point out that Karl Marx, a resident of Brussels in the 1840s, could have drawn on Belgium instead of Britain as his model for *Capital.* In fact, after studying economics in London, Marx himself declared Belgium "the paradise of capitalism," and with its laissez-faire liberal state and powerful industrialists, "the hell of the proletariat." In both Britain and Belgium, industrial strikes—the manifestation of "the current struggle between capital and labor"—frightened reformers. Joseph Dauby, the editor of the official

3. Andrew Mearns, *The Bitter Cry of Outcast London: An Inquiry into the Condition of the Abject Poor* (London: James Clarke, 1883), 9.
4. Emile Vandervelde, *L'exode rural et le retour aux champs* (Brussels: A. Vromant & Co., 1901), 54 and 310.

parliamentary journal, *Le Moniteur Belge* (the *Belgian Monitor*), worried that a workers' violent struggle "threatened at any moment to jeopardize the entire social order."[5]

Dauby, who had risen from the typographer ranks at the *Moniteur Belge,* was a firm believer in Anglo-Saxon self-help, convinced that the door to the bourgeoisie was open to individual workers who saved and practiced moral discipline. Abandoned by their social betters, however, workers bemoaned their poverty, and Dr. De Camps, a Catholic reformer and member of the parliamentary commission on worker unrest, maintained that miserable workers, jostled together in hovels and tenements, were likely to strike, the dreaded "first stage in the insurrectional campaign waged by labor against capital."[6]

Although the manufacturing centers of northern England and southern Belgium surpassed London and Brussels in industrial output at midcentury, the attention of both the British and Belgians was directed to the menace of urban disorder in their overcrowded capitals. "The low parts of London are the sink into which the filthy and abominable for all parts of the country seem to flow," Mearns asserted. "Entire courts are filled with thieves, prostitutes, and liberated convicts."[7] In 1871, one-sixth of all English and Welsh manufacturing workers lived in London working predominantly in the building trades and engineering, with some engaged in metalworking and paper production, and others manufacturing furniture, clothing, and footwear. Brussels was the principal center of Belgian production with more than one hundred thousand laborers employed in clothing, leather, paper and printing, metal, wood working, and construction. These two prosperous and bustling commercial hubs, linked by rail and ship to the rest of Europe, were also the seat of national government, home to the monarch and to parliament. After the Belgians won their independence in 1830, Brussels assumed symbolic importance as the national capital. British leaders, for their part, were less likely to recognize the significance of their own national capital.[8] London, which dwarfed all other nineteenth-century cities, covering more territory than Paris, Berlin, and Vienna combined, instead achieved its renown by its immense size and commercial and manufacturing wealth.[9] Indeed, when the hero of H. G. Wells's novel *Tono-Bungay* visits London at

5. Joseph Dauby, *Des grèves ouvrières: Aperçu sur l'état économique et social actuel des classes ouvrières en Belgique* (Brussels: Imprimerie Delfosse, 1879), v.
6. De Camps, *L'évolution sociale en Belgique* (Brussels: Bruylant, 1890), 48; *Moniteur des Comités de Patronage de Belgique pour les habitations ouvrières* 15 (10 October 1893).
7. Mearns, *Bitter Cry of Outcast London,* 10.
8. E. Gisler, *Embellissement de la capitale et des faubourgs* (Brussels: Simoneau et Toovery, 1862).
9. Roy Porter, *London: A Social History* (Cambridge: Cambridge University Press, 1995), 205; Paul Meuriot, *Des agglomérations urbaines dans l'Europe contemporaine* (Paris: Belin Frères, 1898), 160.

the end of the century, his guide informs him: "It's a great place. Immense. The richest town in the world, the biggest port, the greatest manufacturing town, the Imperial city—the centre of civilization, the heart of the world."[10]

The crisis posed by poor masses in the urban capitals therefore seemed more urgent in Brussels and London than in the other European countries that industrialized later or where industry settled in the countryside. Unruly urban development, a corollary of the industrial revolution, struck observant reformers without ties to commerce and manufacturing as uncontrollable and unnatural. While, in 1851, three-quarters of the British population still lived outside of cities of more than 100,000, by 1911, 43.8 percent inhabited these cities. The number of Belgian "communes" (i.e., boroughs) of five thousand or more residents rose from 112 in 1846 to 191 in 1890, by which time 47.8 percent of the population lived in cities.[11] The rapid growth of London and Brussels can be partially explained by the net rise in births over deaths, but urban immigration also substantially exceeded emigration in this period.[12] Immigrants moved in from nearby rural villages, their homes filled by workers and artisans coming in from the next outer ring of villages in search of higher wages.

Physicians, architects, and municipal officials initially approached the dramatically rising populations of their capital as a public health problem. The 1868 Artizans' and Labourers' Dwellings Act, known as the Torrens Act, enabled British municipalities to inspect and report individual housing as unfit for human habitation, to require repairs, and then, if necessary, to raze dilapidated structures. In 1875, the British Parliament's Artisans' and Labourers' Dwellings Improvement Act authorized local authorities to demolish whole sections of the city that had been identified as "plague spots" and to compensate owners of the condemned property at current use value. After the dust and debris were cleared away, planners enacted building regulations to ensure that air and sunlight could enter remaining and new dwellings, but no government funding was provided for replacement housing. *The Times* celebrated the elimination of London rookeries as a blessing for civilization: "As we cut nicks through our woods, and roads through our forests, so it should be our policy to divide these thick jungles of crime and misery."[13] In Brussels, after the cholera epidemic of 1866 claimed thousands of the poor who lived in the lower floodplain, Mayor Jules Anspach demolished more than a thousand houses and bricked over and canalized the stinking Senne

---

10. H. G. Wells, *Tono-Bungay,* quoted in Porter, *London: A Social History,* 209.
11. John Burnett, *A Social History of Housing 1815–1970* (London: David & Charles, 1978), 139.
12. *Bulletin de la Commission Centrale* (Brussels: Hayez, 1906), 78–79; Camille Jacquart, *Mouvement de l'etat civil et de la population* (Brussels: Hayez, 1906), 112.
13. *Times* (2 March 1861), quoted in H. J. Dyos, "Railways and Housing in Victorian London," *Journal of Transport History* 2 (1955): 14.

River. In 1867, the Belgian parliament extended its 1858 legislation to permit demolition of unsanitary areas by expropriation of entire districts.

Linked to the question of public health was national pride in the capital. Hence, urban planners in Brussels and London followed the lead of Baron Georges-Eugène Haussmann in Paris, replacing the warren of narrow streets and workers' hovels with wide, straight boulevards and public monuments in stone. A few skeptics inquired whether destroying workers' housing to build monuments was in the best interests of the workers themselves. "Don't even speak of the worker's interests, because you are working to thwart them," one Catholic deputy to the Belgian parliament scolded Liberal planners. In reality, he charged: "You just want to build beautiful, large cities."[14]

Despite sizeable sums provided by the municipality and private investors for public health schemes, observers found displaced workers at the turn of the century worse off than before. In London, the clearance of working-class housing in the 1860s and 1870s to make way for new railway terminals had exacerbated the overcrowding of the central city by the poor. To build two miles of track, from Kingsland to Finsbury, for example, the North London Railway Company destroyed nine hundred houses. The London Midland Railway Company demolished ramshackle buildings housing 16,875 people as it extended its lines into Charing Cross and Broad Street and from Shoreditch to New Cross.[15] Urban reform projects in Brussels, such as the erection of the Palais de Justice covering 22,000 square meters, displaced thousands of poor tenants who were chased away to crowd into adjoining, and already overpopulated, neighborhoods. "It is the overcrowding we have to look at—the overcrowding that kills our babies, debases our boys, ruins our girls, enslaves our women, and drives our men to drink and crime," the English writer George Haw despaired in a 1900 treatise, *No Room to Live, The Plaint of Overcrowded London.*[16]

Reformers anguished over the dismal lives of the workers huddled into makeshift dwellings piled one on top of another, none of which the Belgian housing reformer Hippolyte Royer de Dour recognized as a "true home."[17] They saw little evidence of what British Prime Minister Benjamin Disraeli called "homely notions" in the swarms of noisy children who ignored the shouts of their boisterous mothers poised, gossiping, in the decrepit, dingy entryways, or among the carousing men who spilled out of taverns into alleys along which open sewers flowed.[18] Parliamentary commissions in Britain

---

14. Barthélemy Dumortier, quoted by De Camps, *L'évolution sociale en Belgique,* 87.
15. Porter, *London: A Social History,* 231.
16. George Haw, *No Room to Live: The Plaint of Overcrowded London* (London: *The Daily News,* 1900), 20.
17. Hippolyte Royer de Dour, *Les habitations ouvrières* (Brussels: P. Weissenbruch, 1889).
18. Benjamin Disraeli, *Sybil,* quoted in *Les logements de la classe peu aisée dans le ressort du comité de patronage des habitations ouvrières et des institutions de prévoyance pour les*

and Belgium investigated and described in detail the long hours and dangerous working conditions of factory labor, especially for women and children. But, reformers recognized that "the juxtaposition of these massive laboring populations, living badly day after day, piled into narrow spaces, tired, prey to moral misery and ignorance, constitute for society a graver danger."[19] It was at home that reformers in the first two industrial societies located the true source of labor unrest. If industrialization was inevitable—and by the last decades of the century, few British or Belgian reformers envisioned actually returning to a rural past—then Dauby concluded, "improving family life, domestic life, offered the strongest barrier to the dangerous impulses of the worker in the event of conflicts with capital."[20]

A few industrialists offered their workers sanitary, supervised lodging near their new factories. Wealthy entrepreneurs, such as American businessman George Peabody, built tenement blocks in London as models of well-constructed reform for the poor. Belgian mine owners advertised terraced housing for rent near their pits as a lure to draw a labor supply from the fields of Flanders. Yet few workers were enticed into these projects that, although sanitary, prohibited subletting and required the payment of rent in advance. Superintendents of the Rothschild tenements in London regularly inspected their buildings on Friday or Saturday mornings to enforce "Rule 5," which required tenants weekly to wash and whiten the passageways and stairs. They had even more difficulty enforcing "Rule 7," which forbade the six hundred children in residence to play on the stairs or in the corridors. In Belgium, miners who lodged near the pits complained of curfews and other paternal intrusions into their lives. But philanthropists continued through midcentury to construct blocks for workers in the center of the capitals near work sites.

By the last decades of the century, not only the workers, but middle-class reformers, too, were questioning the housing of laborers close to their work in barrack-like blocks where regulations made any concept of home impossible. These urban tenements, constructed by well-intentioned philanthropists, industrialists, and even by the municipality, had substituted vertical overcrowding for the hovel-lined alleys they had cleared in the name of public health. The block dwellings, with their common entrances and long corridors, were transforming residents into animals. Even their "children are part of a flock, there is no more distinction among them than in a flock of sheep," Jack London reported. "If I looked into a dreary future and saw that I would have to live in such a room until I died, I should immediately go down, plump into the Thames, and cut the tenancy short."[21]

Communes d'Anderlecht, Laeken, Molenbeek et Saint-Gilles: Enquêtes & Rapports (Brussels: Imprimerie des institutions de prévoyance, 1892).

19. Dauby, *La question ouvrière en Belgique,* 111.

20. Dauby, *Des grèves,* 184.

21. Jack London, as quoted by Jerry White, *Rothschild Buildings: Life in an East End Tenement Block 1887–1920* (London: Routledge, Kegan Paul, 1980), 32.

Although most reformers acknowledged that the large tenement blocks stifled individuality, the cost of land in the center of Brussels and London prohibited construction of individual houses within reasonable walking distance of work. The reforming British architect Henry Roberts mused: "It must be obvious that in many localities where labourers' dwellings are indispensable, it is impossible to provide them with isolated and altogether independent tenements."[22] The question was where, if anywhere, could individual cottages be built? And who would build them at rents the workers could afford to pay?

In June 1889, reformers convened the first International Congress on Low-Cost Housing in Paris to discuss where to site housing for the poor and to debate the role of charity, private industry, national legislation, and municipal governments in housing them. The "housing reform movement," defined by historians Nicholas Bullock and James Read as "the loose grouping of doctors, architects, economists, philanthropists, sanitarians, and others who attempted to improve housing conditions," looked to their neighbors across national borders for solutions to their common problems.[23] These housing reformers met every few years to compare the housing plans, the building regulations, the inspection of houses, the conflicting goals of commercial and municipal builders, and the value for the community as a whole of ameliorating the lives and health of the working classes.

Like the reformers themselves, some of the urban historians who have studied the housing of the poor, among them Martin Daunton, Anthony Gauldie, Roger Henri Guerrand, Anthony Sutcliffe, Nicholas Bullock, and James Read have discussed this earlier period of housing reform in comparative terms.[24] "There are gains to be made by starting with connections," Daniel Rodgers asserts in the prologue to *Atlantic Crossings*, his monumental history of social politics in a progressive age.[25] *Reforming Urban Labor* explores the "social question" posed by those "cosmopolitan progressives" in London and Brussels whose ideas on the domestication of the working class shaped politics and defined social policy at a municipal and a national

---

22. Henry Roberts, *The Dwellings of the Labouring Classes* (London: Society for Improving the Condition of the Labouring Classes, 1867), 10.

23. Nicholas Bullock and James Read, *The Movement for Housing Reform in Germany and France, 1840–1914* (Cambridge: Cambridge University Press, 1985), 1.

24. Martin J. Daunton, ed. *Housing the Workers: A Comparative History, 1850–1914* (London: Leicester University Press, 1990); Roger-Henri Guerrand, *Une Europe en construction: Deux siècles d'habitat social en Europe* (Paris: Editions La Découverte, 1992); Colin G. Pooley, ed. *Housing Strategies in Europe, 1880–1930* (Leicester: Leicester University Press, 1992); Anthony Sutcliffe, "Environmental Control and Planning in European Capitals 1850–1914: London, Paris, and Berlin," in *Growth and Transformation of the Modern City* (Stockholm: Swedish Council for Building Research, 1979), 71–88; Anthony Sutcliffe, *Towards the Planned City: Germany, Britain, the United States and France 1780–1914* (New York: St. Martin's Press, 1981).

25. Daniel T. Rodgers, *Atlantic Crossings: Social Politics in a Progressive Age* (Cambridge, Mass.: Harvard University Press, 1998), 5.

level in the first two industrial countries of Europe. Rather than comparing broadly across national borders, as Rodgers does, this book focuses on the capital cities, London and Brussels, both the site of municipal reform and the seat of national politics.[26]

Decades ago, the French medieval historian Marc Bloch urged historians to write the history of "two neighboring, contemporaneous societies... that continuously influenced each other."[27] Reformers at the turn of the last century shared a common definition of the overcrowding of urban centers, which they identified as a crisis. They watched each other as they sought to reestablish control over their capital cities and to remake respectable workers into responsible citizens. They compared plans for the British metropolis, a frequent subject of study by historians, with Belgium's much smaller capital, which is largely neglected by historians.

Most European historians of housing reform have both ignored the obvious comparison of the British and Belgian reformers and overlooked this early period of experimentation with state regulation and municipal construction. They focus instead on the boom in municipally constructed housing and the development of garden cities between the two World Wars, the period when municipalities assumed responsibility for housing and built acres of units for workers' families. By then, however, the direction of reform was firmly set. The reforms pioneered in London and Brussels bridged the early nineteenth century, governed by laissez-faire assumptions in the first two industrial nations, and the mid-twentieth century, the heyday of council housing. The London housing reformer William Thompson explained the motivation of the reformers in this experimental period in his guide for workers, the *Housing Handbook:* "Fifty years ago, the 'housing of the Poor' was a burning question. Today it is the Housing of the Working Classes, and it threatens to be the housing of the People."[28]

Belgian and British reformers both concluded, in the last decades before the First World War, that workers and their families stunted by urban

26. The French historian Nancy Green argues that the city makes an ideal unit of analysis for comparative historians because it allows the historian to construct "comparison as similarity." Capital cities in particular allow an analysis of the similar conditions endured by laborers lodged in overcrowded courtyards, although set within the context of the different national politics. Nancy Green, "L'histoire comparative et le champ des études migratoires," *Annales Economies, Sociétés, Civilisations* 45, no. 4 (1990): 1335–1350. On the importance of capitals, see Anthony Sutcliffe, "Environmental Control and Planning in European Capitals 1850–1914: London, Paris, and Berlin," in *Growth and Transformation of the Modern City* (Stockholm: Swedish Council for Building Research, 1979), 71–73; Ken Young and Patricia Garside, *Metropolitan London* (London: Edward Arnold, 1982), 1.

27. Marc Bloch, "Pour une histoire comparée des sociétés européennes." *Revue de synthèse historique* 46 (1928): 19.

28. William Thompson, *The Housing Handbook* (London: National Housing Reform Council, 1903), 1.

overcrowding would thrive again only outside the modern city. The *Railway Register* summed up the two options for rehousing London laborers as if they were vegetables to be transplanted: "either we may *plant out* in the vicinage, or try to make the existing site more fit and commodious" (emphasis in original).[29] The British in particular had tried building housing blocks in city centers, but the workers' families seemed little better off than before. "It is very sad to-day to see the way in which workmen are crowded in block buildings in the central parts of London," George Dew, chair of the National Association for the Extension of Workmen's Trains testified in 1904. "The race is absolutely deteriorating."[30] The answer seemed clear at the turn of the last century: the workers needed to be transplanted to the suburbs.

The garden city planner Ebenezer Howard called for the "spontaneous movement of the people from our crowded cities to the bosom of our kindly mother earth, at once the source of life, of happiness, of wealth, and of power."[31] To counter the "barbaric cities that seemed to have sprung from the earth to cut down human life," European reformers in the second half of the nineteenth century dreamed of static traditional villages.[32] Reformers imagined workers' families tending the gardens of cozy half-timbered individual cottages sited along romantically winding roads following the contours of the rural landscape.

Supported by social scientists, such as Charles Booth in London and Emile Hellemans in Brussels, who had surveyed, counted, visited, and thoroughly investigated the urban poor, reformers on both sides of the Channel targeted the category of regularly employed workers. If they could be separated from the residuum, the unemployed and underemployed with whom they lived in the center cities, then, the reformers imagined, by living like the middle class, they would become orderly, frugal, rooted citizens like the middle class. To domesticate the workers, reformers intended to guide them to emulate the nineteenth-century middle class that had made Belgium and Britain the two most stable and prosperous monarchies of Europe.

But first, they would need to find a way for urban workers to reside in pastoral tranquility while working in the cities. How would these workers get to the city early every morning and away from the cities every night to homes in the suburbs and the countryside? To solve the question of transport,

29. *Railway Register* 2 (1845): 495, quoted in Harold J. Dyos, "Railways and Housing in Victorian London," *Journal of Transport History* 2 (1955): 94 (emphasis in original).

30. George Dew, Select Committee on Workmen's Trains, British Parliamentary Papers 1904, vii.

31. Ebenezer Howard, quoted in Standish Meacham, *Regaining Paradise: Englishness and the Early Garden City Movement* (New Haven: Yale University Press, 1999), 53.

32. A. De T'Serclaes de Wommerson, *La condition du logement de l'ouvrier dans la ville de Gand* (Ghent-Paris: H. Engelcke, 1889), 23.

reformers looked to the railway whose networks crossed the landscape of the countryside. If, Lord Derby argued in an 1864 petition to Parliament, the railways had contributed, as they had, to the overcrowding of London by evicting thousands of workers' families from their urban tenements to build their lines, then the railways should be obliged to run trains at reduced fares to rehouse these displaced families in London's outer rings. In Belgium, the Liberal public works minister and a Catholic deputy joined as allies to set up a system and subsidize workmen's trains that would take the workers to jobs in the cities and back again each evening to the countryside.[33]

The British and Belgian reformers who had decided that the city with its rookeries and impasses marked a dead end in the line of industrial progress looked to the railway, the symbol of technological innovation, to repopulate the countryside and depopulate the cities. Fearing that the collective urban housing constructed in the middle of the century would foster mutual dependency among the poor, a trend not to be encouraged when threats of riots and social crises loomed large at the end of the century, the governments used the train to end migration to the city. Few contemporaries appreciated the irony of harnessing the train to un-invent the industrial city. It did not seem strange to them that the transportation revolution that had contributed so substantially to the dramatic growth of cities was now being harnessed to reduce residential density, to remove the industrial residue. Nor did the reformers pause to ponder the use of trains to reinsert the laborers into bucolic greenery, to reverse the course of the industrial revolution.

The acceleration of locomotion by the railway transformed nineteenth-century perceptions of space on both sides of the Channel in the first half of the nineteenth century. Spaces were no longer fixed and constant, "organically embedded in nature," as they had seemed when travel was by foot, on horse, by barge, or in a stagecoach.[34] Train travel shrank the distance separating the countryside from the city. Although trams, light rail, and buses, too, would come to play an increasingly significant role in workmen's transportation in the twentieth century, trains were the first and remained the major mode of workmen's transportation throughout the period on both sides of the Channel. "Given nominal fares, with rapid, frequent, continuous, and widely accessible means of locomotion, mere distance becomes practically annihilated," Thompson explained.[35]

At the Toynbee Hall Conference held in London in conjunction with the Trades Union Congress, Alderman George Dew of the National Association for the Extension of Workmen's Trains explicitly tied together transit and

---

33. Joseph Kervyn de Lettenhove, 21 April 1869, *Annales parlementaires,* Chambre des représentants (1868–1869), 735.

34. Wolfgang Schivelbusch, *The Railway Journey: The Industrialization of Time and Space in the 19th Century* (New York: Urizen Books, 1977), 43.

35. Thompson, *Housing Handbook,* 221.

housing reform, acknowledging that "rapid, cheap and adequate means of transit are necessary to the solution of the housing problem in many of our large towns."[36] Recognizing this interdependence of the workmen's out-of-city housing schemes and workmen's trains, the Belgian editor of *Le Cottage* commented, "that the question of transportation has an influence on that of housing is one of those truisms, one of the axioms that no one debates."[37] For British reformers to build on less expensive land around the periphery of the capitals, workers had to be able to get out there. But railway companies refused to offer workmen's fares to areas where workmen did not reside. The Belgian government willingly subsidized workmen to ride their national railways, based on the belief that governmental and industrial interests would complement each other. However, the nineteen administratively separate communes of Brussels could not overcome bureaucratic obstacles to building outside the city, leaving most construction to private developers.

In their comparative studies of industrial relations, the labor historians Nancy Green and Laura Lee Downs have charted how "national culture and differences in state structures defined distinctive routes to what were, in many important respects, rather similar outcomes."[38] The divergence in patterns of governmental cooperation intrigued the British and Belgian reformers. Members of the Locomotion Subcommittee of the London County Council repeatedly cited the ever-expanding workmen's service provided by the national Belgian railway as they despaired at the reluctance of the private British railways to carry more workers. Meanwhile, Belgian mayors and architects visited garden cities throughout Britain and the London County Council estates, returning with drawings of model cottages to instruct their colleagues sitting on communal councils and in Parliament.

---

36. *Housing Journal* (September 1902).

37. *Le Cottage* (July 1903). Yet, until the perceptive and provocative studies of H. J. Dyos, historians of urban reform and of working-class housing left the study of railways to transportation historians concerned with questions of infrastructure, rail gauge and boiler fittings, or labor relations within the railways. See also Paolo Capuzzo, "Between Politics and Technology: Transport as a Factor of Mass Suburbanization in Europe, 1890–1939," in *Suburbanizing the Masses,* ed. Colin Divall and Winstan Bond (Hants, England: Aldershot, 2003), 23–48.

38. Laura Lee Downs, *Manufacturing Inequality: Gender Division in the French and British Metalworking Industries, 1914–1939* (Ithaca: Cornell University Press, 1995), 12. See also Nancy Green, *Ready to Wear and Ready to Work* (Durham, N.C.: Duke University Press, 1993). Most other comparative labor historians instead explore divergent "chronologies of change" to understand the "decisive, systematic divergences in the formation of manufacturing practices of industrial relations." They assume difference rather than similarity. Richard Biernacki, *The Fabrication of Labor: Germany and Britain, 1640–1914* (Berkeley: University of California Press, 1995), 1 and 471. These labor historians exemplify what sociologists Theda Skocpol and Margaret Somers categorize as contrast-oriented comparative history. Theda Skocpol and Margaret Somers, "The Uses of Comparative History in Macrosocial Inquiry," *Comparative Studies in Society and History* 22 (April 1980): 181.

Neither the Belgian nor the British reformers expected new residential patterns to develop or to stay in place on their own. They assumed that governments, both municipal and national, must play a role in reshaping the workers' environment. Despite the entrenched laissez-faire convictions that had checked the growth of government throughout the nineteenth century in both Belgium and Britain, reformers proposed national legislation and municipal construction to transport and house the workers outside of their capitals. They intended not only to relieve the density of the cities but also to remake the working class itself in their own image of a provident and law-abiding citizenry.

The crucial leap in housing reform occurred when reformers moved from questions of public health, such as sewers and street width, to consider siting and constructing housing and subsidizing transportation for laborers. The Brussels and London reformers effectively redefined the role of government in a modern, industrial society. In separating home from work, municipal and national governments were demonstrating the reformers' conviction of the critical role of the built landscape in molding the character of citizens. "Social questions preoccupy governments," Prosper Van Nerom, a Belgian reformer observed in 1890. We "are trying to raise the position of the worker and to give him the place he deserves in society."[39]

Workers mobilized, sometimes to adapt to, and sometimes to challenge the housing schemes devised by reformers before the First World War. However, unlike reformers, who meticulously documented their vision, the views of costermongers from the East End with their makeshift vegetable stands, who were driven from their neighborhoods with their barrows loaded with family goods, have to be pieced together from newspaper accounts of their strikes, from journals edited by laborers' organizations, and from the handful of essays written by workers who ascended the political ladder.

By the outbreak of the First World War in 1914, social surveyors in both capitals reported that the commuting laborers had come to resemble, in dress and demeanor, members of the middle classes who shared their daily trains. No longer crowded into "corrupting surroundings, where they are exposed to disease, to infirmities and to all the causes of debility, degeneration, demoralization, that such an environment engenders," the former masses of wretched poor, the reformers assumed, were now saving to purchase their individual cottage with a garden they tended in the evenings.[40] The urban laborers were becoming citizens.

The Belgian and British reformers recognized that they shared a common attachment to family and hearth that they wanted to inculcate among the

---

39. Prosper Van Nerom, *Les lois ouvrières et sociales en Belgique: Epargne, alcoolisme, salaires, conseils de l'industrie, maisons ouvrières* (Brussels: Emile Bruylant, 1890), 1.
40. M. d'Elhoungne, quoted in De Camps, *L'Evolution sociale en Belgique,* 84.

workers. "Like the Anglo-Saxon, whose cousins we are," mused Brussels mayor Charles Buls, "we love our *home,* the family hearth" (emphasis in original). Other Europeans may have been content to live their lives in public and to sleep in large apartment blocks, but not in Britain and Belgium. This bourgeois perspective defined social policy on both sides of the Channel in the decades leading up to the First World War. To British reformers, suburban cottages confirmed their self-image as a nation of quiet, contented, garden-tending home dwellers. They thought large blocks of flats appropriate for the Continent. The mayor of Brussels disagreed. A visitor to London, Buls relegated the massive barracks divided into apartments to Paris. The Bruxellois, as the Londoner "likes to climb his own stairway."[41]

The Belgian and British reformers linked public housing and subsidized rail to take control of their urban capitals and to mold the workers into citizens. The government-sponsored mobility and rehousing of workers in these two industrialized societies domesticated respectable workers in the image of the reformers themselves. Respectable workers would learn to live like, if not too close to, the middle class.

---

41. Charles Buls, *Esthétiques des villes* (1894; Brussels: Sint-Lukasdossier, 1981), 28.

1 A *"Sprawling" City of "Outcast Masses"*

Overcrowded Capitals

> It was a great discovery when men learnt that the best means of saving the individual was to modify his environment.
>
> —B. Kirkham Gray, *Philanthropy and the State*

Teeming, chaotic, and congested cities troubled reform-minded British and Belgian observers at the end of the nineteenth century. In 1883, the secretary of the London Congregational Union, Andrew Mearns, gave readers of a *Bitter Cry of Outcast London* a vicarious tour of the poorest districts, exposing them to the "poisonous and malodorous gases arising from accumulations of sewage and refuse" and to the sights of the shadowy courtyards, where "the sun never penetrates, which are never visited by a breath of fresh air, and which rarely know the virtues of a drop of cleansing water." He invited the middle class to "think of the condition in which they live. We do not say the condition of their homes, for how can those places be called homes, compared with which the lair of a wild beast would be a comfortable and healthy spot."[1] The Reverend Montague Butler, headmaster at Harrow, exhibiting Mearns's twenty-four-page penny pamphlet in his outstretched hand, exhorted parishioners to reflect on the startling revelations of life in the center of their national capital.[2]

The tumbled-down tenements and malodorous hovels, hidden from light and the gaze of passersby, frightened the middle class. Modern civilization

1. Andrew Mearns, *The Bitter Cry of Outcast London: An Inquiry into the Condition of the Abject Poor* (London: James Clarke, 1883), 6.
2. Montague Butler, cited by Alan Palmer, *The East End: Four Centuries of London Life* (New Brunswick: Rutgers University Press, 2000), 86.

Gustave Doré, "Over London by Rail" (1890). Railway in the distance travels over London slum housing. From Gustave Doré and Blanchard Jerrold, *London: A Pilgrimage* (London: Grant & Co., 1872), 121.

had no entry into the quarters inhabited by the urban poor. The middle class had largely abandoned urban industrial centers for the restful greenery of the suburbs and rural villages by the mid-nineteenth century, leaving behind their dwellings to be subdivided to house the legions of industrial workers arriving from the countryside. If they peered through the curtainless windows, the editor of the official parliamentary journal, *Le Moniteur Belge* (the *Belgian Monitor*), Joseph Dauby, cautioned middle-class observers, they would glimpse "a veritable anthill of human beings" lodged between the attic and the cellar.[3] These lodgings were preferable only to the makeshift shelters erected on scraps of vacant land at the center of the expanding urban capitals.

Images of disorderly alleys and impoverished urchins came to represent the city to the bourgeois who rarely ventured from the safety of the major boulevards. These "anthills" of densely packed hovels and tenements rendered the modern city itself suspect. French graphic artist Gustave Doré's

3. Joseph Dauby, *La question ouvrière en Belgique: Causes de nos crises ouvrières; remèdes possibles* (Brussels: Librairie de A.-N. Lebègue et Cie., 1871), 10.

haunting image of the London slums under the railway trestle over which the suburban middle classes rushed on their way to and from work captured the "otherness" of the dark, shadowed urban world.[4] Amidst the stately monuments and broad avenues of industrializing capitals such as Brussels, Berlin, Paris, and London, ever-multiplying populations of laborers dwelt in sordid quarters.

"Tedious Work" and "Foul Garrets": Laborers in the City

Reformers found an antidote to their crowded modern capitals in the greenery of the countryside. Frightened by the urban industrialization of the "barbaric cities that seemed to have sprung from the earth to cut down human life," essayists remembered bucolic peasant villages from the past.[5] In the countryside among the peasants who cultivated the land, they found virtues that the urban poor lacked. Popular Belgian songs such as "Tot Glorie van de Boeren" (To the Glory of the Peasants) paid homage to the hardworking, upright peasants as the foundation of the nation. British yeoman farmers, like the continental peasants, were pictured living peacefully in the midst of nature. However, these idyllic rural villages, formerly populated with hearty, frugal peasants, were being drained by the voracious urban labor markets. Now rootless, laborers were drawn into the congestion of industrial urban slums. With a newfound urgency, the reformers echoed the Genevan Enlightenment philosopher Jean-Jacques Rousseau and contributors to the late-eighteenth-century French *Encylopédie* edited by Denis Diderot, warning that urbanization would precipitate the degeneration of the race.

Writing at the turn of the twentieth century, the oft-cited French essayist Jules Méline marveled at the dramatic changes of the previous fifty years. Industrialization had so transformed European society that trying to remember life before 1850, "one becomes confused before the spectacle of all that has disappeared and all that has replaced it," he mused. Méline warned that the economic transformation threatened to "cast humanity in a new mold." The peasantry was disappearing at an alarming rate, changed overnight into urban laborers. Méline denounced the "splendors of the cities" that attracted peasants like "butterflies to light," luring them away from the countryside he eulogized.[6]

The "sprawling cities" of Brussels and London swelled in the mid-nineteenth century. The city of Brussels experienced its most significant growth in the

---

4. Gustave Doré and Jerrold Blanchard, *London: A Pilgrimage* (London: Grant & Co., 1872).
5. A. De t'Serclaes de Wommerson, *La condition du logement de l'ouvrier dans la ville de Gand* (Ghent-Paris: H. Engelcke, 1889), 23.
6. Jules Méline, *Le retour à la terre et la surproduction industrielle* (Paris: Librairie Hachette et Cie., 1905), 1.

first half of the nineteenth century, with the population rising from 66,000 in 1801 to 150,244 in 1856.[7] The 65 percent growth of Brussels between 1801 and 1856 that so shocked contemporaries, however, was dwarfed by the 146 percent growth of London in the same period. London's population grew from 959,310 in 1801 to 2,633,341 in 1851, increasing by nearly one million people between 1861 and 1881, or by another third.[8] The agglomeration of Brussels—that is, the central pentagon plus the surrounding eighteen communes—mushroomed again in the second half of the century, from 288,400 residents in 1866 to 458,700 in 1890, a growth of 59 percent.[9] London and its inner suburbs grew at the same pace, from 414,226 residents in 1861 to 1,405,852 in 1891.[10] In 1890, 48 percent of Belgians lived in cities with a population of 100,000 or more; 44 percent of the British were urban dwellers in 1911.[11]

In part, the growth of London and Brussels can be explained by the excess of births over deaths—there were 33,685 more births than deaths between 1891 and 1900 in Brussels, for example.[12] But, as contemporaries noted, during this same decade immigration into Brussels exceeded emigration by 70 per 1,000 residents, far higher than any other Belgian city.[13] London's growth between 1841 and 1851 was fueled by an influx of 330,000 migrants. Most of the immigrants came from nearby. In both cities, the migration created a cascading series of moves inward. When one group of residents moved toward the center, they were replaced by another group from neighboring villages in search of higher wages.

When, in the second half of the century, the two capitals reached what contemporaries identified as their saturation points, residents, first the middle class and then artisans and workers, began flowing outward again, this time to the suburbs developing on the outskirts of the capitals. Rising land values at the center of the city, the movement of some commercial and industrial enterprises outward, the development of rapid transit, the desire for the outdoors, city taxes, and the unsanitary conditions of the central cities all combined to convince the middle classes to move to the suburbs in the mid-nineteenth century.

But it was the density of the urban capitals that particularly alarmed reformers. "It is the overcrowding we have to look at—the overcrowding that

---

7. *Les Recensements de 1910* (Brussels: E. Guyot, 1912).

8. John N. Tarn, "French Flats for the English in Nineteenth-century London," in *Multi-Storey Living: the British Working-Class Housing,* ed. Anthony Sutcliffe (London: Croom Helm, 1974), 19–40.

9. Paul Meuriot, *Des agglomérations urbaines dans l'Europe contemporaine* (Paris: Belin Frères, 1898), 160.

10. "County of London," Tables, *Census of England and Wales* (London: H.M.S.O., 1922).

11. John Burnett, *Social History of Housing 1815–1879* (London: David & Charles, 1978), 139; Meuriot, *Des agglomérations urbaines,* 154.

12. *Bulletin de la Commission Centrale* (Brussels: Hayez, 1906), 78–79.

13. Camille Jacquart, *Mouvement de l'etat civil et de la population* (Brussels: Hayez, 1906), 112.

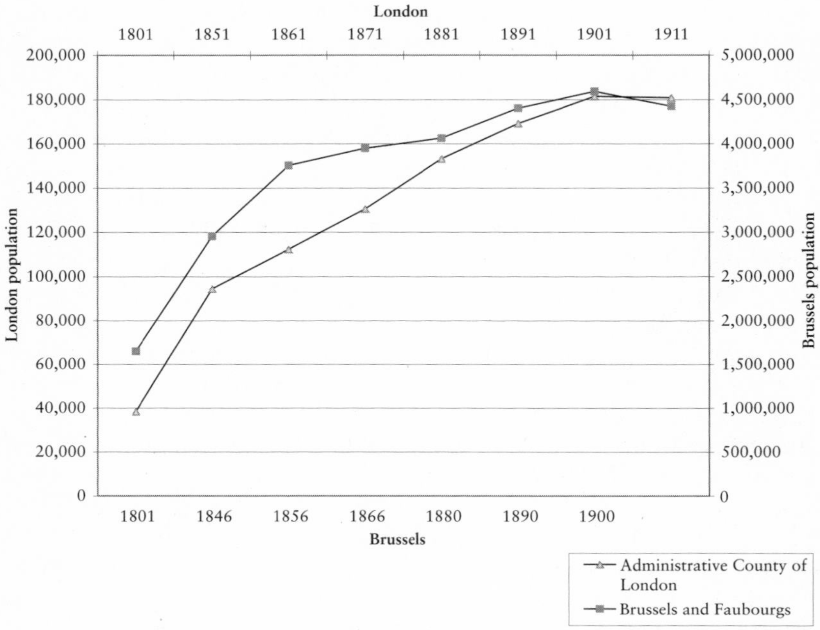

Population growth, London and Brussels, 1801–1911. Data from Royal Commission on London Traffic, *Report of the Royal Commission appointed to inquire into and report upon the means of locomotion and transport in London* (London: 1905–1906), 126; and *Les Recensements de 1910* (Brussels: E. Guyot, 1912), 21.

kills our babies, debases our boys, ruins our girls, enslaves our women, and drives our men to drink and crime," George Haw proclaimed in *No Room to Live.*[14] The inner cores of Brussels and London at the end of the nineteenth century harbored populations at a density almost double that of the first ring of their suburbs. Although according to official figures, only 18.6 percent of the population of London suffered from overcrowded conditions in the 1870s, overcrowding figures for working-class neighborhoods told a different story: For Whitechapel that figure was 48.3 percent, Holborn 29.8 percent, Shoreditch 27.3 percent, Bethnal Green 26.9 percent and Stepney 25.6 percent.[15] Similarly, the density of the center of Brussels rose from 340 people per kilometer in 1846 to 655 in 1890. Most (90.3%) working-class families

14. George Haw, *No Room to Live: The Plaint of Overcrowded London* (London: Wells Gardner Darton and Co., 1900), 20.

15. Gareth Stedman Jones, *Outcast London* (Oxford: Clarendon Press, 1971), 178 and 306. In London, reformers calculated overcrowding by counting the number of families lodged in one and two rooms.

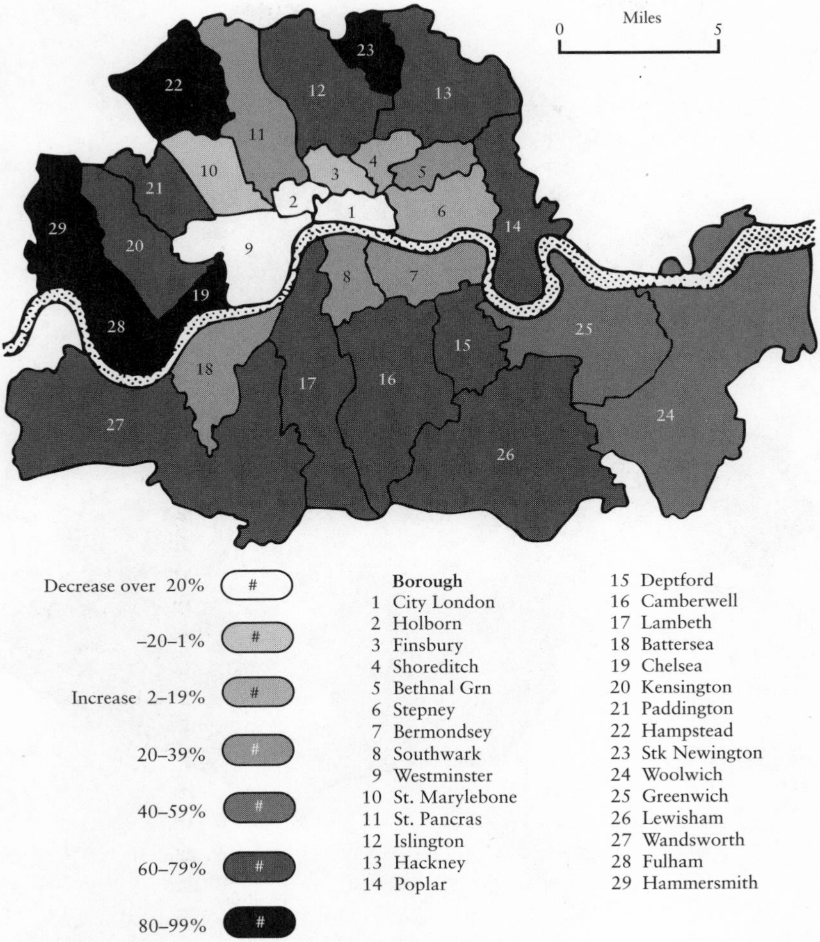

London metropolitan boroughs. Percentage population growth, 1851–1891. Data from Paul Meuriot, *Des Agglomérations urbaines dans l'Europe contemporaine* (Paris: Belin Frères, 1898), 469; "County of London," Tables, *Census of England and Wales* (London, 1922), 4–9.

in Brussels were housed in one- or two-room lodgings in the 1890s.[16] This association of cities with closely packed poverty spawned an intense antiurbanism at the end of the nineteenth century, in Belgium as in Britain.

16. Meuriot, *Des agglomérations urbaines,* 152; Patricia Van den Eeckhout, "Belgium," in *Housing Strategies in Europe, 1880–1930,* ed. Colin G. Pooley (London: Leicester University Press, 1992), 192.

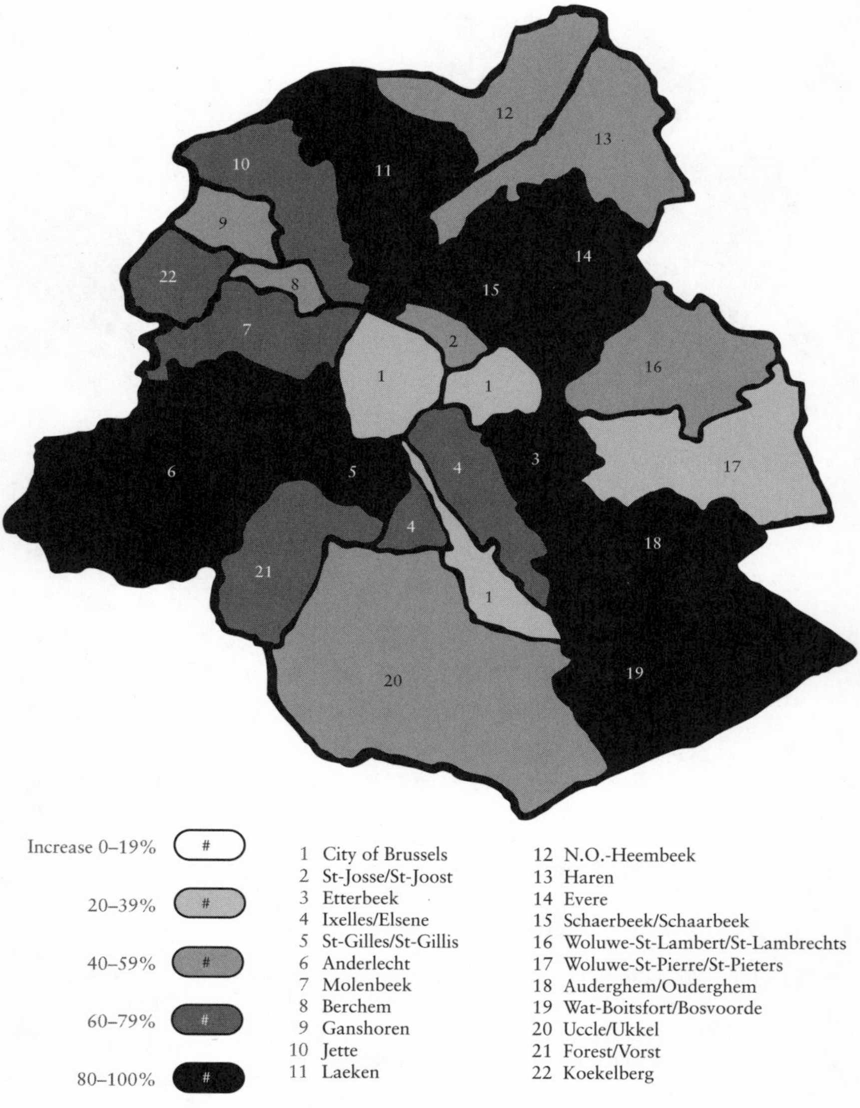

Brussels communes. Percentage population growth, 1851–1891.
Data from Omer Tulippe, *Densité de la population. Atlas de Belgique* (Brussels: Académie Royale de Belgique, 1962), 34.

The Belgian Socialist Emile Vandervelde described the growing city that projected its tentacles—the rail lines—into the countryside to ensnare and draw into itself men and material. In his study of rural exodus, *L'exode rural et le retour aux champs* (The Rural Exodus and the Return to the Countryside), Vandervelde quoted the Belgian poet, Emile Verhaeren, who visualized the tantalizing allure of London in the poem, "La ville tentaculaire" (the sprawling city):

> While the evenings
> Sculpt the firmament of their ebony hammers,
> The city, in the distance, is exposed and dominates the plain
> like a colossal, nocturnal hope;
> It surges: desire, splendor, obsession;
> Its bright lights are projected in mirrors up to the heavens,
> Its myriad gases and golden thicket stirred up,
> its rails are the audacious roads
> towards the deceptive happiness
> that is accompanied by fortune and force;
> Its walls distended, like an army
> And the fog and smoke that comes from it
> Arrives, in clear calls, to the countryside...
> That is the sprawling city![17]

Vandervelde analyzed rural exodus as a result of the push away from the countryside as well as the pull toward the city. Peasants, like animals driven from their natural habitats, were "uprooted from their native soil, chased from the countryside by the agricultural crisis" that led to the disappearance of 84,569 Belgian farms of less than two hectares between 1880 and 1905.[18] They had been swallowed by the larger farms that relied on machinery and modern methods of rational agriculture. Left without an alternative source of work in the countryside, the peasants migrated to cities in search of employment.

Vandervelde saw the future of Belgium in the burgeoning cities of Britain, where he reminded his readers, the industrial transformation began. The English writer, P. Anderson Graham, in his economic study, also entitled *The Rural Exodus,* had explained quite simply: "The prime reason for the majority leaving is that of all the roads to wealth, agriculture is the slowest." He cited the lower profitability of the English farming during agricultural depression and the distaste for rural labor among the youth who complained about the monotonous village life as causes of the ruinous rural migration to the cities. "Our towns are already large beyond precedent and yet they continue to grow at an alarming rate," he worried, and the rural poor continued "to drift into them."[19]

---

17. Emile Verhaeren, *Campagnes hallucinées,* quoted in Emile Vandervelde, *L'exode rural et le retour aux champs* (Brussels: A. Vromant & Co., 1901), 18.
18. Vandervelde, *L'exode rurale,* 193.
19. Peter Anderson Graham, *The Rural Exodus: The Problem of the Village and the Town* (London: Metheum & Co., 1892), 203 and 1.

A multitude of French, British, and Belgian economists corroborated the conclusion that emigration dramatically exceeded immigration in rural districts in the decades before the turn of the century.[20] The population of small villages under five hundred people in Belgium declined continuously between 1846 and 1890. The Belgian government estimated that the average family needed seven to eight hectares to survive, but in the Hageland, a region of northern Belgium, families typically worked two- to three-hectare plots.[21] An English Royal Commission reported in 1893 that the value of agricultural produce had declined by almost half while costs of production remained the same or increased; in 1894, the price of wheat fell to the lowest point in 150 years. The number of agrarian laborers in Britain declined by one-third between 1851 and 1891, their labor done by machines.[22] The final blow on both sides of the Channel was the disappearance of domestic industry from the countryside, making it impossible for peasants to subsist and leading to the migration of unmarried women to the cities.

Anecdotal evidence suggested that young men, especially vulnerable to the lure of the city, abandoned their ancestral villages en masse in search of jobs. Mine owners from the Borinage near Mons and the Liège basin sent scouts in the Flemish countryside to recruit a labor force. They promised good wages, steady employment, and terraced tenements. Contemporaries recounted tales of urban cabarets and dance halls that tempted young men away from their families. Men also migrated away from rural districts in Flanders to cultivate beets in northern France or to dig coal in Wallonia. According to one study, in 1900 between 33 and 42 percent of the active agricultural population of northern Belgium migrated seasonally in search of work.[23] These "Franschmannen" (Frenchmen) took up the most physically demanding, least skilled work for the lowest wages.

---

20. See, e.g., *Bulletin de la commission centrale* (Brussels: Hayez, 1906); Camille Jacquart, "Migrations de la population belge (1888–1897)," *Revue sociale catholique* (October 1899): 358–366 and (January 1900): 11–21; Camille Jacquart, *Mouvement de l'état civil et de la population* (Brussels: Hayez, 1906); J. J. Jacquemin, *De la force de l'attraction des villes* (Liège: Mercenier, 1906); Emile Jottrand, *Le dépeuplement des campagnes* (Mons: Dequesne-Masquillier & Fils, 1895); Edmond Nicolai, *La dépopulation des campagnes* (Brussels: P. Weissenbruch, 1903); Emile Vliebergh, *De Kempen in de 19e en in 't Begin der 20e Eeuw* (Ypres: Callewaert-De Meulenaere, 1908); Benoit Bouché, *Les ouvriers agricoles* (Brussels: Misch et Thron, 1913).

21. Emile Vliebergh, *Het Hageland: Zijne plattelandsche Bevolking in de 19de Eeuw,* Académie Royale de Belgique, Classe des lettres et des sciences morales et politiques, Mémoires, Deuxième serie 13 (Brussels: Marcel Hayez, 1921), 168–181.

22. David Grigg, *English Agriculture: An Historical Perspective* (London: Basil Blackwell, 1989), 145.

23. G. E. Karush, "Industrialisation et changements de la population active en Belgique de 1846 à 1910," *Populations et Familles* 40 (1977): 37–76.

The popular Flemish novelist, Stijn Streuvels, depicted the travails of seasonal workers who commuted by train in *De Werkman* (The Workman).[24] When Manse, the laborer's wife, receives a letter informing her of Ivo's imminent return from France, she prepares to go to the railway station, accompanied by all her children. The men have been away from their families all summer working. The train finally comes into sight, spewing black smoke and droning loudly until it comes to a stop, disgorging the long-absent husbands onto the platform. Spouses greet each other warily, wondering about their lives together again after the long absence. Manse does not even recognize Ivo, who has grown a full, brown beard. Before returning home to the now-overcooked meal, the husbands go out to the café for a parting beer. They then tour the bakeries and shops to repay the debts their wives have been forced to incur in their absence. That evening, Ivo searches for winter work in the village, but finds there are no jobs left. He departs his village immediately, seeking work this time in a factory in Wallonia, the French-speaking southern half of Belgium. Without having slept one night in his own bed, he trudges back out into the cold, autumn rain.

"The peasants of the Flemish countryside are deeply rooted in their native soil," the Belgian Socialist Auguste De Winne observed with obvious pride. "Neither the crisis in the linen industry nor agricultural unemployment and low salaries nor misery seem to be able to chase them from their homes."[25] The Belgian Catholic writer Henri Demain concurred: "the Flemish peasant is not very communicative, not very demonstrative, but with a strongly felt manner, attaches himself to his native soil and to his family."[26] It took severe hardship to convince peasants to move definitively.

Belgian and French novelists and essayists opposed urban degeneration to rural virtues: Industrial workers spent frivolously, subsisting from day to day, while peasants confronting the uncertain nature of harvests budgeted and saved. Working women could not be bothered to cook meals or to clean house in the city, but the peasant wife and mother understood the value of order and of nutrition. Working men escaped the chaos of their overcrowded urban rooms in cafés, cabarets, and pubs, while peasants tended to their families gathered around the fireside each evening.

The rapid industrialization and urban development sent the observers back to the countryside in search of a pastoral, rooted past. Sharing what historian Ray Jonas has called a "preference for the rustic," the middle-class observers of the rural exodus linked their national image to rural populations, to

24. Stijn Streuvels, *De Werkman* (1913; reprint, Amsterdam: L. J. Veen, 1965).
25. Auguste De Winne, *A travers les Flandres* (Ghent: Volksdrukkerij, 1902), 99.
26. Henri Demain, *Les migrations ouvrières à travers la Belgique* (Louvain: Hugues Bomans, 1919), 16.

greenery, and to the land.[27] Peasant families appeared to embody the timeless values that lay at the heart of French and Belgian civilization, in particular. Cities were "rapidly devouring the most robust peasants; tedious work, foul garrets, unhealthy meals, and terrible sicknesses weakening them, making them anaemic and eventually killing them," destroying the age-old foundations of French society, the French writer Pierre Deghilage warned.[28]

"We must stop the rural exodus." The agrarian expert, Paul De Vuyst, feared that uprooted peasants transformed into industrial laborers were fueling the politics of the urban dispossessed. In response to the threat, provincial officials wrote agricultural bulletins for the rural population, encouraged experimental planting, and established a land credit system. Addressing peasant women "whose powerful and fruitful influence extended far beyond their hearth," they directed wives and mothers to dedicate themselves to binding their husbands to the land and to nurturing a love of that soil in their children.[29] Belgian Catholic organizations established schools and "circles" to teach peasant women to cook nutritious meals, to tend kitchen gardens, to heal their families, and to make butter. In the short term they distributed soup, and in the long term sponsored agrarian protectionism. French reformers cited the Belgian efforts to stem rural exodus as a model to be emulated. Deghilage applauded the circles organized to instruct peasant women in cooking, in medicine, in milking, and in tending a garden. That would keep men at home.

London philanthropist Helen (Dendy) Bosanquet was convinced that the rural exodus did not really matter in Britain where fewer people owned land.[30] Without domestic industry to sustain them, landless, unskilled families with no continuity of occupation from one generation to the next—a description of much of the rural population of Britain—were inherently unstable, Bosanquet explained. British reformers were not preoccupied with trying to keep these poorer rural tenants on the land because this shiftless population did not exemplify values the British wanted to preserve. These reformers, instead, focused on the receiving side of migration, on urban overcrowding, rather than on the process of rural exodus. They echoed the director of welfare in Brussels, Charles De Quéker who declared: "It is indispensable to end this immigration of the poor to the cities."[31] They turned their gaze on the city, especially on their capitals.

---

27. Raymond A. Jonas, *Industry and Politics in Rural France. Peasants of the Isère, 1870–1914* (Ithaca: Cornell University Press, 1994), 97; Jean Pitié, *Exode rural et migrations intérieures en France. L'exemple de la Vienne et du Poitou-Charentes* (Poitiers: Norois, 1971).
28. Pierre Deghilage, *La dépopulation des campagnes* (Paris: Nathan, 1900), 4.
29. Paul De Vuyst, *Le rôle social de la fermière* (Brussels: Albert Dewit, 1911), 15.
30. Helen Bosanquet, *The Family* (London: Macmillan, 1906), 197.
31. Charles De Quéker, *La Bienfaisance publique & privée* (Brussels: Imprimerie des institutions de prévoyance, 1894.)

"The Family ... the Only School for the Life of the Citizen": Charitable Visitors

Modern cities played host to disease. Urban illnesses spread at an alarming speed. The epidemics that ravaged the nineteenth-century cities—cholera, typhus, and typhoid—decimated thousands of the malnourished poor who were housed in their path. Civic authorities who followed the doctors on their rounds reported in horrifying detail the misery of the inadequately housed poor huddled in their rags. Having witnessed the devastating effects of epidemics in 1848, 1849, 1853, and 1866, a Dutch physician labeled the popular neighborhoods of Amsterdam "ziektemagazijnen" (disease warehouses).[32]

The middle class not only worried about the poor victims of cholera, typhus, and typhoid but also feared that the epidemics would spread beyond the neighborhoods of the poor. The public health reformer Edouard Ducpétiaux advised his Belgian readers that the diseases that festered in the filthy tenements of the East End threatened to invade the respectable squares and wide streets of West London.[33] It seemed only a matter of time before contagion would spread from low-lying, flood-prone regions at the center of Brussels to the bourgeoisie in villas on the higher ground of their capital.

The epidemics alerted public health reformers to the relationship between the environment and the physical degeneration of the urban working class. No connection between disease and overcrowded dwellings had been scientifically proven by the middle of the nineteenth century, but by then most reformers were convinced that a causal link existed. Cramped quarters and shared beds in particular greatly increased the dangers of contracting influenza, consumption, and a host of other diseases, doctors suggested. Disease, immorality, and rebellion threatened to spread as epidemics and riots out of the overpopulated urban rookeries and the warren of alleyways of the European capitals to the peaceful tree-lined enclaves of the stable middle class.

In Britain, the 1838–39 Poor Law Commission, the 1840 Health of Town Committee, the Royal Commission on the Sanitary State of Large Towns and Populous Districts, and the Statistical Society of London compiled tables showing the relationship between overcrowding and mortality, and linking high death rates from fever to families residing in one- and two-room

32. Quoted in H. F. J. M. Van den Eerenbeemt, "Wat leidde tot de Woningwet 1901," *Spiegel Historiael* 9 (1976): 517.

33. Edouard Ducpétiaux, quoted in Marcel Smets, *L'avènement de la cité-jardin en Belgique. Histoire de l'habitat social en Belgique de 1830 à 1930* (Brussels: Pierre Mardaga, 1976), 17.

accommodations.[34] The British commissioners used infant mortality as a significant indicator of the decline of public health caused by overcrowding. The Belgian government launched its own investigations, exploring conditions in working-class housing in Brussels in 1838 and throughout Belgium in 1843–46 and 1848. Not only did they measure air volume, but investigators also asked about the employment of children, night work of women, gin consumption, and the appeal of cabarets. The statistical findings of the British and Belgian experts reinforced each other.

Investigators on both sides of the Channel discussed the link between sanitation and the morality of the poor in the centers of the cities. The Belgian study of 1846 lamented that the residents of the hovel "did not care about cleanliness. The beds are miserable, disgusting straw litters of dirtiness; too often they are located in stinking rooms."[35] George Godwin, the influential editor of *The Builder,* in his 1854 treatise, *London Shadows: A Glance at the "Homes" of the Thousands,* wrote: "Dirty, dilapidated, and unwholesome dwellings destroy orderly and decent habits, degrade the character, and conduce to immorality."[36] The inquiries revealed that social ills were general, not individual. Poor drainage and inadequate water supplies had far-reaching physical and—so the reformers began to speculate—moral consequences. Revolts broke out in the same streets that the public health officials named as breeding grounds for disease.

The epidemics of the 1860s reminded the reformers, in case their attention had lapsed, of the threat posed by the overcrowded rookeries and impasses or dead-end alleys. Observers rediscovered the poor who lived "with their families in base, corrupting surroundings, where they are exposed to disease, to infirmities and to all the causes of debility, degeneration, demoralization, that such an environment engenders."[37] To reinforce the sense of urgency conveyed by the statistics gathered over the previous decades, novelists, journalists, and essayists in the 1860s and 1870s guided middle-class readers back into the rookeries and impasses. They invited their readers to follow them vicariously as they ventured into the dens of the poor, unearthing an unknown "other" that did not share their morality.

To understand the conditions that contributed to the high mortality rates in Brussels, Ducpétiaux compared disease-ridden families in the low-lying Marolles district in the center of Brussels to healthier peasants. His rural

34. Anthony S. Wohl, *Endangered Lives: Public Health in Victorian Britain* (London: Methuen, 1984), 307.

35. *Enquête sur la condition des classes ouvrières* (Brussels: Imprimerie de Th. Lesigne, 1846), 3:88.

36. George Godwin, *London Shadows: A Glance at the "Homes" of the Thousands* (London: George Routledge & Co., 1854), 45.

37. M. d'Elhoungne, quoted in De Camps, *L'Evolution sociale en Belgique* (Brussels: Emile Bruylant, 1890), 84.

subjects grew vegetables for themselves and had access to healthier meat, while urban workers spent their higher wages on drink and debauchery, not food for their families.[38]

Belgian King Leopold I cited the findings of the 1846 investigation to focus attention on the plight of urban laborers, and, in 1851, Prime Minister Charles Rogier convened a hygiene congress in Brussels. The assembled delegates advocated clearing the decrepit buildings from the center of the cities, enforcing building regulations, and granting exemptions from the land tax for new worker housing projects. They invited charitable institutions to appropriate funds for the construction of the housing. National, municipal, and philanthropic actions must join together, reinforcing each other in the attempt to meet the grave threat, the Belgian congress concluded.

The editor of the Belgian journal *Mon Home* (my home) exhorted his middle-class readers to "leave your sumptuous apartments where you pass more or less useful days and descend into the most remote quarters, penetrate the somber impasses, sit in some cabaret of the sixth order, clamber up black stairs, enter slimy corridors."[39] The time had come to learn more about the others in their cities, he admonished his readers. Gathering information was the necessary precursor to action that could forestall revolution among the urban slum dwellers.

Henry Mayhew's widely read articles in the *Morning Chronicle* described graphically the poverty of the marginally employed inhabitants of central London. Godwin took his readers along on an urban journey to experience "the frightful amount of ignorance, misery, and degradation which exists in this wealthy and luxurious city—this city of 300,000 houses and two million and a quarter of persons."[40] A bevy of other journalists, including John Hollingshead and James Greenwood, made forays into the rookeries to gather copy for their often sensational articles describing the "swarms of wretched, filthy, haggard, dissolute, profligate, careworn, outcast masses" who "inhabit the dingy courts, dingy cellars, and miserable garrets of our great towns."[41] In their accounts, the poor ate like pigs, rooted through refuse, and bedded down together in insect-ridden straw, less than civilized, closer to animals than to the refined bourgeoisie. Within their putrid buildings, breathing the foul night air, the families of the marginally employed could be easily corrupted by the criminal influences of the lowest beings. The poor of London and Brussels, lurking in shadowy slums, were as exotic as the indigenous people of darkest Africa. Unlike the Africans who lived

38. E. Ducpétiaux, *Budgets économiques des classes ouvrières en Belgique: Subsistances, salaires, populations* (Brussels: M. Hayez, 1855), 25.
39. Louis Banneux, *Mon Home* (Brussels: Polleunis et Ceuterick, 1896).
40. Godwin, *London Shadows,* 32.
41. John Knox, *The Masses Without! A Pamphlet for the Times* (London, 1857), quoted in H. J. Dyos, "The Slums of Victorian London," *Victorian Studies* 9, no. 1 (September 1967): 13–14.

far away, the urban poor festered in the heart of their European capitals, threatening civilized society.

Illegitimate births soared in the cities, "the seat of all immorality," the Belgian Emile Jottrand claimed in his study of rural depopulation and urban overcrowding.[42] Edmond Nicolai, the author of another study of migration from farms to factories, saw cities as "the refuge of repeat criminals, of old offenders, of vagabonds with suspicious morals, of the déclassés, etc,... the center of alcoholism with all its excesses and of debauchery with its often dangerous and always hideous parade of hangers-on and depraved." As a result of their density and promiscuity, he explained, "cities are the endemic host of tuberculosis, syphilis and other illnesses that, if they are not shameful, are at least contagious."[43] There, fathers drank to excess, allowing their daughters, tempted by night life, to fall prey to vice.[44]

The earliest commentaries had attributed the misery of the slum dwellers to individual moral defects—to alcoholism, restlessness, and improvidence. By the 1860s, a number of observers suspected that the physical overcrowding of the slums itself weakened the already degenerating moral fabric of working-class families. The reformer Henry Davies asked the Earl of Derby if morality could prevail when parents had to share a bedroom with their children, "in the filthy dens which are so rife in the crowded districts of the Metropolis?"[45]

In London, individuals from the middle class came forward to ameliorate the conditions of the urban poor. The Charity Organisation Society organized their efforts to introduce morality to the London poor, sending out volunteer visitors to observe and to instruct the poor in their homes, to make them self-reliant individuals like the middle class. The visitors looked to bad character as the cause of poverty and considered domestic economy the key to improving the working class. Helen Bosanquet, the daughter of a Unitarian minister and wife of the philosopher, Bernard Bosanquet, instructed working-class mothers in living within their means. Poverty was preventable, she believed. It all depended on the organization of the family. She complained continually about the disorder of the workers' dwellings, especially bothered that no one seemed to mind the chaos: "It is a peculiarity of these places that the house doors always stand hospitably open,

---

42. Emile Jottrand, *Le dépeuplement des campagnes* (Mons: Dequesne-Masquillier & Fils, 1895), 9.

43. Edmond Nicolai, *La dépopulation des campagnes* (Brussels: P. Weissenbruch, 1903).

44. Louis Bertrand, *Le logement de l'ouvrier et des pauvres en Belgique* (Brussels: Chez l'auteur, 1888), 68; P. Van Nerom, *Les lois ouvrières et sociales en Belgique. Epargne, alcoolisme, salaires, conseils de l'industrie, maisons ouvrières* (Brussels: Emile Bruylant, 1890).

45. Henry D. Davies, *The Way Out: A Letter Addressed (by permission) to the Earl of Derby, K. G. in which the Evils of the Overcrowded Town Hovel and the Advantages of the Suburban Cottage are Contrasted* (London: Longman, Green, Longman & Roberts, 1861), 12.

inviting attention to a confusion of chaotic dirt within, and letting out into the street an indescribable odour which at once betrays the class of the inhabitant."[46] Sturdy mothers with red elbows simply turned their heads, looking toward the streets as they yelled at their children swarming down the doorsteps. Margaret Loane, who had been trained as a nurse at Charing Cross Hospital, surveyed the cooking, marketing, child rearing, and cleanliness of working-class homes. She noticed the inordinate strength of these robust laboring women and disparaged their unseemly dominance. Were these really women? the charitable visitors asked. They bore so little resemblance to the middle-class mothers the visitors idealized.

Appointed district secretary for the Charity Organisation Society in Shoreditch in the East End, Bosanquet took up residence for several months among the poor to "feel the burden of their irresponsibility."[47] She recounted stories of the children's games that she observed over her back garden wall, noting that "here human nature displays naturally and off guard." The future held little for these "ugly, half-starved, cross little things." Her assessment of responsibility was clear. "They owe their lot to nothing so impressive as an inherited doom, but to a very commonplace carelessness and stupid selfishness on the part of the family and community into which they are born."[48]

Individual irresponsibility, especially the mother's, was to blame for the plight of the family. But that also meant that with instruction, their lot could be improved. The visitors were on the lookout for signs of respectability—women "who could keep a home together."[49] They noticed when working-class women scrubbed their doorways and front steps, put up starched white curtains, and washed their windows. The visitors' pastoral images of the ideal wife and mother did not include the reality of working-class women's lives outside of the home, so convinced were they that "the Family, with its mingled diversity and identity of interests, is the best, if indeed the only school for the life of the citizen."[50] They left work itself to parliamentary commissions to investigate; their concern was the family. That was where they believed change could be induced.

The English visitors had few followers on the Continent. In Belgium, charity was funneled through Catholic organizations such as the Societies for Mutual Assistance and the workers' clubs. The Société de Saint-Vincent

46. Helen Dendy, "The Children of Working London," in *Aspects of the Social Problem by Various Writers,* ed. Bernard Bosanquet (London: Macmillan, 1895), 40.
47. Helen Dendy, "The Industrial Residuum," in Bosanquet, *Aspects of the Social Problem.*
48. Dendy, "Children of Working London," 29 and 39.
49. Margaret E. Loane, *The Queen's Poor: Life as They Find It in Town and Country* (London: Edward Arnold, 1910), 27; A. Bulley and M. Whitley, *Women's Work* (London: Methuen & Co., 1894); Bosanquet, *Aspects of the Social Problem.*
50. Bosanquet, *The Family,* 245.

de Paul, founded in 1842 in Brussels, engaged men from the nobility, the upper bourgeoisie, industrialists, and businessmen in missionary visits to those poor families judged most susceptible to improvement. Their conception of charitable assistance was clear: "The goal of charity... is not to raise up the poor man from his misery each day, to let him fall back down in the evening to the depths of despair; but it is to teach him to pull himself up to live the life of God and to reclaim his dignity as a man and as a Christian."[51] Otherwise comparatively few members of the bourgeoisie emerged from the comfort of their villas to engage in alleviating the suffering of the poor.

Belgian reformers in the 1880s, surveying the results of what they identified as four decades of neglect, asked how their forefathers (and mothers) could have observed the growing misery of the urban workers and yet failed to respond.[52] Dr. De Camps complained that in Belgium, unlike Britain, the investigations just followed one after another. "Always studies, groping, but never action."[53] Nor was the lack of intervention to resolve the inadequacies revealed by in-depth studies limited to housing. It took over thirty years for the recommendations of the Hygiene Congress of 1851–1852 to be considered and partially implemented, for example. Similarly, on the question of child labor, the Belgian government accumulated volumes of statistics but concluded that limiting child labor would restrict the freedom of industry and of heads of households.

Contemporaries explained what they identified as the dearth of Belgian philanthropists by pointing to the Anglo-Saxon traditions of charitable engagement. They suggested that the differences between Britain and Belgium could be traced to the Protestant benevolence that spurred charity volunteers in Britain. Many of the British philanthropists and visitors did volunteer under the aegis of an evangelical benevolent society. The most famous of these "missionising philanthropists," William Booth, organized soup kitchens and promised "Heaven in East London for everyone."[54] The Protestant missionaries visited the poor and the sick to save their own souls as well as to rescue the poor, some historians suggest, echoing nineteenth-century Belgians who argued that active Catholic associations on the Continent

---

51. Etienne-Constantin de Gerlache, quoted in Gunter Bousset and Marie-Thérèse Delmer, "La Société de Saint-Vincent de Paul à Bruxelles (1842–1992)," in *De Vincentianen in Belgie 1842–1992*, ed. Jan De Maeyer and Paul Wynants (Louvain: Universitaire Pers Leuven, 1992), 244.

52. Conseil supérieur d'hygiène publique, *Habitations ouvrières* (Brussels, 1887). The same questions are posed today as Belgian television commentators and newspaper editors continue to probe the striking lack of volunteerism and of charitable contributions in their country.

53. De Camps, *L'Evolution sociale*, 82.

54. William Booth, quoted in Alan Palmer, *The East End: Four Centuries of London Life* (New Brunswick: Rutgers University Press, 2000), 80; Roger-Henri Guerrand, *Une Europe en construction: Deux siècles d'habitat social en Europe* (Paris: Editions La Découverte, 1992); Frank K. Prochaska, *Women and Philanthropy in Nineteenth-Century England* (Oxford: Clarendon Press, 1980), 120–123.

concentrated instead on the spiritual and moral well-being of their subjects. These Protestant missionaries worked individually and in associations to improve the lodging conditions of the respectable poor, but they did not advocate interference with "the laws of political economy" by offering charity as a long-term solution or by looking to the government for assistance.

The Belgians were also more willing to look to the government for assistance. A number of public health reformers, such as Ducpétiaux, considered the government a crucial supplement to individual initiative and employers' paternal responsibility.[55] After the church, they expected the state, not to intervene in the home, which should remain free from government interference, but to encourage private initiatives and to facilitate assistance to the poor. Many Belgian Catholic reformers staked out a position in favor of "the providential state" that called into question the assumptions of the "laissez faire, laissez passer" of Liberals on both sides of the Channel.[56] The unchallenged Catholic control of the Belgian government after 1885 meant that legislation at a national level in Belgium reinforced the actions of Church philanthropists. In Prime Minister William Gladstone's Britain, few of the charitable visitors expected to remake the urban poor by their individual efforts alone, but they did not look to the state. They hoped to inspire like-minded individuals and institutions to follow in their benevolent footsteps.

"Knowledge That Gives a Broad Basis for Reform": Social Classification of the Urban Poor in "Pest-stricken Regions"

Workers' unrest on both sides of the Channel in the 1880s refocused attention on the workers' plight. In Britain, the unemployment crisis of 1885–1886 that spurred massive demonstrations on the streets of London in February 1886, followed by the 1888 London match girls' strike, the gas workers' strike of August 1889, and two weeks of dockers' strikes, raised the specter of class warfare. In 1886, strikes erupted in Amsterdam and a

55. Charles Woeste, "Les Catholiques belges et les intérêts ouvriers," *Revue générale* 65 (April 1897): 481–501; Charles Cambier, *Het Boek der goede Werklieden: Handboek van Voorzienigheid of Middelen tot Verbetering van den Toestand der Werkersklassen* (Ghent: Algemene Boekhandel van Ad. Hoeste, 1887); Emile Vliebergh, *De Boeren en de maatschappelijke Zaak* (Eernegem: Laga- van de Casteele, 1894), 12–13; Paul Berryer, *De 1884 à 1900* (Bruxelles: J. Goemaere, 1900); Leen Van Molle, *Katholiken en Landbouw: Landbouwpolitiek in Belgie, 1884–1914*, Symbolae facultatis literarum et philosophiae lovaniensis, series B/vol. 5. (Louvain: Universitaire Pers Leuven, 1989).

56. Arthur Vermeersch, *Manuel social: la législation et les oeuvres en Belgique* (Louvain: Uystpruyst, 1904), 14. See also Molly de Spoelberch de Lovenjoul, Mme. Charles Vloeberghs, and August Beernaert, *La Belgique charitable* (Brussels: Dewit, 1904).

wave of Belgian strikes originating in the mining and industrial regions of Wallonia spread to Brussels and Ghent.

Investigators of all political persuasions anxiously launched studies to explain this growing antagonism between capital and labor. The Belgian Catholic periodical *Le Travail Chrétien* (Christian labor), worried by the contagion of socialism, published scores of articles asserting that "the Church is very concerned with the fate of the worker."[57] British journals such as *Nineteenth Century, Contemporary Review,* and *National Review* and the Belgian *Revue générale* featured articles on the slums of London and Brussels at the end of the nineteenth century. The descriptions of criminality and hints of revolution and rampant disease fueled the pages of the popular press as well.

British novelists rediscovered the poor herded together in the "unknown" and "dark" regions of East London. These were not the isolated neighborhoods of the poor that observers had visited just a decade earlier. The size of the cities and the depth of the despair overwhelmed individuals. In George Gissing's novel *The Nether World,* pubs and domestic disorder in the end ensnare all of the residents of "the Court," where "like any other slum; filth, rottenness, evil odours, possess these dens of superfluous mankind." The characters—no matter how personally admirable, even those who dabble in philanthropy—squander fortunes, lose their jobs, seek casual employment, and fall into criminal schemes. Girls fail to learn housekeeping from their dissolute mothers and households fall apart in this unstable, ever-moving morass of casually employed workers. Poverty, that "hostile force of nature" eventually fells even Sidney Kirkwood, the one character who stood above the rest in the beginning of the novel. No character emerges in tact from the "pest-stricken regions."[58]

British novelists and essayists were particularly intrigued by the working-class women they found clustered in doorways. In the poorest families, where the mothers and children all worked for wages, the father had lost his authority as a breadwinner. He commanded no respect in these households run by women. Poor women defied their physically diminutive husbands and neglected their sniveling children at play in the streets. These large, raucous figures barring the entrance to their unkempt hovels symbolized the threat of urban poverty to civilization as the middle class knew it.

In the words of historian Gareth Stedman Jones, the British novels and essays of the 1880s, in contrast to earlier works, revealed not "pauperism but chronic poverty."[59] Walter Besant's *Children of Gibeon* (1886) and Arthur Morrison's *Tales of Mean Streets* (1894), among others, chronicled the dire

57. *Le Travail Chrétien* (Seraing: Revue Mensuelle, 1896 to 1902).
58. George Gissing, *The Nether World* (1889; reprint, London: Dent, 1973), 74 and 164.
59. Gareth Stedman Jones, *Outcast London* (Oxford: Clarendon Press, 1971), 286.

poverty of the tenements, drawing the conditions to the forefront of readers' social consciences. George Sims reported on his "journey through Outcasts' Land" for the *Pictorial World* and the *Daily News,* reprinted as *How the Poor Live* (1883). Arthur Morrison's London, as described in *A Child of the Jago* (1896) and *The Hole in the Wall* (1903), seethed with criminality and violence.[60]

Despite the flourishing realist movement in Belgian literature, most Belgian novelists focused on rural rather then urban life, perhaps reflecting the significance of the peasant and the theme of rural exodus.[61] The novels that were set in cities, such as those of Violette (Florence Gillo-Deros), Camille Lemonnier, Emile LeClercq, Caroline Gravière, and Hermann Pergameni dealt with the travails of the petit bourgeoisie, rather than the workers. The characters drawn by Gillo-Deros, for example, looked out their window at gardens full of flowers.[62] Marriage served in many of the novels to reconcile social classes in a world not yet pulled apart by class conflict. In Lemonnier's "Le Polichinelle," even though the scene is one of absolute misery—the husband having died leaving the family without material resources—the reader's attention is focused on the sentiments of the devoted mother who will prevail against all odds.[63] On this side of the Channel, issues of sentiment and the struggle with Catholicism loomed large while urban poverty lay beyond the concern of novelists. There seems to have been little interplay between the British and Belgian authors whose works, unlike reformers' essays, remained untranslated and unavailable across the Channel.

Ignored by Belgian novelists, the poor families residing in the center of the industrial cities obsessed Belgian political observers in the 1880s. The implied contrast of working women with the cheerful serenity of peasant and middle-class families formed the implicit backdrop to the oft-repeated urban tales of whining children and shrieking, gossiping wives. The failure of working women to maintain domestic order had immense social consequences. How many laboring men would have remained at home and resisted the temptations of drink and socialism, one observer asked, "if they had found a gay, amiable, sprightly wife to greet them when they returned, if they had found clean and laughing children, a warm foyer, a well served

60. Walter Besant, *Children of Gibeon* (London: Chatto & Windus, 1886); Arthur Morrison, *Tales of Mean Streets* (London: Metheun & Co., 1894); George Sims, *How the Poor Live* (London: Chatto & Windus, 1883); Arthur Morrison, *A Child of the Jago* (London: Metheun & Co., 1896); Arthur Morrison, *The Hole in the Wall* (London: Methuen & Co., 1902).

61. Philip De Pillecijn, *Sociaal Probleem en verhalend Proza, 1830–1886* (Antwerp: De Standaard, 1967).

62. Florence Gillo-Deros, "Tante Julienne."

63. Camille Lemonnier, "Le Polichinelle," *En Brabant* (Verviers: Ernest Gilou, 1878).

meal?"[64] Instead, the working man returned from the factory or the mine to a disorderly house, a boisterous wife, and unruly children. Forced to forage for a cold meal, he sought refuge in the pub or café, a sure sign of moral degradation in the eyes of the writers on both sides of the Channel.

Married at an early age, the urban working girl lacked the "disciplined habits of mind" and domestic skills necessary to set up a house. By the time she turned thirty-five, her "voice has grown more shrill, her patience declines; she learns to whine and nag," one set of investigators recounted. Working different schedules, often into the night, husbands and wives never sat down to a common meal with their children. They passed through the shared abode, each adding "to the litter of dirty cups and crumb-covered plates on the table."[65]

The Belgian Socialists echoed Catholic concerns about the plight of young working girls who sank into the depraved life of prostitution as their fathers drank themselves into a stupor. Observing women attempting to cook a meal in the filth of the single room where piles of rags doubled as beds, Socialist leader Auguste De Winne asked incredulously: "Are these really human beings who live here?"[66] De Winne's solution echoed that of British philanthropists: Women should be relieved of the burden of working outside of the home so they could partake of the joys of domesticity. The middle-class visitors and writers, Socialists as well as Conservatives, in Brussels and London had uncovered a world radically different than the one they knew in their cozy bungalows and suburban villas.

As corroboration of these anecdotal impressions, social scientists throughout Europe in the last decades of the nineteenth century documented the deepening urban poverty. Tramping through the slums, they filled their notebooks with the details of the plumbing, ventilation, child-rearing practices, marriage expectations, and diets of the working poor. They counted, subdivided, and categorized. They charted the migration of workers, recorded their diet, compared the rents they paid to the wages they earned, counted the number of inhabitants per rooms, and calculated the amount of air available per inhabitant.[67] The volumes of statistics and studies collected on both sides of the Channel allowed the classification and segregation

---

64. Dauby, *Des grèves,* 186. See also De Camps, *L'évolution sociale;* Paul Gemahling, *La femme ouvrière et la maternité* (Reims: L'Action populaire, nd); Edward Cadbury, Cecile Matheson, and George Shann, *Women's Work and Wages* (London: Fischer Unwin, 1906).
65. Amy Bulley and Margaret Whitley, *Women's Work* (London: Methuen & Co., 1894), vi, 31, and 23.
66. Auguste De Winne, *A Travers les Flandres* (Ghent: Volksdrukkerij, 1902); L. Bertrand, *Le logement de l'ouvrier et des pauvres en Belgique* (Brussels: Chez l'auteur, 1888), 68.
67. See, e.g., Charles De Quéker, *Cent budgets ouvriers à Bruxelles en 1897* (Brussels: N. De Bremaeker-Wauts, 1897); Hippolyte De Royer de Dour, *La condition du logement de la classe peu aisée et les institutions de prévoyance à Saint Gilles-lez-Bruxelles* (Brussels: Alfred Vromant, 1891).

of the workers who could help themselves from the amorphous mass of the poor.

Perhaps the most meticulous and influential of all social surveyors, Charles Booth, measured and mapped London poverty. Booth complained that East London "lay hidden from view behind a curtain on which were painted terrible pictures:—starving children, suffering women, overworked men; horrors of drunkenness and vice; monsters and demons of inhumanity; giants of disease and despair" and asked what relation these terrible images bore to reality.[68] A Unitarian and entrepreneur, Booth had been trained in the office of Lamport and Holt's Steamship Company and had launched a business with his brother. Well-steeped in the late nineteenth-century debates on the causes of poverty, Booth wondered about the connections between individual poverty and social conditions. A pragmatist, like many of his contemporaries, Booth believed that this "problem of all problems" could be fixed by knowledge, by the collection of facts.

In his multivolume study of the London poor, Booth broke up the all-inclusive Victorian category of the "laboring poor," categorizing and classifying his subjects according to their work and mapping their lodgings by class, distinguishing streets by color. Like many of the visitors affiliated with the Charity Organisation Society, Booth took up residence among his subjects. Usually he lived with families in the slightly more affluent districts who took in boarders, but occasionally he found unfurnished spare rooms on the meaner streets. On his maps of London, he colored the streets inhabited by workers earning regular wages pink, the streets inhabited by casual laborers dark blue, and used black for semi-criminals. Eating his meals with the families, Booth came to know them quite intimately, which allowed him to describe their work and their family relations in great detail. Booth commented: "Of Shoreditch, or rather Hoxton, which is the most characteristic part of Shoreditch, I am tempted to recall a description by Mr. Besant, which will be remembered by all who have read 'The Children of Gibeon.' There is, he says, nothing beautiful, or picturesque, or romantic in the place, there is only the romance of life in it, sixty thousand lives in Hoxton, every one with its own story to tell."[69] Poverty, was less pervasive than earlier writers like Bosanquet had assumed, but their private philanthropy had not begun to alleviate the misery of the lowest orders.

Booth then turned his attention to work, a subject that was often neglected by reformers focusing on families and their homes. His first survey led him to the conclusion that 55 percent of his subjects were poor as a result of

68. Charles Booth, quoted in Phillip J. Waller, *Town, City and Nation: England 1850–1914* (Oxford: Oxford University Press, 1983), 44.

69. Charles Booth, *Life and Labour of the People in London* (1889; reprint, New York: Augustus M. Kelley, 1969), 1:72.

insufficient wages. In his study of industry, Booth noted the increased separation of the place of residence from the place of work, especially for the middling classes. As immigrants migrated outward to the suburbs, generations of London-born poor deteriorated in the center without the possibility of escape. That was especially true in the East End where casual laborers struggled to find work when industries closed up shop or moved outside of the city.

It took seventeen years for Booth to complete his research. A staff of fifteen researchers, including a number of women, assisted him. Booth's cousin by marriage, Beatrice Potter, the daughter of the chairman of the Great Western Railway, served an apprenticeship with him as a researcher. Tutored as a child by Herbert Spencer, she worked for a short time for the Charity Organisation Society and as a rent collector for the housing reformer Octavia Hill, before joining Booth. "Practical work does not satisfy me," she lamented. "It seems like walking on shifting sand, with the forlorn hope that the impress of one's steps will be lasting."[70] Potter married Sidney Webb in 1892; together Beatrice and Sidney Webb pursued "the life history of institutions."[71]

Legions of other social surveyors categorized and classified the British poor, perhaps most notable among them Benjamin Seebohm Rowntree. His categorization of the poor in York confirmed Booth's conclusions about the poverty line. However, Rowntree distinguished between primary and secondary poverty, the first defined by wages so low as to prevent a family from rising out of poverty, and the second marked by improvident spending.[72] Rowntree argued that the "deserving poor" could be pulled up to the morality of the middle class, away from the unemployed residuum in "the hell of savagery."[73] These British studies separated out categories of the poor that could be counted and classified. At the top, the "deserving poor" rarely caused trouble and seemed to possess human qualities, while at the bottom of industrial society, "the mass of social wreckage" was beyond help.[74] The respectable working class in between the middle class and the residuum could be reformed.

70. A. M. McBriar, *An Edwardian Mixed Doubles: The Bosanquets versus the Webbs: A Study in British Social Policy, 1890–1929* (Oxford: Clarendon Press, 1987), 29.
71. Jane Lewis, "The Place of Social Investigation, Social Theory, and Social Work in the Approach to Late Victorian and Edwardian Social Problems: The Case of Beatrice Webb and Helen Bosanquet," in *The Social Survey in Historical Perspective, 1880–1940*, ed. Martin Bulmer, Kevin Bales, and Kathryn Kish Sklar (Cambridge: Cambridge University Press, 1991), 149.
72. Asa Briggs, *Social Thought and Social Action: A Study of the Work of Seebohm Rowntree. 1871–1954* (London: Longmans, 1961).
73. Robert A. Woods, quoted in H. J. Dyos, "The Slums of Victorian London," *Victorian Studies* 9, no. 1 (September 1967): 18.
74. Bosanquet, *Aspects of the Social Problem*, 116.

Charles Lagasse and Charles De Quéker conducted a survey of workers' housing in 1890 for the Housing Committee of Brussels. Visiting 19,284 families, they divided the city into divisions and the divisions into series, compiling statistics on the average rent, salary, number of rooms occupied by each family, and the volume of air available to be breathed in the rooms. They explained, "before wanting to remedy conditions alleged to be unsatisfactory, we must come to understand it down to its smallest details."[75] Belgian investigators, in contrast to the British studies, refrained from moral commentary, leaving it to their readers to digest the tables of statistics.

A decade later, the Brussels Housing Committee commissioned Emile Hellemans to conduct an even more precise scientific study. Like Booth, the architect Hellemans devoted a number of years to his multivolume study. He collected information on "the siting, the orientation, the dimensions, the measure of the inhabited rooms, examining them from the point of view of their livability, their sanitation, weighting the proportion of their size to the number of inhabitants, the condition of the furniture" so that he could sketch "a picture of the material and hygienic situation of the working population of the capital."[76]

Lagasse, De Quéker, and Hellemans did not categorize the poor as they observed and counted. The Brussels Housing Committee lumped together "our brothers and sisters of the popular classes" as a group to be pitied. In contrast to Booth's proposals for the provision of insurance, education, and limited government welfare, when they asked themselves, "How will we be able to improve conditions?" they answered: "We are still thinking!"[77] The Liège professor Ernest Mahaim called on the Belgian government to intervene by collecting more data so that reformers could target their subjects more effectively.[78] New scientific studies would yield the public understanding that would favor reform. Louis Bertrand, a leader of the Belgian Socialists, concurred, appealing to the government to collect statistics on poverty that would guide legislation to meet the intensifying urban crisis.

---

75. Charles Lagasse and Charles De Quéker, *Ville de Bruxelles, Enquête sur les habitations ouvrières en 1890* (Brussels: N. de Bremaeker-Wauts, 1891); Patricia Van den Eeckhout, "Enquête sur l'habitat ouvrier à Bruxelles au début du 20e siècle," *Les Cahiers de la Fonderie* 6 (June 1989): 26–33.

76. Emile Hellemans, *Enquête sur les habitations ouvrières en 1903, 1904, 1905* (Brussels: Imprimerie des institutions de prévoyance, 1905), 3:vi.

77. Hellemans, *Enquête sur les habitations ouvrières,* xi and ix.

78. Ernest Mahaim, "De l'organisation d'une enquête statistique permanente. Rapport sur la VIe question," *Congrès international des habitations à bon marché. Actes du Congrès* (Brussels: Hayez, 1897); Ernest Mahaim, "La statistique des logements au point de vue hygiénique, économique et social. Exposé critique des méthodes et des résultes."

The historian H. J. Dyos marveled that in a society so divided and faced with such overwhelming poverty, the middle-class novelists, essayists, visitors, surveyors, and reformers who took on the urban crisis of London in the last half of the nineteenth century remained so steadfastly optimistic.[79] The journalist George Sims, for example, testified that the years he spent investigating the poor, collecting stories for his series of articles, made him "think better, and not worse of human nature."[80] Observers and investigators on both sides of the Channel were convinced that the data they collected and published would empower legions of reformers "with a feeling of responsibility" to go forth and improve. Empowered by "the knowledge that gives a broad basis for reform," the enlightened middle class would address urban problems that were ultimately capable of resolution.[81] None of these investigators expected their carefully collected facts to lie dormant on the page. "Knowledge is never 'mere' knowledge, and the knowledge which is able to touch the springs of conduct is indispensable to right conduct," the philosopher B. Kirkham Gray reasoned.[82]

The Belgian parliament responded to the 1886 riots when miners from Liège to Charleroi went out on strike, marching, pillaging, and setting fires in a social movement that threatened to turn revolutionary by enlisting the Commission du Travail (Labor Commission) to undertake a substantial investigation into working and living conditions.[83] The Commission traveled throughout the country, collecting volumes of testimony from workers, philanthropists, manufacturers, provincial governors, artisans, and landlords on industrial relations and work conditions. It also investigated housing conditions, inquiring into the number of families who squeezed into one room, two rooms, or entire houses, examined the relation of rent to wages, and probed the moral condition of workers.

In Britain, Queen Victoria pressed the prime minister, William Gladstone, to supply "more precise information as to the true state of affairs in these overcrowded, unhealthy and squalid abodes," and in response, a Royal Commission on the Housing of the Working Classes was appointed.[84] Allotted several years to complete its study, the Royal Commission findings were more detailed than those of the Select Committee on Artizans'

79. Dyos, "Slums of Victorian London," 5–40.
80. Sims, *How the Poor Live,* 86.
81. A. Paterson, *Across the Bridges, or Life by the South London Riverside* (1912; reprint, New York: Garland, 1980), 271.
82. B. Kirkham Gray, *Philanthropy and the State* (London: P.S. King & Son, 1908), 14.
83. Commission du Travail, *Questionnaire relatif au travail industriel* (Brussels: Ministère de l'Agriculture, de l'Industrie et des Travaux publics, 1887).
84. Queen Victoria, quoted in Lynn Hollen Lees, *The Solidarities of Strangers: The English Poor Laws and the People, 1700–1948* (Cambridge: Cambridge University Press, 1998), 247; Select Committee on Artizans' and Labourers' Dwellings Improvements. British Parliamentary Papers, vol. 7 (1881 and 1882).

and Labourers' Dwellings Improvement that had met from 1881 to 1882. The Royal British Commission collected evidence from specialist witnesses and from surveyors of the London parishes other large cities and town in England. Its report echoed Booth: immorality did not cause poverty. Many poor working families not given to drink or gambling or frivolous spending simply could not afford healthy dwellings.

The urban reformers, buttressed by the volumes of statistics, successfully propelled questions of social policy and societal responsibility for the poor to the center of progressive debate at the end of the nineteenth century on both sides of the Channel. Gradually, overcrowding had come to be viewed as the result of poverty, not intemperance. The problem was that costs of rent and food were higher than wages, especially in Belgium where salaries lagged behind Britain. The visibility of urban poverty called into question the liberal economics that informed the assumptions of politicians. In Brussels as well as London, the Victorian solutions were beginning to seem woefully inadequate. Despite their contrasting earlier histories of charitable intervention, the push for urban renewal as part of the "many-sided project for social reform" developed simultaneously in London and Brussels, and also in Berlin, Amsterdam, and New York.[85] Styling themselves professional experts, many of the newest generation of reformers, especially in London, distanced themselves from politics. Unlike the ideologically divided philanthropic movements, these conservative, liberal, and socialist reformers adopted a shared pragmatic language. The urgency of the social question as verified by scientific studies set it above party squabbles.

The investigators' conclusions were informed by their memories of their "native town," of the idyllic life before "hurry and poverty, and the geographical separation of rich and poor... dragged down the ideals of a London street."[86] Both the Belgians and the British expected confidently that they could remedy the urban crisis by restoring the regularly employed workers to habitable spaces, by separating them from the residuum. But the reformers' optimism did not completely assuage their contemporaries' fears about urban poverty. Doubts lingered, especially in Britain, about the future of a civilized society harboring the poor in its capital. In language reminiscent of the earliest bestial metaphors, Charles Masterman pictured the poor as "the locust horde... the swarm," inhabiting the "stagnant marshland" at the center of the city, susceptible to epidemics and criminal elements, but he too shared a new environmental understanding of causation with Seebohm Rowntree whom he quoted at length.[87] The plethora of studies on both sides

85. Christian Topalov, "From the 'Social Question' to 'Urban Problems': Reformers and the Working Classes at the Turn of the Twentieth Century," *ISSI* 125 (1990): 319–335.
86. Paterson, *Across the Bridges*, 8.
87. C. F. G. Masterman, "The Social Abyss," *Contemporary Review* 81 (1902): 30.

of the Channel had convinced the experts that the slums themselves were responsible for urban degeneration. Entombed in pestilential rookeries and impasses, respectable workers and the unemployable poor alike languished without the benefit of sunlight, beyond the gaze of the middle class. They needed to be removed from the dark, stinking hovels at the center of their capitals.

2 *"Give Men Homes, and They Will Have Soft and Homely Notions"*

Reformers' Schemes for Housing Urban Workers

> The whole social question is contained in the four rooms of several meters that form workmen's housing.
>
> —*Le Cottage* (June 1903), 37

In the wake of industrialization, domestic disorder spilled out of the wretched lodgings inhabited by workers and their families fomenting social chaos. Civilization, like breathable air and sunlight, had failed to penetrate these enclosed spaces in which the poor lived and bred. Malnourished infants perished, unschooled children misbehaved, gossiping women neglected their families, and men drank up their earnings in cafés and pubs. Drawn to the cities to build the infrastructure of an industrial society, the laborers and their unruly families threatened to undermine public order.

The middle class feared that laborers, newly arrived in the cities, were being lured into lives of crime in the promiscuity of the slums. Brussels reformer Hippolyte Royer de Dour warned that "the absence of a true home engendered drunkenness, profligate spending, misery, debauchery, immorality."[1] It seemed clear, in the words of another Belgian reformer, that "the origin of all the vices, all the evils that afflict the workers" could be traced to "the terrible condition of their lodgings."[2] After a visit to London, Charles Buls, the mayor of Brussels from 1881 to 1889, summarized the call to housing reform: "In our opinion it seems obvious that a working population...living in dark, dirty, and miserable lodging and passing most of their time seeking pleasure in public places or in the cabaret, would be

1. Hippolyte Royer de Dour, *Les habitations ouvrières* (Brussels: P. Weissenbruch, 1889), 9.
2. Ed. Roselli-Mollet, *Des logements à bon marché* (Brussels, 1866).

more easily led to trouble public order than others who owned an attractive and agreeable home where they found rest and could restore their laboring powers."[3] These reformers looked to improved housing not only to cleanse their capitals of the festering "fever nests," but to transform the working class into responsible citizens. Workers and their families would be segregated from the impoverished and improvident who were to be left behind, isolated in their pernicious impasses.

Reformers were convinced that snugly housed workers in their own homes would learn to be frugal, responsible fathers providing for loving families like themselves. The 1892 annual report of four Brussels communes cited Benjamin Disraeli's 1845 novel *Sybil:* "At home, so the people. Give men homes, and they will have soft and homely notions."[4] This middle-class domestic dream shaped the first social reforms aimed at controlling workers through the redesign of the built environment of Europe's crowded urban capitals.

The industrial revolutions had drawn the workers into the cities. Graphic artist Gustave Doré and journalist Blanchard Jerrold depicted these "black objects against the deep gloom,...the vanguard of the army of Labour who are...to add a new story to a new terrace; the cornerstone to another building; bulwarks to another frigate; another station to another railway; and tons upon tons of produce from every clime to the mighty stock that is for ever packed along the shores of the Thames."[5] The "army of Labour" crowded into makeshift shelters, threatening the very civilization they had been summoned to build. Newly arrived workers and their families lodged in any roofed-over space they could find and afford. With few building regulations, a second overbuilt city, with rows of identical, dank rooms stretching along tunnel-like alleys sprang up between the streets of the urban capitals of Europe. Rents escalated in urban centers already suffering from rising land prices, even during the 1870s and 1880s when other prices fell. Workmen's wages failed to keep pace.

The London reformer, Charles F. G. Masterman, who had taken up residence himself in a tenement block in East London, observed within these "imbedded cities of poverty, dingy, stagnant and lifeless," a proletariat huddled in "numbers that defy humanity, a kind of colossal ant-heap of stunted life, pent up in crowded ways."[6] In 1866 in Brussels, 27,273 people crowded into

3. Fonds Charles Buls III 20 A-D, Habitations ouvrières et à bon marché 1887–1914, Archives de la Ville de Bruxelles, Brussels.

4. These four communes (boroughs of more than 5,000 residents) ringed central Brussels on its industrial western side. *Les logements de la classe peu aisée dans le rapport du Comité de patronage des habitations ouvrières et des institutions de prévoyance pour les Communes d'Anderlecht, Laeken, Molenbeek et Saint-Gilles. Enquêtes & Rapports* (Brussels: Imprimerie des institutions de prévoyance, 1892).

5. Gustave Doré and Blanchard Jerrold, *London: A Pilgrimage* (London: Grant & Co., 1872), 114.

6. C. F. G. Masterman, "The Social Abyss," *Contemporary Review* 81 (1902): 23. Masterman joined a coterie of other journalists and observers of industrial England that included Friedrich Engels.

388 of these "ant-heaps."[7] A door separated the dark world of the impasse, the alley without an exit, from the street and the bourgeoisie beyond. The British architect George Godwin, editor of a housing reform journal, *The Builder,* condemned the closed-off courtyards and blind alleys as sources of both "immorality and physical suffering," warning: "The means of escaping from public view which they afford generate evil habits, and even when this is not the case, render personal efforts for improvement unlikely."[8] Reformers suspected these hidden courtyards because the sweltering masses who lived there were never seen. With their own makeshift cabarets and small stores squatting at the entrance to the alleyways, the poor had little need to venture outside, except to work, and much time to smolder.

Public health officials recounted stories of visits to families who subsisted in a single room with one bed for the parents and a pile of straw for eight sleeping children. The director of communal welfare for Brussels, Charles De Quéker, and the director general of public works, Charles Lagasse, reported on one household where three daughters had been impregnated by a half brother with whom they were forced to sleep by lack of space.[9] "How could you expect that pure morals could be preserved in these places where the most frightening promiscuity inevitably exists even among the members of the same family, and between the families in which the miserable lodgings all open onto a common landing or shared corridor?" asked a contributor to a Belgian Catholic journal.[10]

Other newly arrived laborers and their families sought refuge in houses in the industrializing urban centers that had been abandoned by the bourgeoisie when they retreated to the suburbs in the mid-nineteenth century. Godwin complained that "the streets of houses originally erected for the 'merchant princes' are now in ruins...now the abodes of the improvident, the vagrant, the vicious, and the unfortunate."[11] The principal tenants, often artisans, subdivided the villas into smaller and smaller units, maximizing the rent they collected. Subletting became the rule in an overcrowded housing market. Many marginally employed families could afford to pay rent for only one room in the houses, typically lacking water and sanitation.

"It would probably startle nine-tenths of the wealthy residents of Kensington to discover that 25 percent of the total inhabitants of their Sanitary Area live under crowded conditions," at least two to a room, the author of *Life in West London: A Study and a Contrast* wrote. In the East End of London, 55 percent of the population of St. George's-in-the-East, 54 percent of

7. Louis Verniers, "Les Impasses Bruxelloises," *Le Folklore Brabançon* 14 (August 1934): 91.
8. George Godwin, *London Shadows: A Glance at the "Homes" of the Thousands* (London: George Routledge & Co., 1854), 12.
9. Raoul Mangot, *Les habitations ouvrières en Belgique* (Paris: Recueil Sirey, 1913), 23.
10. *Travail chrétien* (1897): 322.
11. George Godwin, *Town Swamps and Social Bridges* (1859), quoted in John Burnett, *A Social History of Housing 1815–1970* (London: David & Charles, 1978), 65.

IMPASSE DU MUGUET

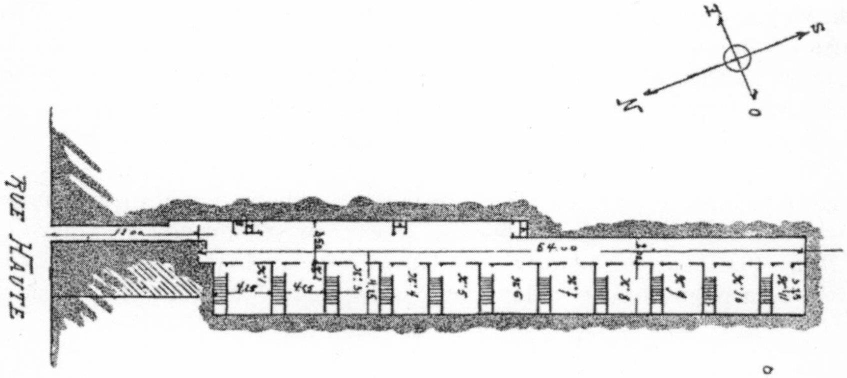

Impasse du Muguet, 1905. Mother and children posed outside their house in one of the dead-end alleys of central Brussels. Photograph from Emile Hellemans, *Enquête sur les habitations ouvrières en 1903, 1904, 1905* (Brussels: Imprimerie des institutions de prévoyance, 1905).

Whitechapel, and 54 percent of Clerkenwell lived two or more to a room.[12] Middle-class reformers who valued privacy calculated that housing units required at least two rooms, one for living and one for sleeping accommodations for a couple, three rooms if there were children so they could sleep separately from the parents, and four rooms if children were of opposite sexes. In Brussels, 90 percent of workers lived in one- or two-room lodgings in 1897.[13] Yet, reformers acknowledged, privacy was not a compelling issue for the tenants themselves who lived quite publicly in the streets, courtyards, and public houses. The workers did not complain about shared rooms.

A series of laws enacted in the 1860s and 1870s in Britain gave municipalities the right to inspect, regulate, and eventually raze the suspect rookeries. Belgian legislation passed in 1858 likewise permitted the demolition of buildings deemed to be unsanitary. After the cholera epidemic of 1866 that claimed 3,467 victims, the law was extended to cover the expropriation of entire districts such as the low-lying region along the Senne River. François d'Elhounge of Ghent, the author of the law, voiced his hope that the legislation would allow reformers to "transform the cities by suppressing the unhealthy sections and creating new quarters that would facilitate the migration of the population from wherever it is too crowded to a place where there is more space."[14] British laws served as the model for this 1867 legislation. However, when d'Elhounge proposed going a step further than the British and requiring the replacement of razed houses, a group of conservative Belgian deputies intervened. The assumption behind the early British and Belgian public health legislation was that adequate housing already existed or would be provided by the market once the decrepit sections were excised.

"Brick Boxes with Slate Lids": Urban Blocks, Industrial Estates, Utopian Villages, and Scattered Suburban Cottages

Most of the middle-class reformers who decried the horrendous living conditions in overcrowded lodgings that "demoralized" the poor in the middle of the nineteenth century interpreted the workers' plight in their own terms. They reasoned that if working families budgeted as their own wives did and lived more frugally, they too could afford better housing. Small-scale solutions, pockets of lodging to house regularly employed laborers, held promise.

12. Arthur Sherwell, *Life in West London: A Study and a Contrast* (London: Methuen & Co., 1897), 29 and 30.

13. Comité officiel de patronage des habitations ouvrières et institutions de prévoyance de Schaerbeek, Saint Josse ten Noode et Evère, *Premier Rapport annuel sur les travaux du comité en 1901* (Brussels: L. G. Laurent, 1902), 42–44.

14. François d'Elhounge, quoted in Marcel Smets, *L'avènement de la cité-jardin en Belgique: Histoire de l'habitat social en Belgique de 1830 à 1930* (Brussels: Pierre Mardaga, 1976), 43.

Philanthropists in London, industrialists in Brussels, and the market on both sides of the Channel were expected to provide housing for the poor. The Peabody Trust, established in 1862 with funds from the American merchant-banker George Peabody purchased its first construction site in Spitalfields in East London from the Commission of Public Works. Two-room flats arrayed along a central corridor were stacked four stories tall. Communal laundries and baths were located on the top floor, washing facilities and sculleries on the landings. Caretakers monitored all of the common spaces, including the shared lavatories. The Trust set aside a common area for children to play away from the streets under the watchful eye of their mothers. The design of the urban blocks met the public health standards that had motivated these early housing reformers and satisfied philanthropists' demands for moral control. By 1887, Peabody Trust had constructed 5,014 dwellings, mostly in the center of London.

To build suitable dwellings of flats charging reasonable rents and at the same time return 5 percent to their investors, the philanthropic trusts of London rented their model housing only to regularly employed heads of households, tenants who would pay their rent, and who were deemed capable of self-restraint. Less promising, marginally employed laborers were left behind in the low-lying rookeries, but only until, in a trickle-down sequence, the poorest residents would eventually inherit the dwellings abandoned by the favored workers chosen to move up to the model housing.

Trustees of philanthropic building societies, such as the Peabody Trust, the Improved Industrial Dwellings Company, the Society for Improving the Condition of the Labouring Classes, the Metropolitan Association for Improving the Dwellings of the Industrious Classes, and the East End Dwellings Company assumed responsibility for uplifting their new tenants. They rigidly enforced stringent codes of regulations, prohibiting subletting and taking in lodgers and banning home industries such as matchbox making. Contrary to working-class practice, rents were to be paid in advance of occupancy. The trusts forbade hanging out washing, keeping dogs, painting or papering rooms, and hanging pictures, and they required sweeping every day before ten and washing halls, steps, and lavatory windows every Saturday. Tenants had to be vaccinated and to report births, deaths, and infectious diseases to the superintendent of their building. The philanthropist Octavia Hill justified the paternalist regimentation: "It is a life of law, regular, a little monotonous, and not developing any great individuality," but supervised tenement life was at least "consistent with happy home-life, and it promises to be the life of the respectable London working-man."[15]

---

15. Octavia Hill, quoted in Charles Booth, *Life and Labour of the People in London* (1889; reprint, New York: Augustus M. Kelley, 1969), 3:31–32. Hill otherwise disapproved of the block dwellings that she judged incapable of transforming residents into worthy tenants.

Many residents resented this social control, especially the rules designed to ensure their morality, such as the locking of outside doors at 11 p.m. and the shutting off of the gas at night to get the tenants to bed at a reasonable hour. Workers refused to move from their neighborhoods with their shared sculleries, pubs, and gossip into the regimented blocks. Despite their laundries and lavatories, a number of model flats stood empty because few tenants could afford even the "reasonable" rent in the philanthropic blocks.

The construction of these massive blocks of flats, "brick boxes with slate lids" in the center of London, raised objections among the middle class as well; they idealized the self-contained family residing in a separate home of their own.[16] "It is impossible in such blocks to give any expression to homeliness," the British planner Raymond Unwin complained in a 1905 report to the International Congress on Low Priced Housing, adding "there is no place for childhood in such dwellings."[17] A growing chorus of reformers worried aloud about the lives of the families in the block dwellings with their common entrances and long corridors. The novelist George Gissing called the blocks built by the Metropolitan Association for Improving the Dwellings of the Industrious Classes a "terrible barracks... An inner courtyard, asphalted, swept clean—looking up to the sky as from a prison." He asked his readers to "picture the weltering mass of human weariness, of bestiality, of unmerited dolour, of hopeless hope, of crushed surrender, tumbled together within those forbidding walls." In their dilapidated hovels in the slums of Shooter's Gardens, the poor at least had enjoyed "independence, that is to say, the liberty to be as vile as they pleased." They lost that freedom in the Farringdon Road Buildings, "acres of these edifices... housing for the army of industrialism."[18] Rather than molding civilized individuals, the blocks massed men and their families, standing them on top of one another.

Philanthropists in London generally agreed that individual houses were preferable to blocks of flats, in terms of hygiene and morality, but argued that the housing block was the most evident means of providing for large numbers of people densely crowded in cities beset by escalating land prices. As the architect Henry Roberts reasoned: "It must be obvious that in many localities where labourers' dwellings are indispensable, it is impossible to provide them with isolated and altogether independent tenements."[19]

---

16. Henry Aldridge, Report of the Society for National Housing Reform Council for England and Wales, *Actes du VIIme Congrès International des Habitations à bon Marché tenu à Liège, du 7 au 10 Août 1905* (Liège: Imprimerie industrielle et commerciale, M. Thone, 1906).
17. Raymond Unwin, *Actes du VIIme Congrès International des Habitations à bon Marché tenu à Liège, du 7 au 10 Août 1905* (Liège: Imprimerie industrielle et commerciale, M. Thone, 1906), 81.
18. George Gissing, *The Nether World* (1889; reprint, London: Dent, 1973), 274 and 74.
19. Henry Roberts, *The Dwellings of the Labouring Classes,* 4th ed. (London: Society for Improving the Condition of the Labouring Classes, 1867), 10.

Visitors from the Continent sometimes complained about the utilitarian facades of the "vraies casernes" (true barracks), but more often they were impressed by the British philanthropists' initiative.[20] The French reformer Georges Picot's essay "Social Duty and Workers' Housing," describing British philanthropists' projects eventually inspired some French industrialists and architects to launch building projects in Paris and in Rouen. In Belgium, although Parliament had passed legislation in 1849 and 1867 to authorize investment by philanthropic organizations in worker housing and to grant building societies the stature of limited companies, few philanthropists came forward to build and supervise such housing. In part that can be explained by differences in Catholic and Protestant benevolent traditions. The Belgian typographer Joseph Dauby explained in a widely distributed advice manual addressed to workers in his Catholic country that charitable assistance destroyed the crucial initiatives of self-help, discouraging the poor from seeking work, and, as Belgian Liberals argued, threatened the natural order. In Protestant Britain, philanthropy acted as a complement to the market; in Belgium it was seen as an obstacle to individual initiative. On the Continent, it was primarily the industrialists, not the philanthropists, who took the initiative in constructing workers' housing. They built in rural areas rather than in center cities. French entrepreneurs pioneered the construction of workers' housing near rural industrial sites. In 1835, the industrialist André Koechlin built thirty-six semi-detached dwellings to lodge his employees in the rapidly expanding provincial industrial center of Mulhouse. Based on the plans of the architect Emile Muller, the Société des Cités Ouvrières (Society of Housing Estates) subsequently constructed another eight hundred houses along wide, tree-shaded streets on the estate. The individual houses surrounded by small gardens were designed to inculcate stability and frugality in their inhabitants. About 5,500 workers eventually moved to the twenty-hectare estate, which included public baths, a swimming pool, a laundry, schools, shops, and a library.

If the French could construct Mulhouse, why not "the Belgians who were so enlightened, so economically developed, and free?" a Belgian visitor to the French workers' estate asked.[21] As if in response, the Belgian architect Bruno Renard designed Le Grand Hornu, a cluster of four hundred houses,

---

20. Léonce du Castillon and Fernand Bansart, *La question des habitations et des logements à bon marché en Belgique et à l'étranger* (Brussels: Etablissements généraux d'imprimerie, 1914); Commune de Schaerbeek, *Construction d'habitations à bon marché par la commune* (Brussels: Becquart-Arien, 1898); A. Raffalovich, *Le logement de l'ouvrier et du pauvre, Etats Unis, Grande Bretagne, France, Allemagne, Belgique* (Paris, Librarie Guillaumin, 1887); *Les logements de la classe peu aisée dans le ressort du comité de patronage des habitations ouvrières et des Institutions de prévoyance pour les Communes d'Anderlecht, Laeken, Molenbeek et Saint-Gilles*, 7.

21. A. Vergote, *Amélioration des logements d'ouvriers, Rapport fait à M. le Ministre de l'Intérieur* (Brussels: l'Imprimerie de Deltombe, 1866).

around a factory near the Belgian industrial city of Mons. In addition to providing gardens and basements for each individual house, Le Grand Hornu had two public squares with fountains, a professional school for girls, a library, a bakery, and a number of other common buildings.[22] Belgian industrialists built similar groupings of workers' housing in Bois-du-Luc (Bosquetville), Mariemont, Verviers, Ghent, and Seraing, emphasizing communal structures that reproduced the hierarchy and the paternal control of the factories and mines. In 1885, a Dutch industrialist built a workers' city in a park in Delft, Agneta Park. His motto—"the factory for all, all for the factory"—made clear his paternalist goal. As in philanthropic housing, a number of workers protested against the paternal control of their employers' housing, but industrialists hailed the housing that secured a complacent labor force.[23] Middle-class visitors to these model industrial communities applauded their cleanliness and order, a marked contrast to the filth and tumult of the industrial cities.

Driven by principles quite different from those of the early industrialists, utopian socialists in France and Belgium also planned and built a number of workers' communities. Jean-Baptiste Godin, a radical republican who had been inspired by utopian socialists, organized his first utopian community at Guise, a phalanstery, a cooperative community housed in buildings constructed between two branches of the Oise River. Godin had criticized industrialists' housing estates for workers such as Mulhouse that segregated workers from the rest of society. His plan would bring together people from all walks of life in a beautiful village. The Familistère, completed in 1880, housed 1,170 people. In 1887, Godin built a second Familistère in the suburb of Laeken, on the northern edge of Brussels where he had established a foundry. This "social palace," squeezed between his foundry and a gasworks, housed seventy-five families. While less ambitious than the utopian housing estate at Guise, it provided a laundry, primary school, and nursery facilities. Communal social life, including festivals with orchestras and marches of well-behaved children, took place in the central courtyard. In accord with Godin's plans, the residents were drawn from diverse backgrounds and freed of the regimentation imposed by philanthropists on their tenants.

Both utopian socialists and industrialists anticipated restoring physical health and improving the moral behavior of the workers by removing them from their overcrowded urban neighborhoods. Their projects, unlike those of the British philanthropists in the center of London, however, did little to

22. Marinette Bruwier, Anne Merant, and Christiane Pierard "Les ateliers et la cité du Grand-Hornu," *Industrie* (January 1968): 39–56.

23. Association des maîtres de verreries belges, Commission du Travail, *Questionnaire relatif au travail industriel* (Brusssels: Ministère de l'Agriculture, de l'Industrie et des Travaux publics, 1887).

recast urban space other than to relieve the density of the urban neighborhoods. The industrialists and utopian socialists in France and Belgium effectively abandoned the city.

A third alternative to the philanthropists' urban blocks and rural workers' estates—cottages beyond the central core of the capital—gradually attracted attention on both sides of the Channel as a means of extending the ideal of separate homes to workers. In Brussels, two building associations, l'Immobilière bruxelloise (Brussels Property), composed mainly of Catholic aristocrats, and the Société anonyme des habitations ouvrières dans l'agglomération bruxellois (Limited Society for Workers' Housing in the Brussels Region), which enjoyed the support of the royal family, experimented with building outside of central Brussels. Promising a return of 4 percent per year on their investment, l'Immobilière bruxelloise enlisted subscribers to assist "honest and hard-working laborers" by providing them "the means of lodging, without paying a rent that would sap their spirit."[24] These Catholic investors financed the construction of small dwellings for laborers by building commercial establishments and housing for purchase by the middle class adjacent to the workers' housing; they assumed that the bourgeoisie would be good neighbors for the workers. The Société des habitations ouvrières built three hundred houses outside of the capital in the communes of Molenbeek and Schaerbeek/Schaarbeek and fifty houses in St.-Gilles/St.-Gillis, closer to the urban center.

In Britain, several nonprofit housing societies, including the Artizans, Labourers and General Dwellings Company, experimented with building cottages for workers on the edges of London. Unlike the Belgian housing societies that scattered their cottages, Lord Shaftesbury, a Tory and Anglican evangelical, declared his intention to create a "workmen's city." In suburban Battersea, the tree-lined Shaftesbury Park Estate provided a common recreation ground and a cooperative store but intentionally excluded pubs. The architect and editor George Godwin wrote skeptically: "We are not quite certain that we desire to see workmen's cities established. We have no desire to segregate classes."[25] The Belgian reformer Royer de Dour echoed the objection to isolated workmen's housing with its resulting social segregation. Housing estates, like the philanthropists' blocks, exacerbated tensions building between the social classes, by limiting occasions for intermixing, he explained.[26] Belgian senator and president of the Commission de

24. Cited by André-Claude Content, "L'habitat ouvrier à Bruxelles au XIXe siècle," *Belgische Tijdschrift voor nieuwste Geschiedenis/Revue belge d'histoire contemporaine* 3–4 (1977): 511.

25. George Godwin, quoted in Arthur Edwards, *The Design of Suburbia* (London: Pembridge Press, 1981), 59.

26. Hippolyte Royer de Dour, *Les habitations ouvrières* (Brussels: P. Weissenbruch, 1889), 62.

la Justice, Jules Lammens, concurred: "This separation between classes, if it really comes to pass, will result in the reversal of all that is good, human, and fraternal in Christian civilization."[27] Like other Belgian Catholics, he preferred to site small pockets of workers' housing into existing mixed neighborhoods throughout the capital.

Belgian Liberals, for their part, saw nothing wrong with the British designs for cottage estates. The British-born engineer and managing director of a number of Belgian railway companies, Georges Montefiore Levi, proposed new workers' quarters around Brussels separate from but near the middle-class districts. Removed from the shadowy promiscuity of the slums, the respectable workers could be publicly observed in their new homes, but the bourgeoisie would continue to enjoy their own privacy. The Liberals assumed that the free market would properly redistribute housing as increased industrialization lowered the price of housing and made it available and affordable for workers.

Throughout this experimental housing period of the 1860s and 1870s, as the condition of the poor in the cities became increasingly dire, philanthropists, industrialists, and public health officials watched each other intently across the Channel, drawing lessons from the setbacks of those who ventured before them. Reformers noted the differences in philanthropic initiative. Belgian reformers observed with envy the profusion of British building societies actively engaged in housing the poor in the British capital. Over three decades, British philanthropists spent about 6,500,000 pounds to house 29,700 families on 254 sites in London, about 4 percent of the entire population of London.[28] By 1886, all of the Belgian housing societies together had constructed only 1,093 houses for 8,484 people, many of them artisans, not workers. Even the industrialists seemed to have lost interest in their workers. Reformers in France and Belgium protested: "Talk to them of the social crisis, of the misery of the working class... they ask what it has to do with them?... Ask them to contribute to a philanthropic or social work, and they will invariably respond, 'What do I stand to gain from it?'"[29] Economic liberalism prevailed on both sides of the Channel at the end of the nineteenth century.

In neither country was there much tolerance for direct governmental intervention. Reformers in Belgium and Britain had been able to justify action by municipalities in such recognized public arenas as sanitation, but not in the

27. M. Lammens, *Congrès des oeuvres sociales*. Liège, 26–29 September, 1886 (Liège: Imprimerie et Lithographie De Marteau, 1886), 276.

28. Burnett, *Social History of Housing*, 178. See also Susannah Morris, "Organizational Innovation in Victorian Social Housing," *Nonprofit and Voluntary Sector Quarterly* 31, no. 2 (June 2002): 188.

29. *Moniteur des Comités de patronage et des sociétés d'habitations ouvrières* (25 August 1899).

housing market. On matters of public health such as the provision of water and sewage, medical professionals had weighed in with expert opinions, providing reformers with a solid rationale for legislation in national parliaments and for enforcement of regulations by municipal councils. Housing, however, was too closely tied to private concerns, too intimately linked with the individual, too readily supplied by the market, at least in theory. Frustrated Belgian reformers grumbled that "the exaggerated respect for private property has caused public authorities to tolerate the most glaring abuses."[30] In London, as in Brussels, until the 1880s, "the real crisis years of the housing movement," reformers assumed that individual workers and their families could be salvaged from the slums through individual efforts.[31] That labor force, arriving in ever-increasing numbers in the national capitals, overwhelmed the pockets of blocks and cottages constructed and overseen by philanthropists, industrialists, and utopian socialists.

Ernest Dewsnup from Britain despaired of the difficulty of the task: "The diagnosis of a disease is one thing, its cure another, and so of housing evils their identification is simple, the tracing of their origin comparatively easy, but their amelioration remains a matter of singular perplexity."[32] By the end of the nineteenth century, few reformers still assumed that if left to their own devices, the market—private housing developers and speculators—would solve the problems of the urban environment. The building trades clearly preferred to build for the more lucrative middle-class market.[33] But what were the alternatives?

"Demolished, Embellished, but Little Improved": Government Commissions

The more housing conditions in the capital were investigated, the more statistics were collected on overcrowding, "the more terrible and appalling

30. Ville de Gand, *Proposition du Collège concernant la construction d'habitations pour les ouvriers* (Ghent: Annoot-Braeckman, 1868).
31. John Nelson Tarn, *Five Per Cent Philanthropy: An Account of Housing in Urban Areas between 1840 and 1914* (Cambridge: Cambridge University Press, 1973), 114.
32. Ernest Dewsnup, *The Housing Problem in London* (Manchester: Manchester University Press, 1907), 211.
33. British historians disagree about the pace of the new construction and whether the British building industry was to blame for the shortage. Andrew Wohl explains that no building industry could have kept up with population growth. In particular, the nineteenth-century British builders operated on a small scale and preferred to construct for the middle class. John Burnett suggests that the rate of housing construction kept pace with a population growth in Britain. The problem was one of distribution. See Anthony S. Wohl, *Endangered Lives: Public Health in Victorian Britain* (London: Methuen, 1984), 290; John Burnett, *A Social History of Housing* (London: David & Charles, 1978), 139.

does the problem appear," one London housing reformer lamented.[34] Francis Rivington, another reformer, opened his exposé of the London housing crisis by acknowledging: "The wretched condition of the dwellings of the lower classes in the metropolis and other populous places has been so fully and frequently described, and has attracted such general sympathy and regret, that it appears superfluous at the present time to enlarge upon it or enter into the distressing details now so widely known and so deeply deplored."[35] Nonetheless, Rivington set off on his own investigation, convinced that additional information would alert the poor to their misery and prod the better off to lend assistance.

The first response to the deteriorating housing crisis on both sides of the Channel was to compile more statistics; the "multitudes of social fears seemed to require a numerical scaffolding for containment," the historian Lynn Lees explains.[36] In the 1880s, the British and the Belgian governments commissioned national panels of experts to collect additional facts to document the squalid conditions of workmen's housing. The French housing reformer, Emile Cheysson, lauded the two national investigations that revealed the conscience of these pioneering reformers.[37] The official Belgian and British reports inspired the French Société d'Economie Sociale (Society of Social Economy) and the German Verein fur Sozialpolitik (Association for Social Politics) to launch their own investigations of working-class housing. The crowding of workers into cellars and hovels in the center of Amsterdam led the Dutch Maatschappij tot Nut van 't Algemeen (Dutch Society for the Benefit of the Community) to issue a report in 1890 on workmen's housing that called for national housing legislation.

In 1880, the defeat of the Tory government empowered the British Liberals to chart a new course that would call into question the last twenty years of British housing legislation. In May 1881, Prime Minister William Gladstone named a Select Committee on Artizans' and Labourers' Dwellings Improvement followed in 1884 by the appointment of a Royal Commission on Housing of the Working Classes. In Belgium, after riots in 1886 threatened to spread from the mines of southern Belgium to cities throughout Belgium, the Catholic government also appointed a commission to study the condition of the working class. This Belgian Commission du Travail (Labor

34. Arthur Sherwell, *Life in West London: A Study and a Contrast* (London: Methuen & Co., 1897), 34–35.

35. Francis Rivington, *A New Proposal for Providing Improved Dwellings for the Poor upon an Adequate Scale in the Metropolis and Other Populous Places* (London: W. Skeffington and Son, 1880).

36. Lynn Hollen Lees, *The Solidarities of Strangers: The English Poor Laws and the People, 1700–1948* (Cambridge: Cambridge University Press, 1998), 247.

37. Emile Cheysson, "Trois lois récentes sur les habitations ouvrières en Belgique, en Angleterre et en Autriche," *Revue d'hygiène et de police sanitaire* (1892): 291.

Commission) consciously emulated the British in its study of workmen's lodging, but they diverged in their recommendations, launching the two countries on a different course of reform.

The British Select Committee first solicited reports from local medical officers who detailed the unsanitary conditions of London districts previously condemned as "fever nests." The officers testified that it would not be worth "the powder and the shot" to repair the dilapidated housing and that slums should be razed to the ground.[38] On the other side, the Reverend Canon Gilbert pointed out that tenants displaced by earlier clearance schemes had crowded into single rooms in the center of London, near their families, friends, and work, rather than moving to available suburban cottages or into philanthropists' urban blocks. Gilbert had heard a great deal of grumbling about the clearance and rehousing schemes among the tenants and warned "with all respect, that the way in which the poor are treated, and the want of consideration shown them, is tending to drive the poor of London to democracy and republicanism."[39]

When Sir Sydney Waterlow, a member of the Select Committee, asked Samuel R. Lovett, the medical officer for St. Giles, if it was not a good idea to build housing for unskilled laborers near their work, Lovett replied blithely: "Yes; but these people, I say, can get a living anywhere; you are not throwing any great responsibility upon them by shifting their lodgings."[40] Like a number of other witnesses, Lovett looked toward the suburbs. Waterlow pursued his line of questioning: "Have you any knowledge of the nature of the suburbs of London; do you think people of this class can get their living in the suburbs where there are very few shops, and where 19 houses out of 20 are private houses?"[41] Another committee member, William Torrens, author of earlier housing legislation, interrupted a medical officer who had advocated commuting by train but could not cite the price of the workmen's tickets, suggesting sarcastically that workers would enjoy riding in hansom cabs, too, but for the question of cost.

Most witnesses before the Select Committee were middle-class professionals, but workers, too, testified, adding arguments not heard from the medical officers and public health officials. They explained that neighbors depended on each other. While it was true that workers moved often, they stayed within the same neighborhood. They shared a strong sense of place, and, that place was the center of London.

---

38. Select Committee on Artizan's and Labourers' Dwellings Improvements, British Parliamentary Papers (1881): 7:3.
39. Rev. Canon Gilbert, 16 March 1882, Select Committee on Artizan's and Labourers' Dwellings Improvements, British Parliamentary Papers (1882): 7:75.
40. Mr. Lovett, 27 June 1881, Ibid., 32.
41. Sir Waterlow, 27 June 1881, Ibid., 32.

Members of the Select Committee pressed witnesses for information about transportation and work available for family members forced to move out of their neighborhoods by slum clearance. Dock workers and costermongers hawking produce from the carts had to live in central neighborhoods close to their work because trains from the suburbs would not get them to the gates at the docks for the daily 6 a.m. workers' call. The wives of these "casual laborers" also relied on wages from work in the city center, unlike the wives of the better-paid workers who did not need to work to supplement the family income. Select Committee members also inquired about the supply of food in outlying neighborhoods, given the poor's dependence on the cheap markets of central London.

In the end, despite all the testimony to the contrary, the British Select Committee advocated suburban development as the only feasible solution to rehouse the workers displaced by city clearance schemes, its basic assumption that "dispersion is healthy, and aggregation is a great intensification of the evil."[42] The Select Committee's final report called for the provision of better train transport for workmen at reasonable fares and for stricter regulations on suburban construction. The Committee recommended not a complete overhaul of the complex existing legislation, but its amendment. The Artisans' Dwellings Act of 1882 was the result.

The report of the Royal Commission on Housing of the Working Classes of 1884 went further than the Select Committee in dispelling any remaining comfortable assumptions that the overcrowding of London had been solved by the efforts of philanthropists. Lord Salisbury testified that two to three hundred people still lived in the long, dark alleys where he was shocked to find, "there was but one accommodation for the whole of that number."[43] Walking through the narrow alleys, he could reach out his arms and touch both sides; the sunlight never penetrated the "foul" space. The Commission acknowledged that improvements had been made, especially for skilled laborers, but concluded that, in general, "the overcrowding has become very serious, much more serious than it ever was." The slums had been swept away, but not the people, especially "the classes that live hand to mouth, large numbers of whom rise every morning and do not know what job they will do in the day."[44] The Royal Commission underscored the mounting skepticism that the housing trusts alone could alleviate the suffering of the urban poor. There was not sufficient housing available at affordable rents. Even workers who did not drink and who worked regularly were forced to

42. Mr. Torrens, 27 June 1881, Ibid., 48.
43. Lord Salisbury, Royal Commission on Housing of the Working Classes, First report of Her Majesty's Commissioners for Inquiring into the Housing of the Working Classes, Minutes of Evidence (London: Eyre and Spottiswoode, 1885), 2:44.
44. Ibid., 2:5 and 44.

seek shelter for their families in the slums; their housing problems were not caused by a lack of individual responsibility.

The Belgian Commission du Travail of 1886 followed the British example in gathering data, distributing an extensive questionnaire, and interviewing workers, employers, union officials, philanthropic associations, and public health officials. Even more vociferously than in Britain, reformers in Belgium acknowledged the total failure of philanthropic societies to alleviate the housing crisis. Belgian witnesses lauded the work of the British philanthropists in building tenements, noting that all the while, the Belgians had merely "demolished, embellished, but on the whole, from the point of view of sanitation, little improved."[45] Most troubling, the Belgians had built little housing to replace what had been torn down. Dauby, editor of the official state journal, *Le Moniteur Belge,* argued that, in Brussels, the clearance of slums had made worker housing worse than when he began to protest conditions decades earlier. Workers still sought lodging in single rooms in the impasses, but now were paying a much larger share, 25 to 30 percent of their salaries, for the privilege of subsisting in squalor. One Brussels building society, frustrated by the limited provisions of Belgian housing legislation, grumbled: "In a word, we are in favor of any means at all that has as its goal the improvement of workers' housing, it is quite simple."[46]

Workers themselves testified that it was now absolutely impossible to find affordable housing in the Belgian capital. A Brussels printer, Gustave Conrardy, explained that exorbitant rents forced families to seek lodging in truly miserable impasses "where the air is tainted and corrupted by all sorts of emanations, where light barely penetrates and the sun never shines."[47]

He acknowledged that lodging was cheaper outside of Brussels but, echoing British workers, reminded commissioners that commuting workers had to leave at 4:30 in the morning to get to work by 6:00. That was no life. Commuting laborers corroborated his testimony, describing their exhaustion after a fifteen-hour day of work and travel. Workers who walked long distances to work complained about the expense of eating a midday meal in a restaurant because they could not return home to eat. The additional cost of transport in trams, buses, and trains made living outside the city even less affordable for the commuting laborers.

On the other hand, as in London, Belgian reformers cited the benefits in dispersing workers through the countryside away from the immoral influences of the city. A number of officials commented favorably on the comparatively low cost of workmen's fares on the national Belgian railways. The

45. Commission du Travail, *Questionnaire relatif au travail industriel* (Brussels: Ministère de l'Agriculture, de l'Industrie et des Travaux publics, 1887).
46. Société anonyme de Marcinelle et Couillet, Commission du Travail, *Questionnaire,* 610.
47. Gustave Conrardy, Commission du Travail, *Questionnaire,* 582.

overwhelming majority of Brussels employers agreed with British reformers that, ideally, workers would live in the countryside and be linked to their work in the city by train.

Delegates to the Belgian Commission split along party lines in their recommendations for action. One Catholic legislator identified "the problem of popular housing as the social question that elicits the most passionate debate. . . . It is connected to the most essential interests of nations and individuals. Health, morality, temperance, the spirit of family, patriotism, in short all of the major virtues that constitute the force of a race are tied up in it."[48] On the other side of the ideological divide, the Belgian Socialist Hector Denis, quoting French housing reformers, Emile Muller and Emile Cacheux, and British economists such as Henry Fawcett, argued that private capital had done little to resolve the housing crisis on either side of the Channel. Denis proposed the organization of a national administration to coordinate public and private initiatives in Belgium.[49]

The Belgian Commission disbanded without proposing a plan of legislative action. But that had never been its intention, according to the minister of agriculture, industry, and public works, le Chevalier de Moreau d'Andoye. A disciple of the French sociologist Fréderic Le Play, the Catholic minister had cautioned at the outset: "The government does not exaggerate the influence that its intervention through legislation could have in the domain of worker questions. In this question the role of particular individuals is more important than that of the state and measures realized by individual initiative will always have a greater success than those where public powers try to impose obligations."[50] For Belgian Catholics and Liberals alike, housing remained an issue to be resolved by individuals, despite the dearth of philanthropic ventures. The frustrated Belgian Socialist leader César de Paepe inquired why the Socialists had agreed to serve on a commission alongside "the flowers of the Belgian plutocracy, government bureaucrats, and landlords?" Did they really expect the powerful men who had "shot dead rioting workers" to approve a plan of government action?[51]

---

48. Jules Derbaix, cited by Annick Stélandre, "Contribution à l'histoire des habitations ouvrières 1889–1919," Mémoire présenté en vue de l'obtention du grade de licenciée en philosophie et lettres group histoire, 1982–1983, Université libre de Bruxelles.

49. Hector Denis, Commission du Travail, *Comptes Rendus des Séances plénières: Mémoires, rapports, lettres, etc. envisageant la question ouvrière dans son ensemble* (Brussels: Société belge de librairie, 1888), 4:169.

50. Jean-Pierre Nandrin, "La laborieuse genèse du droit social belge: Un utopie récupérée?" in *La question sociale en Belgique et au Canada,* ed. G. Kurgan-van Hentenryk (Brussels: Presses de l'Université libre de Bruxelles, 1988), 124.

51. César De Paepe, quoted in Etienne Fourier, "La Commission du Travail et l'amorce de la legislation sociale," in *La révolte des damnés de la terre,* ed. Etienne Fourier and Daniel Pector (Charleroi: Le Progrès, 1986), 55. For a breakdown of the membership of the commission, see Eliane Gubin, "Les Enquêtes sur le travail en Belgique et au Canada à la fin du 19e siècle,"

In Britain, the Workmen's National Housing Council followed a similar line of reasoning, questioning the need for further reports and the gathering of more statistics. It argued that the solution to the housing problem was not nearly as complex as all of the middle-class "statesmen," whether reformers or industrialists or politicians, seemed to think. The Council quoted the chief sanitary inspector for Bethnal Green, who had finally, after a great deal of study, endorsed "the position we have always taken," proclaiming: "It seems such useless, tiresome repetition to report year after year that so many of the poorest and most wretched of our people have again been driven about pillar to post, hunted out of one wretched 'home' into another, and each one more squalid than the one before, all because of their inability to pay rents impossible to their straitened circumstances."[52] No more studies were needed. Overcrowding clearly resulted from poor peoples' inability to pay the required rents, the Housing Council asserted; slums were the result of poverty.

"A Healthy, Respectable, Independent Lodging": National Legislation

The official British and Belgian investigations providing further evidence of the urgency of the housing crisis spurred legislative action throughout Europe. The Belgian and British parliaments passed radically different housing acts in the 1890s, laying the groundwork for a European wave of legislation to encourage slum clearance, regulate private speculation, and facilitate the construction of housing to accommodate the ever-expanding urban labor force.

Two years after publication of the Belgian Commission's report, in 1889 the Catholic majority in the Belgian parliament enacted legislation that would define the course of Belgian housing policy through the First World War. The ultimate goal of the Belgian legislation was not to provide rental accommodation, as the British philanthropists had done, but instead to make available housing for purchase by frugal working families. One year later, the British Housing of the Working Classes Act of 1890, taken together with the Reform of Local Government Acts of 1888 and 1894, encouraged British municipalities to intervene directly, clearing land and constructing housing for rental.

These radically different paths inspired study, if not emulation, by French, Dutch, Italian, and German housing reformers. The Siegfried law passed in

in *La question sociale,* ed. Kurgan-van Hentenryk (Brussels: Presses de l'Université libre de Bruxelles, 1988), 93–113.

52. John Foot, *Housing Journal* (April 1907).

France in 1894 promoted the construction of inexpensive housing by associations with credit and tax exemptions from the national government. French housing reformers consciously rejected the British example. Modeled on Belgian legislation, the Siegfried law spurred the organization of new housing societies, which constructed 1,400 houses between 1895 and 1902. French housing reformer Georges Picot compared the five million francs invested in housing by the French to the fifty million invested by the Caisse générale d'épargne et de retraite (CGER; the semi-public savings and loan bank) in Belgium: "A small country six times less populated than ours has accomplished a project ten times larger," he declared.[53] In contrast, the Dutch Woningwet (housing law) of 1901 required municipalities to draft and enforce building codes, pledging financial assistance to nonprofit housing associations and to local authorities to build inexpensive housing for the working class. The municipality assumed a much more direct role in regulating construction; the code of Amsterdam issued in 1905 filled 340 pages.

The Belgian housing legislation of 1889 established Comités officiels de patronage des habitations ouvrières/Beschermingscomiteiten der Werkmanswoningen (Official Patronage Committees for Workmen's Housing) to oversee existing nonprofit housing societies and to encourage the creation of new ones. Rather than building workmen's housing themselves, the Patronage Committees were empowered by Parliament to review plans submitted by private housing societies. These committees were to recommend projects to the CGER, which, in turn, extended loans to the private housing societies at a rate of 2.5 percent. That allowed housing societies to use their capital for construction rather than holding it in reserve and to set rents that guaranteed their investors a 4 to 5 percent profit. Even though the Belgian housing societies and charitable bureaus had built comparatively few houses by the end of 1886, Liberals and Catholics in Parliament believed that these private reformers held the key to solving the intensifying housing crisis.

The new law effectively revitalized the all-but-moribund housing construction programs in Belgium, especially in rural areas. Before 1889, charitable institutions had contributed only about 8,864,000 francs to Belgian workers' housing; between 1889 and 1911, the CGER advanced 99,342,117 francs for construction of 3,850 workers' houses.[54] Within the Brussels agglomeration, eight housing societies and four cooperative credit societies worked with the Patronage Committees.[55]

53. Georges Picot, quoted in Roger-Henri Guerrand, *Une Europe en construction: Deux siècles d'habitat social en Europe* (Paris: Editions La Découverte, 1992), 81.

54. F. Hankar, A. Van Billoen, and A. Van Melle, *Les Habitations ouvrières en Belgique. exposition internationale de Milan en 1906* (Brussels: Imprimerie A. Lesigne, 1906).

55. Annick Stélandre, "Les habitations ouvrières dans la région bruxelloise: l'application de la loi de 1889," *Bulletin Trimestriel: Le Crédit Communal* (1991): 71–96. The eight housing societies were the Société anonyme des Prêts Etterbeek, the Société Anonyme Crédit Watermael,

The Belgian housing legislation of 1889 also extended fiscal privileges directly to workers to purchase land and to construct housing. By law, individuals claiming these tax exemptions had to obtain a certificate from their local Patronage Committee declaring them to be workers as defined by the 1889 legislation; that is, as employees who depended on their wages and who worked with their hands. The law made no distinction between agricultural and industrial workers, but it explicitly excluded artisans and small businessmen. Legislators assumed that their housing needs would be met by the private market. Between 1892 and 1900, the fifty-two Patronage Committees issued 60,064 certificates to individual workers for loans from the CGER to construct housing throughout Belgium.[56]

"It is a true crusade that must be undertaken in Brussels and throughout the country," one Brussels housing society proclaimed as it launched a campaign "to restore family life and to improve the home."[57] The Brussels Patronage Committees and housing societies took their duties to improve the workers' lives seriously, regularly visiting urban families housed in two or fewer rooms. "We intend to accomplish good works, not just offering simple charity, but securing the moral and physical rehabilitation of the tenants," the Patronage Committee of Brussels East vowed.[58] The visitors recorded wages earned against rent paid and savings invested in mutual societies. Much like the British philanthropists, the Belgian housing societies evaluated and instructed the wives in budgeting and in cleaning, and noted and approved of children attending school or serving apprenticeships.

The Committee awarded annual prizes "for order, cleanliness and savings" to superior households, the "elite" of the working class, in competitions designed to stimulate improvement among "the worthy mothers of families, the hope of the nation."[59] The ceremonies were attended by communal representatives, mayors, members of the Patronage Committees,

---

Travail et Propriété, 't Eigen Huis Best, Le Coin de Feu, La Familie, and Prévoyance Molenbeekoise. The four cooperative credit societies were the Société Crédit, the Société Cooperative de Laeken, Le Foyer Bruxellois, and the Société Ixelles.

56. Marcel Smets, *L'Avènement de la cité-jardin en Belgique. Histoire de l'habitat social en Belgique de 1830 à 1930* (Brussels: Pierre Mardaga, 1976), 49.

57. Association pour l'amélioration des logements ouvrières. Comité de Bruxelles Est, Fonds Fauconnier, Boîte 46, Archives de la Ville de Bruxelles/Stadsarchief, Brussels.

58. Ibid.

59. *Moniteur des Comités de patronage et des sociétés d'habitations ouvrières* (10 October 1893): 1; Ville de Bruxelles, Comité de patronage des habitations ouvrières et des institutions de prévoyance, *Enquêtes sur les logements, les ressources & la prévoyance des ouvriers à Bruxelles* (Brussels: Imprimerie des institutions de prévoyance, 1897); *Compte rendu de la remise officielle des prix d'ordre, de propreté de d'épargne* (16 February 1896) (Brussels: Alliance typographique, 1896); Comité officiel de patronage des habitations ouvrières et des institutions de prévoyance pour les communes Ouest de l'agglomération bruxelloise, *Compte rendu de la remise officielle des prix d'ordre, de propreté et d'épargne* (9 December 1894) (Saint-Gilles: J. B. Schaumans, 1895); "Bulletin de renseignement sur les ménages participant au concours

government ministers, and even Prince Albert. In a typical address to an audience of assembled dignitaries and working women, the Belgian minister of agriculture preached the rewards of domestic virtue to the assembled model working-class families: "If your husband, your son, exhausted from his work comes home and finds everything clean, in order and shining, if the food is delicious, then he will not go elsewhere to find his pleasure, but he will stay home." He rhapsodized: "Oh, in such a house it is so pleasant to gather around the hearth! Men will readily sing the old song, that you all know so well: Where could men better be, it is truly there that men shall sing: East, West, house best!"[60] The Committee, acknowledging the efficacy of prize competitions as propaganda, cited "the authority of the English" as "our model on this question as on so many others."[61]

In contrast with British reformers, who sought to expand affordable rental options for the working poor, expecting to domesticate them by controlling their environment, the Brussels Patronage Committees believed that frugal, hard-working laborers ought to aspire to home ownership. Instead of lodging workers in rented "barracks," they sought to house them in individual cottages they could one day hope to buy. Dauby summarized the hopes of the housing reformers: "Locate a healthy and comfortable lodging for the worker[, and] you inculcate in him the joys of family life, . . . you attach him to the industrial factory, . . . and in the end you inspire in him the desire and give him the possibility of becoming a property owner."[62] Workers who aspired to own property would not make the improvident expenditures so characteristic of the poor; they would not be dependent on charitable assistance. By encouraging the goal of home ownership, the housing societies would "inculcate little by little into the working populations, the special faculties that have distinguished the bourgeois classes, the moral forces that have come through a long series of struggle, the traditions of a series of meritorious generations."[63] The Belgian Patronage Committees and housing societies distributed house plans and found plots of land for

et/ou correspondance divers," Fonds "Maisons Ouvrières," Boîte 10, Archives de la Ville de Bruxelles/Stadsarchief, Brussels.

60. Quoted in Annick Stélandre, "Contribution à l'histoire des habitations ouvrières 1889–1919;" "Les Habitations ouvrières," *Vers l'Avenir* (Brussels: Société anonyme belge d'imprimerie, 1912); Hippolyte Royer de Dour, *Les habitations ouvrières* (Brussels: P. Weissenbruch, 1889), 79; Alex Bidart, *L'exposition du mobilier ouvrier à Saint-Gilles* (Brussels: L.G. Laurent, 1901).

61. Compte rendu de la remise officielle des prix d'ordre, de propreté de d'épargne, Saint-Gilles, 16 février 1896 (Brussels: Alliance typographique, 1896); Comité officiel de patronage des habitations ouvrières et des institutions de prévoyance pour les communes ouest de l'agglomération bruxelloise, *Rapport annuel, 1894* (Bruxelles: Alliance typographique, 1895).

62. Jean Dauby, *La question ouvrière en Belgique: Causes de nos Crises ouvrières; remèdes possibles* (Brussels: Librairie de A.-N. Lebègue et Cie., 1871), 45–46.

63. Royer de Dour, *Les habitations ouvrières,* 79; Alex Bidart, *L'exposition du mobilier ouvrier à Saint-Gilles* (Brussels: L.G. Laurent, 1901).

Invitation to the Awards Ceremony from the Molenbeek Committee for the Association pour l'amélioration des logements ouvriers (Association for the Improvement of Workers' Housing). Reproduced with permission from the Archives de la Ville De Bruxelles/Stadsarchief, Brussels.

individual workers, as directed by the 1889 legislation. "Procure for him a healthy, comfortable, independent lodging, that will moralize him," a progressive Catholic group concluded.[64]

Home ownership prevailed in the dreams of French and Belgian planners in a way that it did not elsewhere in Europe. Reformers from around Europe traveled to Belgium to study the results of the 1889 law. French reformer Jules Siegfried wondered: "Who can fail to see to what extent the hope of becoming a proprietor makes a man more hard working, more thrifty, more regular in his habits."[65] Rooted in the earth, home-owning workers, like the bourgeoisie, would live frugally, avoid the carnival, and eschew the comradeship and disorder of the café. Similarly, his fellow countryman, Emile Cheysson, rhapsodized: "Owning his own house completely makes a

64. *Rapport sur la Question des habitations ouvrières, présenté à l'assemblée générale de la fédération des sociétés ouvrières catholiques belges tenue les 3 et 4 décembre 1878.*

65. Jules Siegfried, quoted in Nicholas Bullock and James Read, *The Movement for Housing Reform in Germany and France, 1840–1914* (Cambridge: Cambridge University Press, 1985), 323.

"This is my house. I am king here." Pride in home ownership.
One workman showing another his cottage.
From K. Beyaert, "Helpt u zelf," pamphlet (1901).

man. . . . It is in truth the house that possesses him, that moralizes, and stabilizes him, that transforms him."[66]

A housing reformer from Liège, Ernest Mahaim, pointed out rather smugly, "the legislation was perfectly conceived to fit the Belgian spirit." The state had eased the way for private enterprise to tackle the social problem, he explained, in conscious contrast to the British. This was the Belgian way, because it "encouraged liberty."[67] The 1889 legislation did not infringe on the rights of private property; it encouraged private development.

In the hope of achieving such a property-owning electorate, some British Tories advocated programs like the Belgian one that allowed local authorities to advance money to private individuals for the purchase of homes. These Tories argued not only for giving the working man a stake in society but also for removing the middleman from the housing market. Their proposals did not command a consensus since few British reformers assumed that workers, even the most elite, would be prepared to assume the risk of a mortgage.

It could be argued that the British Housing of the Working Classes Act of 1890 and the reform of local government acts of 1888 and 1894 carried

66. Emile Cheysson, quoted in R. Butler and P. Noisette, *De la cité ouvrière au grand ensemble: La politique capitaliste du logement social, 1815–1975* (Paris: Maspero, 1977), 52.
67. Ernest Mahaim, "La législation sociale en Belgique, 1869–1919," 167.

out the goals of the British Royal Commission of 1884, just as the 1889 Belgian legislation was the Belgian parliament's response to the 1886 Belgian Commission. A growing number of reformers in Britain were beginning to suspect that: "Private enterprise unstimulated, unregulated, unassisted, undirected, has hopelessly failed."[68] British consensus on the housing question, which had shifted earlier from reliance on the market to reliance on philanthropy, was moving toward a consideration of municipal action to supplement the market and philanthropy.

The Housing of the Working Classes Act of 1890 made it possible for municipalities to intervene to resolve the housing crisis, giving the newly created London County Council authority to purchase land for redevelopment. The legislation authorized the British equivalent of the Belgian CGER, the Public Works Loan Commission, to make advances for the construction of workmen's housing, but it went further in providing for building of this housing directly by local authorities or by charitable enterprises. The Council was required to submit an improvement scheme for expropriated lands demonstrating that it would rehouse at least as many people as had been displaced by the improvement scheme itself. Subsequent laws passed in 1891, 1894, and 1903 facilitated the inspection and encouraged the clearance of housing deemed a public health nuisance, and recognized the role of municipal authorities in building and in managing rental housing for the working class.

While in Belgium the activist CGER offered loans to housing and credit societies at 2 percent, the British Public Works Loan Commission was consigned by law to a more marginal position. Before the British parliament's passage in 1899 of the Small Dwellings Acquisition Act, it was impossible for municipalities to advance funds to tenants for purchase of homes.[69] In Britain at the turn of the century, renting remained the most viable option for workers as well as for vast segments of the middle class. Fewer than 10 percent of all British households owned their own house at the end of the nineteenth century.[70] In 1870, 57 percent of Belgian households owned their own home, although that percentage declined gradually over the next three decades.[71] Brussels printer Gustave Conrardy testified to the

68. W. Thompson, *The Housing Handbook* (London: National Housing Reform Council, 1903), 9.
69. It could be argued that the difference in rates of home ownership reflected the land holding systems in the two capitals. London development followed the building-lease system in which plots belonged to landlords, including institutions such as the city or church commissioners. Plots were rented to builders, typically on ninety-nine-year leases. In contrast, the free-hold system operated in Brussels, whereby the land for a building was purchased outright. On the other hand, property sold without the added cost of land, as in London, presumably should have been less expensive and so in fact more affordable than in Brussels.
70. Colin G. Pooley, "England and Wales," in *Housing Strategies in Europe, 1880–1930* (London: Leicester University Press, 1992), 73–104.
71. Eric Vanhaute, "'Chacun est propriétaire ou espère le devenir.' Het Grondbezit in Vlaanderen begin 19de-begin 20ste eeuw," *Belgisch Tijdschrift voor nieuwste Geschiedenis/ Revue belge d'histoire contemporaine* (1996): 114.

Belgian commission in 1866: "For those who think that simple workers could become owners of their houses, I think that would be a bitter irony to believe in such a possibility."[72] Of the 6,756 very poorest households surveyed in Brussels, only 26, or 0.4 percent, owned their own dwellings.[73] Brussels officials Charles Lagasse and Charles De Quéker calculated that at the average wage of a Brussels worker of 960 francs per year, 1,174 francs including the money brought in by a working wife and children, few if any workers would ever be able to buy a house or flat within the cities.[74] Most workers would remain renters, both in Brussels and in London, Lagasse and De Quéker conceded.

Nevertheless, most Belgian reformers appear to have been satisfied with the early results of their national legislation that emphasized home ownership. The law of 1889 overcame "the inertia and the obstacles that had previously blocked urgent and important reform."[75] The Belgians had also avoided a semi-collectivism that would impose obligations and expenses on the municipality and bestow on the state direct paternal control over workers and their families. Between 1889 and 1911, the Belgian government advanced 41,191,717 francs worth of tax reductions and exemptions for construction of housing overseen by semi-private Patronage Committees.[76]

British and Belgian reformers both claimed at the turn of the twentieth century to have learned the lessons of their earlier reliance on the market alone and on limited charitable endeavors. Ironically, while the Belgian law of 1889 was premised on the assumption that charitable endeavors encouraged by the government would effectively render assistance to the poor, it was the British not the Belgians who had the wealth of experience with philanthropic involvement in housing. The British by the 1890s had found charitable activism wanting and looked to the municipality for assistance in alleviating the deepening housing crisis in their capital. Over the next two decades, Belgian reformers observed the differences that separated their experience from that of the British, many proudly declaring that they had

72. G. Conrardy, Commission du Travail. *Questionnaire relatif au travail industriel* (Brussels: Ministère de l'Agriculture, de l'Industrie et des Travaux publics, 1887), 582. It should be noted that in the 1905–1910 housing census of Brussels, only 26 of the 6,756 worker households owned their own dwellings. Patricia Van den Eeckhout, "Belgium," in *Housing Strategies in Europe, 1880–1930,* ed. Colin G. Pooley (London: Leicester University Press, 1992), 197.
73. Emile Hellemans, cited by Patricia Van den Eeckhout, "Belgium," in Colin G. Pooley, *Housing Strategies in Europe, 1880–1930* (London: Leicester University Press, 1992), 197.
74. MM. Lagasse and De Quéker, Comité officiel de patronage des habitations ouvrières et institutions de prévoyance de Schaerbeek, Saint-Josse-ten-Noode et Evère, "Deuxième rapport annuel sur les travaux du Comité en 1902," (Brussels: L.G. Laurent, 1902), 49.
75. Albert Soenens, *Les habitations ouvrières en Belgique: Extrait des Pandectes Belges* (Brussels: Veuve Ferdinand Larcier, 1894), 3; Comité de patronage, Bruxelles (16 March 1906), Habitations à bon marché, Boîte 6, Archives de la Ville de Bruxelles/Stadsarchief Brussel, Brussels.
76. F. Hankar, A. Van Billoen, and A. Van Melle, *Les Habitations ouvrières en Belgique: Expostion internationale de Milan en 1906* (Brussels: Imprimerie A. Lesigne, 1906), 166.

found a very Belgian—that is, a more private—alternative to the British plan of municipal intervention in housing.

In June 1889 the first International Congress on Low-Cost Housing convened in Paris, gathering together municipal officials, architects, and physicians, among others, to discuss the roles of charity, private industry, national legislation, and municipal governments in housing the poor. Dutch municipal officials read Belgian sanitation reports, Belgian architects looked to German land legislation, and the German physicians visited philanthropic blocks constructed in London. A British delegate to the congress, William Thompson, cited the investment of the CGER for emulation by his countrymen; a Belgian delegate, Charles De Quéker, told Belgian architects to study the efficient housing plans designed by British planners. Delegates subsequently convened congresses in Antwerp, Bordeaux, Brussels, and, again, in Paris to report on new strategies for assuring order in collective dwellings and for planting gardens alongside workers' dwellings. Highlights of the 1905 meeting in London included excursions to housing projects constructed by the London County Council and to garden cities, such as Bourneville and Port Sunlight, the first outside Birmingham and the second near Liverpool.[77] Built by philanthropic industrialists, these new urban centers were planned and built in open spaces away from congestion, offering residents a healthy environment. Delegates returned from the Continent full of admiration for the activism of British housing reformers.

"A Workman's Paradise": Municipal Housing

The London County Council was created in 1889, built on the rising tide of national reform. It had a mandate to establish a municipal identity for London and to tackle the urgent social problems left untouched by national legislation. Brussels was less successful, though no less energetic, in its struggle for self-government. Despite a century of attempts to annex the suburban *faubourgs*—the eighteen communes surrounding the central, pentagon-shaped commune of Brussels retained their status as autonomous villages. There was no central municipal administration linking them as there was in London.

Alfred Smith, the head of the Housing Committee of the newly organized London County Council argued in 1900 that there was more than enough room for municipal intervention alongside private development in this "city teeming with slums and rookeries, the outcome of generations of apathy and neglect."[78] The Council appointed medical investigators, cleared unsanitary slums, and planned blocks of flats and lodging houses to accommodate the

77. Standish Heacham, *Regaining Paradise: Englishness and the Early Garden City Movement* (New Haven: Yale University Press, 1999).
78. Alfred Smith, *The Housing Question* (London: Swan Sonnenschein, 1900), 29.

"vast population of toilers." Carefully calculating the gross income from rents against construction costs, the Council downplayed the new municipal housing initiative as "the only practical way out of the difficulty."[79] Their intervention made it clear, however, in the words of historian John Tarn, that "a new kind of local government organisation, more positive and willing to act for the public good, had sprung into existence," opening up "a new era of public responsibility."[80]

The London County Council built its largest project, the Boundary Street Estate on fifteen acres in the East London neighborhoods of Bethnal Green and Shoreditch where the death rate stood at twice the London average.[81] Arthur Morrison, in his 1896 novel, *A Child of the Jago,* described the impoverished tenants set apart from civilized society and subsisting on crime and charity.[82] Razing the slums, the Estate displaced 5,719 tenants, 2,118 from 752 single-room tenements. Laid out on a radial system of tree-lined streets around a central garden and bandstand, Boundary Street Estate was designed as a community of five-story dwellings. The *British Architect* hailed it as a "workman's paradise," complete with laundry and club room.[83] It was designed as a community rather than a collection of buildings. The Council architects envisioned strolling couples listening to a band on summer evenings. Reformist architects praised the project for its open space and its humane design in contrast to the prevailing barracks-type working-class developments. The Prince of Wales himself opened the new twenty-three-block estate, begun in 1893 and completed in 1897.

Contemporary critics of Boundary Street, however, were less sanguine, deploring the demolition of the East End to build the new flats. Arthur Jay protested in *A Story of Shoreditch* that "there can be no more pitiable way of 'improving' an area than by driving its inhabitants away and substituting others of a nominally superior type."[84] With their houses demolished, the reformer Lord Shaftesbury observed, the poor "are like persons possessed—perplexity and dismay are everywhere;...they rush into every hole...all struggle to be as near as possible to their former dwellings."[85]

---

79. London County Council, *Housing of the Working Classes in London* (London: Oldhams, 1913), 27.
80. Tarn, *Five Per Cent Philanthropy,* 129.
81. John Joseph Clark, *The Housing Problem: Its History, Growth, Legislation and Procedure* (London: Sir I. Putnam & Sons, 1920), 40.
82. Arthur Morrison, *A Child of the Jago* (London: Metheun & Co., 1896).
83. *The British Architect* 47 (18 May 1907): 383–384, cited in Susan Beattie, *A Revolution in Housing: LCC Housing Architects and Their Work, 1893–1914* (London: The Architectural Press, 1980), 54.
84. Arthur Osborn Jay, *A Story of Shoreditch* (London: Simpkin, Marshall, Hamilton, Kent & Co., 1896).
85. Lord Shaftesbury, James A. Yelling, *Slums & Slum Clearance in Victorian London* (London: Allen & Unwin, 1986), 143.

Central bandstand on Arnold Circus of the Boundary Street Estate (1903).
London Metropolitan Archives 91/226.
Photo courtesy of London Metropolitan Archives.

Arthur Morrison complained that the Council had, in effect, created a new ring of slums in a circle around the development.

A 1907 editorial in the *Times* of London noted that the London County Council had not had much success in rehousing tenants evicted by demolition projects, despite its attempts to phase in housing.[86] The Council itself acknowledged that evicted tenants had not moved into the new dwellings. Few tenants from Shoreditch could afford the high rents, and fewer still would put up with the regulations of Council housing. The Progressive councillor Edward Pickersgill condemned the Council for charging rents that earned a 3 percent return on their investment, arguing that if it was willing to pay to clear away the slums, it should accept the principle of subsidizing rents as well.

The Council purchased two and three-quarters acres of land between Clerkenwell Road and Portpool Lane, building Bourne Estate to house 2,642 people displaced by urban renewal projects and smaller projects at Brookes Market, Mill Lane, Ann Street, Norfolk Square, London Terrace,

86. *Times* (London), 13 February, 1907.

and Queen Catherine Court. These housing estates grouped dwellings according to rent, isolating workers and their families from the middle class, instead of encouraging social intermixing as in Belgian schemes.

Reformers on the Continent followed the London County Council projects closely, noting that other cities plagued by overcrowded slums had shied away from municipal construction. In Brussels, a few Liberals joined the Socialists in asking if the Belgian housing legislation, the so-called Catholic law of 1889, was not better suited for rural areas than for their urban capital. Few houses had been built in Brussels, leaving workers poorly housed in cramped, dark hovels lining impasses with rents three times higher than comparable bourgeois rents. Brussels administrator De Quéker concluded that the municipality needed to get involved in housing its citizens, citing an old Flemish proverb: "Kooken moet kosten" (you get what you pay for).[87] What made the Boundary Street Estate unique, the *Moniteur des Comités de Patronage* (Monitor of the Patronage Committees) explained was not the beautiful tree-lined streets, the lighting, the heating, or the schools, but the fact that the Council itself had planned and built the housing for working families.[88]

The Brussels commune of St.-Gilles/St.-Gillis decided to build its own apartments to avoid what the councillors identified as the corruption of private interests. In 1894, the commune borrowed from the CGER to construct five houses, three to be sold to tenants, and two to be rented. It also built fourteen lodging houses for poorer workers, projects that earned St.-Gilles/St.-Gillis a mention in the French housing reform discussions of municipal initiatives, just under the discussion of London where "we find vast enterprises, most of which are succeeding."[89]

The Brussels commune of Schaerbeek/Schaarbeek, located just east of the center of Brussels, lacking both joint stock companies and private housing societies, had seen little new construction of workmen's housing. In 1898, Socialists Louis Bertrand, alderman for finances, and Emile Vanden Putte, alderman for public works, proposed that the Communal Council of Schaerbeek/Schaarbeek undertake the construction of housing blocks itself, justifying their proposal by citing the report presented by the representatives of the London County Council at the most recent international meeting on affordable housing: "Look at what is happening in England, the classic site of *laisser faire* and of *laisser passer,*" Bertrand urged the Liberals on the Council. "In four years, the [London County] Council had spent more than twenty-five million" on workers' housing.[90] After extensive debate, the Socialists

87. Charles De Quéker, *Des maisons ouvrières à appartements en ville* (Brussels: Imprimerie des institutions de prévoyance, 1904), 12.

88. *Moniteur des Comités de Patronage* (25 October 1998): 115.

89. Henri Turot, *Le surpeuplement et les habitations populaires* (Paris: F. Alcan, 1907).

90. Louis Bertrand, Commune de Schaerbeek, *Construction d'habitations â bon marché par la commune* (Brussels: Becquart-Arien, 1898), 38 and 45.

of Schaerbeek/Schaarbeek agreed to a compromise proposed by the Liberals, whereby two hundred thousand francs in public funds would be channeled through a separate institution, the Foyer Schaerbeekois/Schaarbeekse Haard. The Schaerbeek/Schaarbeek Council expected housing constructed by the Foyer/Haard to stimulate private industry as they believed that the London County Council construction had done in London.

Liberals and Socialists clashed over the siting of the new model housing. The Liberal members of the Council wanted to build exclusively on cheaper land on the periphery of Schaerbeek/Schaarbeek, and instead of large apartment blocks, they advocated construction of single-family houses. They planned to build cheaply so that houses could be demolished when demand for worker housing in the central city ebbed, as they assumed it would. The Socialist Bertrand countered that scattered single-family houses would not even begin to solve the housing crisis; building apartment blocks within the city made more financial sense.

Compromising, the Foyer Schaerbeekois/Schaarbeekse Haard bought three plots of land dispersed throughout the Schaerbeek, investing half of their funds in the construction of single- and two-family houses that might be purchased and half in multiple units to be rented at lower prices. The flats shared common services, such as a library, shower rooms, and a meeting hall. The Schaerbeek/Schaarbeek Council set as its goal the construction of "model accommodations whose general appearance would contribute to the beautification of the quarter by its monumental aspect, while still maintaining the character of inexpensive housing."[91] While critics wondered whether the blocks of flats designed for workers making two francs a day really gave the same benefits as small cottages built for higher-paid workers, supporters pointed to the benefits of municipal as opposed to private construction: the availability of gas, electricity, and water, the private gardens, the terraces, and the iron stairways. Inspired by the example of Schaerbeek/Schaarbeek, the Foyer Anderlechtois, organized in 1907 by the Brussels commune of Anderlecht, built a block of workers' housing on K. Marxstraat (K. Marx Street) called "Fraternité."

In the central commune of Brussels, Liberals proposed to meet the housing crisis by channeling funds through a private housing society, the Société Anonyme des Habitations à Bon Marché de l'Agglomération Bruxelloise (Society for Affordable Housing in the Brussels Region). The Socialists on the Communal Council complained that the private Société had built only fifty houses in the fifteen years from 1891 to 1905, and that these had not alleviated the misery of the poorest workers.[92] The Liberals urged

91. Le Foyer Schaerbeekois, *Historique de la société* (Schaerbeek: Le Foyer Schaerbeekois, 1905), 27.

92. Camille Lemonnier, "Logements ouvriers—emplacements," *Bulletin communal, Bruxelles 1906* 20 (July 1906): 19.

patience, pointing to the success of private initiatives, such as London's Peabody Trust. The Socialists reminded them, in turn, that the London County Council had picked up the slack by constructing its own housing.[93] After extensive discussion, in 1907, the Liberal-Socialist coalition finally launched its own housing project, the Cité Hellemans. The Council dispatched a commission to visit workmen's housing in London, Manchester, Liverpool, Sheffield, Paris, Cologne, Cassel, Quedlinburg, Berlin, Dusseldorf, and Elberfeld.[94]

The Liberals would have preferred to look to the suburbs where land was cheaper, but the Socialists had convinced them to build within the commune on the site of demolished tenements. De Quéker lauded the decision to build in the center of the Belgian capital, contending that not all apartment blocks needed to fall under attack as "vertical impasses." Given the impracticality of constructing individual cottages in the city itself, he urged architects to design multifamily buildings that avoided the worst features of philanthropic blocks such as common corridors where unrelated families had to meet on their way in and out of their own flats. The Cité Hellemans, completed in 1912, housed two thousand tenants in apartments, each with a kitchen, a common room, and bedrooms, usually three, to allow parents and children to sleep separately.[95] Tenants had access to a shared nursery and common laundry facilities. The open stairs leading to the apartments allowed for public inspection from the broad courtyard below while the spacing between the seven blocks allowed sunlight to penetrate each apartment. Although loosely modeled in design on the impasses of Brussels, the architects did not intend the courtyards to mimic the public life of the worker neighborhoods that had been razed. Underlying construction plans was the goal of creating the conditions for independence for each family with the explicit aim of dissipating the sociability of worker neighborhoods. The family's outdoor life was to be channeled instead onto private balconies.

Tenants of Brussels municipal housing were expected to conform to a battery of rules that differed little from the much-maligned London philanthropic regimentation. In the Cité Hellemans, for example, tenants were forbidden to sublet apartments, to have pets, to play on the stairways, or to modify their lodging by painting or hanging pictures. Any tenant found "guilty of disorder or of committing an immoral or unworthy act" was to be immediately evicted. The Foyer Schaerbeekois/Schaarbeekse Haard also had regulations against talking on the stairways or drying clothes in the

---

93. G. Grimard and Max Hallet, "Habitations ouvrières, Proposition," *Bulletin communal Bruxelles 1899* (1899).

94. See *Moniteur des Comités de patronage et des sociétés d'habitations ouvrières* (25 February 1907) for a discussion of the visits.

95. *Bulletin communal de Bruxelles* (13 February 1899, 27 March 1899, 29 April 1907, 4 November 1907). See Bruno De Meulder, "De 'Cité Hellemans,' 1906–1915," *Wonen TABK* (November 1985): 27–36.

Cité Hellemans. Workers' housing constructed by the Municipality of Brussels in the center of Brussels. Family life was to be centered on the individual balconies. Stairs were open to the outside. Photo by author (2002).

halls. Steps were to be washed every Wednesday and Saturday. The Foyer/Haard required renters to give access three times a year to members of the Société.

The Schaerbeek/Schaarbeek and Brussels housing projects had few imitators in Belgium, with a number of Belgian Liberals and Catholics denouncing them as examples of "municipal socialism," a dangerous import from London. Private initiative, they asserted, stimulated by national regulation was working on their side of the Channel. Large-scale construction by local governments, they argued, would only disrupt the balance of supply and demand, driving private builders out of the capital. Brussels mayor Charles Buls added that Brussels workers were not all that poorly housed, especially compared with those of London, Paris, or Berlin. None of the continental capitals had followed the path of the London County Council.

On both sides of the Channel, municipalities were thwarted in implementing their more innovative housing projects by conservative opposition at the national level. When they initially proposed to build municipal housing, the governing Liberal-Socialist coalitions of Brussels and Schaerbeek/Schaarbeek encountered stiff resistance from Catholics in the national government and in Parliament. Similarly, the British secretary of state intervened to deny the London County Council permission to seek alternative housing sites for rehousing displaced tenants and involved himself in detailed criticism of specific building plans. At most, local authorities in Britain were supposed to draw up plans for the improvement of slum areas, to pave streets and construct sewers, and to lease land for building to private persons. The legislators did not expect either local or national governments to intervene directly into housing construction, nor did they intend any municipal schemes to burden local rate-payers.

Neither London nor Brussels before the First World War offered examples of straightforward struggles opposing market forces and a monolithic government as described by historians of twentieth-century social housing.[96] There were debates among political leaders juxtaposing market and government forces, just as there were arguments over the effect of philanthropy on individual initiative. But most of the struggles over housing reform pitted national against municipal governments. In London and in Brussels, housing reformers preferred the construction of municipal housing to national intervention, in Britain because they distrusted it and in Belgium because national programs were not forthcoming. The London County Council housing committee justified municipal intervention in housing as a way to "provide an efficient collective response" without requiring "undue dependence on the state." Addressing the 1905 International Congress on Low-Cost Housing, Albert Soenens depicted Belgium as the classic land of local franchise and administrative decentralization.[97] In both countries, municipalities intervened to supplement not to replace philanthropic and private housing.[98] It was not that the market had failed, but that the municipality

96. Guy Vanthemsche argues in *Les paradoxes de l'Etat: L'Etat face à l'économie de marché XIX & XX siècles* (Brussels: Editions Labor, 1997) that it is the liberal and neoliberal economists who have created this myth of a government separate from the market.

97. Albert Soenens, Actes du VIIme Congrès International des Habitations à bon Marché tenu à Liège, du 7 au 10 Août 1905 (Liège: Imprimerie industrielle et commerciale, M. Thone, 1906).

98. The historian Martin Daunton reminds us that in Britain, although subsidized municipal housing prevailed in the long run as the solution to the housing question, before 1914 most working-class housing was still supplied by private landlords. Daunton, *House and Home in the Victorian City* (London: Edward Arnold, 1983). Susannah Morris adds that thirty-one of the forty-three philanthropic institutions formed between 1840 and 1914 to address

was better equipped to supply social housing. Except for the Belgian Socialists, theirs was a pragmatic, not an ideological decision.

Housing: "The Reformers' Reform"

After visiting housing projects on the other side of the Channel, Belgian reformer and administrator Ernest Mahaim commented, "One must travel to England to meet men who combine dreaming and a practical spirit, balancing the most realistic positivism with the highest idealism."[99] It was a characterization that could be applied to most Belgian housing reformers at the turn of the last century. The Belgians, like the British, took on the reform of worker housing "because everyone—moralists, public health officials, sociologists, economists—all agreed it held the key to any social conservation and renovation, it was the reformers' reform."[100] They directed their reforms toward those workers and their families who seemed capable of transformation, of redemption.

Delegates to the Belgian National Congress on Workmen's Housing recognized at their annual meeting in 1910 that the Belgian legislation of 1889 had succeeded principally in allowing an elite group of workers to buy their own homes.[101] They acknowledged that the poorer, more marginally employed workers who were not in a position to take advantage of the provisions of the law remained behind. That troubled the Belgian Socialists. "One trembles before the seriousness and the extent of the problem revealed again by the most recent studies, despite all of the generous efforts, before the admirable devotion, and the considerable results that no one could deny have come from the law of 1889," the Belgian Socialist Hector Denis declared. To assist the most needy, he called for "public intervention in a much stronger vein than that extended by the Savings Bank [CGER] in response to solicitations of private initiatives."[102] Some of the Social Catholics and a few Liberals joined Denis. The "Catholic legislation" of 1889 may have served the provinces well, but it had made little difference in large cities such

the housing problem in London provided more than 35,000 dwellings, more than twice the amount provided by governments. Morris, "Organizational Innovation," 196.

99. Ernest Mahaim, *Le Congrès des habitations a bon marché de Londres* (Brussels: E. Daem, 1908), 10–11.

100. Jules Simon, quoted in the *Compte rendu de la remise officiel des Prix d'Ordre, Saint Gilles* (February 1896); Comité officiel de patronage des habitations ouvrières et des institutions de prévoyance pour les communes Ouest de l'agglomération bruxelloise, *Compte rendu de la remise officielle des prix d'ordre, de propreté et d'épargne* (Saint Gilles: J. B. Schaumans, 1896).

101. "Rapport de MM. A. Soenens et A. Merckx," *Congrès National des habitations ouvrières* (1910), 72.

102. Hector Denis, cited by Stélandre, "Contribution à l'histoire des habitations ouvrières."

as Brussels, they asserted. The Belgian capital in particular lacked economical municipal transport and affordable land, two assumptions behind the legislation.[103] These reformers, who believed the working class susceptible to improvement, recognized that marginally employed laborers had been ill served by both private enterprise and municipal construction. A few reformers in Britain echoed their complaints, appealing to the municipality to help the most desperate.

In neither capital, however, did the calls for intervention on behalf of the impoverished raise a significant response. De Quéker rationalized that those workers who could not afford to pay between two francs and two francs fifty a week in rent probably spent that much on drink. They did not deserve to be called workers, he explained, but instead were just "the poor." They needed a completely different kind of housing, one with control such as that provided by the philanthropist Octavia Hill in London.[104] By the first decade of the twentieth century, as a result of the extensive collection of statistics and categorization by social scientists such as Charles Booth, the attention of the housing reformers had shifted decisively to the improvement of the skilled and semi-skilled workers, not the amorphous mass of the poor who had first enlisted the sympathy of reformers in the middle of the century. They were housing workers who could be respectable citizens. Abandoned in the center of the cities, the so-called residuum, now separated from the working poor, no longer appeared to pose a revolutionary threat to the middle class.

---

103. Charles Buls, cited by Bruno De Meulder, "'A bas les taudis!' Taudisards et logements sociaux à Bruxelles (1920–1960),» *Les Cahiers de la Fonderie* 6 (June 1989): 6; Rapport de MM. A. Soenens et A. Merckx, *Congrès National des habitations ouvrières* (1910), 72; Charles Lagasse and Charles De Quéker, Comité officel de patronage des habitations ouvrières et institutions de prévoyance de Schaerbeek, Saint-Josse-ten-Noode et Evère, "Deuxième rapport annuel sur les travaux du Comité en 1902," (Brussels: L.G. Laurent, 1902), 49.
104. Charles De Quéker, *De la manière de construire les habitations à bon marché à logements multiples* (Brussels: Imprimerie des institutions de prévoyance, 1906).

3 *"Network of Iron Rails"*

Workmen's Trains

> At a time when we are deeply concerned and worried about the industrial classes, at a moment when we are legitimately troubled by strikes, we would do well to recognize that one of the most effective means of improving the lot of the industrial classes would be to discourage them from moving to the large cities where they contract the habits of immorality and disorder.
>
> —Joseph Kervyn de Lettenhove, 1869, 735

On 21 April 1869, Joseph Kervyn de Lettenhove, a Catholic deputy from the Belgian village of Eeklo, introduced a scheme to reduce railway fares for laborers riding to work on the national railways. He proposed government subsidies to encourage laborers to travel daily by train from their homes in rural villages to employment in industrial centers throughout Belgium. Workmen's trains running on the state rails would remove the industrial classes each evening from the large cities where "they contract the habits of immorality and disorder." The Belgian railways would root laborers in their ancestral villages away from the promiscuous cities where they worked.

Kervyn de Lettenhove invoked images of "what the English call 'home'" to justify subsidizing cheap railway fares for Belgian workers. Preserving "the foyer would assure the respectability of the family and the order of society," quelling the strikes spreading through the industrial regions, he explained.[1] These were crucial virtues for the Catholic deputy.

1. Joseph Kervyn de Lettenhove, 21 April 1869, *Annales parlementaires,* Chambre (1868–1869), 735.

The Liberal minister of public works, Alexander Jamar, lost no time in replying to the opposition deputy. With a speed and an assurance that suggests prior consultation, Jamar announced on 22 April 1869 that workmen's trains would be running in Belgium before the next parliamentary session. In language almost identical to that used by Kervyn de Lettenhove, Jamar agreed that this measure to improve the laboring classes served the national interest. The government had a duty, the Liberal minister declared, to bring the working men back each night to their families, removing them from "the unhealthy influences of large population centers."[2]

The Belgians were not the first to run workmen's trains. Kervyn de Lettenhove and Jamar had European models on which to draw for their experiment. The French Compagnie de l'Est (Company of the East) established workmen's train service to the workers' community in Mulhouse along the railway lines stretching from Saint-Louis and d'Altkirch in 1883. But it was the example of workmen's trains on the private British railways that convinced the Belgians to experiment with subsidizing workmen's fares. The Stockton & Darlington Railway operated the first workmen's trains in Britain on their line between Middlesbrough and Eston in 1852 and workmen's trains also served mining districts. These modest British attempts to transport workers between their homes and workplaces convinced Jamar and his staff that Belgian laborers could be induced to commute from their villages, rather than moving permanently to the cities where they worked. The Belgian inspector general based Belgian workmen's fares on the Mulhouse service.[3]

In Britain, with its competing private railways, Parliament required the competing railway companies that served the capital to run workmen's trains at reduced fares. Over the last half-century, "railways have advanced into the dense parts of the metropolis," the *Illustrated London News* reported, sweeping away "large masses of squalid and filthy houses." As they extended lines and built stations in the center of London, the railways had destroyed workmen's housing. No provisions were made for rehousing the laborers dislodged by the wide swathes they cut through the capital, leaving the "miserable and now homeless inhabitants to flock for shelter to the buildings that do remain."[4] The dispossessed, seeking shelter where they could find it in adjacent neighborhoods, added to the overcrowding. To remedy the housing crisis, some London reformers concluded, the railways

2. Alexander Jamar, 22 April 1869, *Annales parlementaires,* Chambre (1868–1869), 765.
3. Workmen traveling to Mulhouse from neighboring villages purchased more than twenty-five thousand "weekly cards." Alain Faure, "A l'aube des transports de Masse: L'exemple des 'trains-ouvriers' de la banlieue de Paris (1883–1914)," *Revue d'histoire moderne et contemporaine* (April–June 1993): 229.
4. *Illustrated London News* 42 (17 January 1868): 83.

would have to run trains to the suburbs at reduced fares. That would encourage the migration of working families out of London.

Belgian and British reformers watched each other across the Channel, comparing their bold experiments at government intervention—one a direct subsidy at the behest of industry and the other a parliamentary regulation of competing private industries. Both harnessed the railway, the "harbinger of civilization" that had made possible the concentration of industry in their capitals to root laborers outside of the urban centers.[5] Within thirty years of the inauguration of government-subsidized workmen's trains, one of every five Belgian workers was commuting by train. The Belgian Socialist Emile Vandervelde observed that workmen's trains had effected "a profound social revolution" in Belgium by the turn of the twentieth century.[6]

"Let the Railways Bring us Backwards and Forwards for a Trifle": Subsidizing Workmen's Fares

Any collaboration between Catholics and Liberals would have struck the nineteenth-century Belgians as unusual, but the partnership that launched the workmen's trains was especially surprising. Jamar, the Liberal minister who organized the workmen's trains—a Brussels native, editor, and printer—was elected to Parliament in 1859 where he vigorously defended workers' causes. During his two-year stint as minister of public works (1868–1870), Jamar was known for his investigation into the conditions of mines and metal factories. Joseph Kervyn de Lettenhove, born in the Chateau de Saint-Michel-les-Bruges, had studied history at the Sorbonne where he befriended François-René Chateaubriand and Adolphe Thiers whose ultraconservative political views he shared. Elected as a Catholic deputy from Eecloo in 1861, Kervyn de Lettenhove achieved renown as one of the most outspoken conservative spokesmen on questions of educational requirements for voting.[7] Throughout the 1860s this impenitent polemicist steadfastly opposed all Liberal initiatives and later, as a government minister, obstinately refused to cooperate with the Liberals whom he blamed for most political crises.

Three years before he pioneered the national scheme for workmen's trains in Belgium, Kervyn de Lettenhove proclaimed, "the true mission of the government is to favor the development of local liberties and to appeal to individual initiative." He vehemently denounced government subsidies, "a

5. Charles E. Lee, *Passenger Class Distinctions* (London: London Railway Gazeteer, 1946), 49–58.
6. Emile Vandervelde, *L'exode rural et le retour aux champs* (Brussels: A. Vromant & Co., 1901), 155.
7. "Joseph Kervyn de Lettenhove," in *Le Parlement belge, 1831–1894: Données biographiques*, ed. Jean-Luc De Paepe and Christiane Raindorf-Gérard (Brussels: Académie Royale de Belgique, 1996); Nelly Thiry, "Joseph Kervyn de Lettenhove," *Biographie nationale* 29:734.

deplorable system that tempts governments with corruption and complacency and that leads the governed fatally towards moral degeneration because it destroys their sense of honor and private initiative."[8] His son did not even mention the railway scheme in his otherwise meticulously detailed two-volume biography of Kervyn de Lettenhove and instead focused on his father's six-volume *History of Flanders*.

A medieval historian and fervent Belgian patriot, Kervyn de Lettenhove professed his belief that nineteenth-century Belgium should be understood not as a nation, but rather as a collection of decentralized communes. In the government, Kervyn de Lettenhove was determined to preserve the Belgian peasant heritage. The peasants had remained faithful to the family, according to Kervyn de Lettenhove, and they could be counted on to resist the revolutionary temptations swirling through nineteenth-century Europe. To keep peasants on the land, Kervyn de Lettenhove founded the first Belgian agrarian institute in Gembloux as well as a horticultural school in Ghent.

The Catholic deputy proposed workmen's trains to forestall the threatened rural exodus in Belgium. Jamar, on the other hand, stewarded the workmen's fare schemes through Parliament at the urging of Belgian industrialists desperate to increase their labor pool. Employers in mines and industrial centers had been trying since the 1850s to lure workers from rural areas to come work for them but could tempt few peasants to follow higher wages to industrial centers. The Liberal government worked together with industry to organize the scheme in this otherwise laissez-faire state.

Minister Jamar set his staff to work on implementation of the workmen's train scheme in the spring of 1869. The first tentative proposals put forward by his staff were designed as an experiment on the railroad between Charleroi and Namur, limiting workmen's travel to distances under thirty-five kilometers. Supported by the inspector general for railways, the minister asked for a broader experiment in his report of 22 August 1869. He wanted laborers to travel in worker cars attached to ordinary trains as well as on the special workmen's convoys originally proposed. On 30 August 1869, the Conseil Permanent de l'Administration des Chemins de Fer (Permanent Advisory Board for the Administration of the Railways) examined the revised proposal for workmen's trains, and, after some discussion of whether the government or the industries served by the workmen's trains would be responsible for subsidizing potential losses resulting from the half-priced fares, the report was approved and submitted to the king. The government would cover the subsidy. Jamar signed the royal decree on 8 September 1869 authorizing special trains to transport workers to and from their work

8. Joseph Kervyn de Lettenhove, 1 April 1866, *Annales parlementaires,* as quoted in H. Kervyn de Lettenhove, *Le Baron Kervyn de Lettenhove (1817–1891): Notes et souvenirs réunis par un de ses Enfants* (Bruges: K. Van de Vyvere-Petyt, 1900), 244.

at hours fixed by the railway administration. Additional trains were to be established on demand from any industrialists or companies constructing workmen's housing who could prove that fare receipts would cover the cost of the train.

Despite the earlier start, it took longer to launch workmen's trains in Britain. Lord Shaftesbury, an evangelical conservative, had proposed in 1853 that the railways serving London be required to rehouse the laborers and their families they had displaced in new tenements, but his suggestion elicited few adherents. In 1864, Lord Derby presented the British parliament with a petition to require that all railways in the metropolitan area run cheap trains to accommodate the displaced workers and their families. Instead of forcing the railways to build new housing for the displaced tenants in adjoining neighborhoods—a measure widely viewed as infringing on the rights of private property—he suggested that the railways run workmen's trains to the suburbs where working families would find cheaper housing. Backing up these proposals, the *Fortnightly Review* pointed out that the North London Railway had demolished nine hundred houses to build two miles of track from Kingsland to Finsbury and the *Working Man* charged that the Midland Railway had leveled four thousand homes housing thirty-two thousand predominantly working class persons in Somers, Camden, and Agar Town for its metropolitan extension.[9] Even the dead were threatened when the construction of St. Pancras station not only displaced twenty thousand people from their homes but also took a part of the St. Pancras churchyard and burial ground.

The railway acts passed by Parliament in 1868 required the railways to provide the working families they had displaced with affordable means of traveling between their work in London and new residences in the suburbs. Applied to the Metropolitan Railway, the North London Railway, the Great Eastern, the Metropolitan District, and the London, Chatham, and Dover companies, they required the running of one morning workmen's train before 7 a.m. and one evening return train after 6 p.m. at a fare of one penny each way. The other railway companies serving London did not come under statutory obligations. Consequently, the London and South Western, the London North Western, and the Great Western issued few, if any, workmen's tickets. They continued to cater exclusively to the middle and upper classes.

This system of workmen's fares supplemented legislation passed in 1844 that required all British passenger railway companies to run at least one reduced-fare train each weekday down the length of their lines at a speed of at least twelve miles an hour and stopping at every station. Parliament

9. H. J. Dyos, "Railways and Housing in Victorian London," *Journal of Transport History* 2, no. 1 (1955): 12.

exempted the railways from paying duty for these trains. The reformer George Holyoake called the 1844 fares "a merciful invention, though a tedious benefit," given the frequent stops and slow speed of the parliamentary trains that made them impractical for regular commuters.[10]

Although not under statutory obligation, the Metropolitan Railway Company voluntarily introduced workmen's fares in May 1864 on its Moorgate extension—the first workmen's fares in London. Initially, Metropolitan Railway trains carried two thousand workmen weekly in each direction on two trains starting at 5:30 and 5:40 a.m. Workers were permitted to return by any train for a round-trip fare of three pence. In 1865, the company added workmen's trains at four pence return to Hammersmith. The London, Chatham, and Dover railway company introduced workmen's fares a year later on the Metropolitan extension—the first workmen's trains to run under statutory obligation. The *Illustrated London News* captured the event in a cartoon published on 22 April 1865 depicting hordes of male and female workers, some with pickaxes, others carrying lunch pails, arriving at Victoria from Brixton.[11] The railway strictly monitored the applications of artisans, mechanics, and daily laborers, both male and female, for the weekly shilling tickets.

Parliamentary legislation required the Great Eastern Railway to add twopenny return trains to Walthomstow and Edmonton for the many tenement-house dwellers displaced by the construction of the railway line to its new terminus at Liverpool Street. Although the Great Eastern ran a significant number of trains, introducing workmen's fares from Stoke Newington to Bethnal Green Junction, the company persistently complained that it lost money on the service. Their protests notwithstanding, the Great Eastern Railway's extensive workmen's service earned it the title "the workmen's railway."[12]

The South Eastern Railway voluntarily issued workmen's tickets on the Woolwich line for four pence a day at the end of 1868. A few years later, the London County Council condemned their workmen's service on the North Kent line as "inadequate and unsatisfactory."[13] Workers had to stand on the trains, an exception to the practice in Victorian London. The London, Brighton and South Coast Railway ran a daily train between New Cross and Liverpool Street at a fare of one penny. Their service also occasioned complaints from the passengers. Seventy postal workers who had to travel to London Bridge petitioned for earlier trains in 1889, but their requests were refused.[14]

---

10. George Jacob Holyoake, *History of the Travelling Tax* (London: A. Bonner, 1901), 5.
11. *Illustrated London News*, 22 April 1865.
12. London County Council Report on Workmen's Trains, *London Statistics* 2 (1891–1892): 325, 299–317.
13. Edwin Course, *London Railways* (London: B. T. Batsford, 1962), 205.
14. Ibid., 206.

Workmen's train arriving at Victoria Station, from the *Illustrated London News* (1868).

Other commuters complained that service from the thirty-seven stations on the lines was more expensive than the London average.

In contrast to the steady, persistent growth of workmen's train service to Brussels over the first decade, the history of the development of workmen's trains around London is a chronicle of dissatisfaction, of petitioning by pressure groups and resistance by the railways. Workers repeatedly asked for more frequent train service, for trains arriving in London after 7 a.m., and for less expensive tickets sold more conveniently. Petitioners also requested that workmen's fares be available not only from the end of the line but from intermediate stations.[15] Typically, the railway commissioners considering the petitions denied them, convinced by the railways' protestations that it would be impossible to meet the workers' demands and make a profit. The Metropolitan Association for Procuring Cheap and Regular Railway Accommodation for the Working Classes and the Association for the Repeal of the Passenger Duty on Railways reminded Parliament that the British railways had a special obligation to transport the workers because, in building their terminal and laying their tracks through workers'

15. Mr. Tilley, 21 December 1887, RAIL 410 367, Public Records Office, London, and Railway Commissioner to London and Northwestern Railway, 7 March 1888, RAIL 410 367, The National Archives.

neighborhoods, they had contributed significantly to the overcrowding of London.[16]

In 1883, the British parliament responded to the mounting pressure from workers and their lobbies by passing the Cheap Trains Act. The Act required the railways to run a "proper and sufficient" number of workmen's trains between 6 p.m. and 8 a.m., although it was left to the Board of Trade to define what was "proper and sufficient." If the Board of Trade judged the number of trains operated by a particular railway to be insufficient or the fares to be prohibitive, the Act directed the Board of Trade to conduct inquiries into the conditions of the workmen's trains and fares and to refer problems to parliamentary commissioners. The number of workmen's trains on railways serving London increased from 110 in 1883 to 478 in 1894 to 756 in 1899. The most significant train service for workmen in 1899 was provided by the London and South Western with 145 trains; the Great Eastern provided 104 trains, the Metropolitan 100, and the London, Brighton and Southern 66.[17]

As a concession to the railways, Parliament remitted passenger duties on all Cheap Train fares, resulting in a decline in receipts from the railway duty from 810,467 to 392,398 pounds. When asked by a parliamentary select committee about the substantial loss of revenue received by the government from the railways, the Inland Revenue Department replied that by providing cheaper fares for workers, the railways were in effect returning to the public the duty they had formerly paid the government.[18] Sir Edwin Watkin of the Great Eastern Railway, though, denounced the Cheap Trains Act as unwarranted state interference and immediately marshaled a campaign against the act through the Association of Railway Shareholders. Other railway spokesmen complained that unprofitable workmen's fares were forcing the railway companies to charge higher fares on the other trains to make up for the lost revenue.[19]

In contrast to the vigorous British debate that preoccupied the Railway Commission, the annual reports for the Belgian railway include no mention of the workmen's fares, not even when the fares were introduced.[20] That

16. Association for the Repeal of the Passenger Duty on Railways, "On the position of the Railway Passenger Duty Question, September, 1876" and "On the Necessity of Forming an Association for its Repeal," British Library, London; Charles Dobson Collet, "Reasons for the Repeal of the Railway Passenger Duty," Paper read in the Rooms of the Society of Arts, 26 February 1877 (London: Waterlow and Sons, 1877), British Library.

17. Sir Francis Hopwood, Appendix 6, Select Committee on Workmen's Trains, British Parliamentary Papers, 1903–1905.

18. James B. Meers, 30 July 1903, Select Committee on Workmen's Trains, British Parliamentary Papers. Some rail historians have echoed the nineteenth-century reformers argument that the Cheap Trains Act of 1883 was passed as a bargain between the government and the railways to remove the passenger duty on penny-per-mile trains.

19. Edwin A. Pratt, *Railways and Their Rates* (London: John Murray, 1906), 40.

20. Annuaire Statistique de la Belgique 1870–1871 (Brussels: Lesigne, 1872).

the new rail fares did not merit notice either in the 1869 or 1870 *Annuaire/Jaarverslag* of the Belgian railways suggests that few, if any, other political leaders at the time appreciated the significance of the legislation. The trains started running and service was expanded. Few complaints about the Belgian service made their way to Parliament. Requests for additional stations, for example, appear to have been promptly met by the government. Once the workmen's trains were running, the rare parliamentary critics of the half-fare service virtually disappeared from public debates. Everyone recognized the success of the workmen's trains.

Over the course of the last three decades of the nineteenth century, the Belgian government oversaw the construction of branch railroad lines, employers adapted their shifts to train schedules, and additional worker cars lined with wooden benches were coupled onto the trains leaving each morning for the industrial and mining centers. With little parliamentary discussion, the government reduced workmen's fares on the trains in 1876, 1880, and 1897 and increased the range of the round-trip tickets from twenty to one hundred kilometers. In 1887, seven-ride tickets were also introduced to facilitate travel.

Most of the railway data that have survived are national, making it very difficult to isolate out the statistics for commuting for an individual city. In contrast, the British railways did calculate commuting into and out of London. While the Belgians counted passengers on the national network, the British railways initially recorded the number of trains they ran to each destination. Managers of the private British railways refused to furnish figures on the number of tickets issued, believing that would open them up to the expectation that they transport a certain number of workers each day. As a business venture, not a public service, they needed to know how far the train had traveled, not how many passengers it had carried. Instead of passenger miles, they kept statistics on train miles. One frustrated economist complained: "In plain English our railway managers have landed us completely in the dark as to the passenger traffic from which nearly one-half of our railway revenue is derived."[21] In a curious turnaround, the *Railway Gazette* responded in 1910 to this criticism by charging that the Belgian State Railways overburdened them with too many figures in their reports.[22] Nevertheless, as the British railways testified repeatedly, the number of workmen's trains consistently exceeded the number of trains required by law at the end of the nineteenth century and workmen's trains serving London increased significantly, from 257 in 1890 to 1,731 in 1911.[23]

---

21. W. R. Lawson, *British Railways: A Financial and Commercial Survey* (London: Constable & Co., 1913), 106.
22. *Railway Gazette*, 25 February 1910, 209.
23. John Nelson Tarn, *Five Per Cent Philanthropy: An Account of Housing in Urban Areas between 1840 and 1914* (Cambridge: Cambridge University Press, 1973), 120.

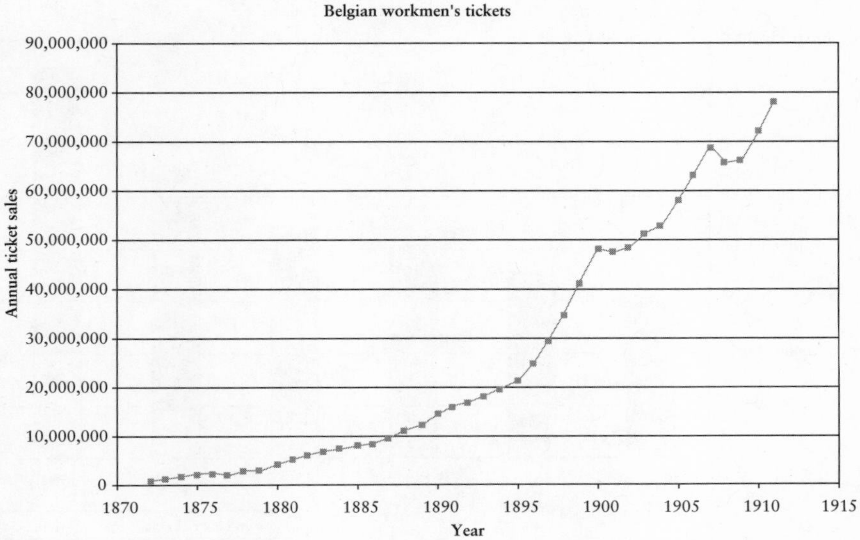

Annual sales of workmen's train tickets in Belgium, 1872–1911. Data from *Compte rendu des opérations de chemins de fer* (Brussels: Goemaere, 1911), A 142, table 30.

A comparison of the development trends of the British and Belgian systems of workmen's trains reveals that from very different starting points in the last third of the nineteenth century, the ticket sales had begun to converge in the first decade of the twentieth century. The lobbying efforts of reformers in London for more government regulation are reflected in the increase in the number of workmen's trains serving the British capital, in real terms and as a percentage of trains run.

By 1912, about 25 percent of all suburban London passengers were traveling with workmen's tickets. Within the six- to eight-mile zone of the center of London, 40 percent of the suburban railway passengers were workers traveling with workmen's tickets.[24] In 1911, the proportion of workmen's tickets to total sales varied by railway, ranging from 33.2 percent on the Great Eastern Railway to 8.8 percent on the Great Central.[25] By 1907, one of every five (20%) Belgian workers was commuting by train and 43 percent of all travelers on the Belgian national railway used worker

24. Anthony S. Wohl, "The Housing of the Working Classes in London, 1815–1914," in *The History of Working Class Housing,* ed. Stanley D. Chapman (Newton Abbot: David and Charles, 1971), 35.

25. London County Council, "Housing Development and Workmen's Fares," Leicester University Library, Leicester.

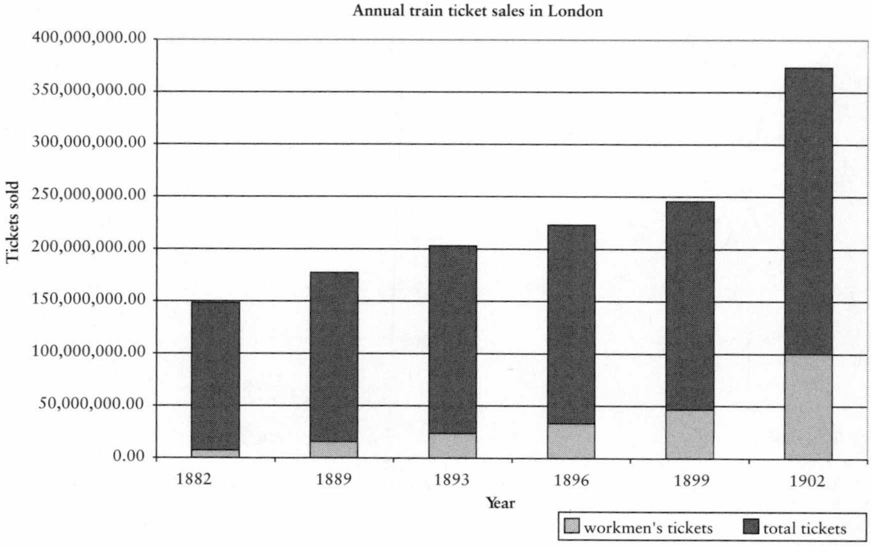

Annual sales of workmen's and total train tickets in London, 1882–1902. The figures are calculated differently in London for 1911 than in earlier years. Data from Hubert L. Smith, *The New Survey of London Life & Labour* (London: P. S. King & Son, 1930–1935). Vol. 1, Royal Commission on London Traffic. Report of the Royal Commission appointed to inquire into and report upon the means of locomotion and transport in London (London: HMSO, 1905–1906); London County Council, "Housing Development and Workmen's Fares." Report by the Valuer to the Housing of the Working Classes Committee (1913), London Metropolitan Archives.

tickets in 1907.[26] Of the total increase of 111,843,914 tickets over the thirty-two-year period in Belgium, 70,750,730, or 63 percent, were for subscription tickets.[27] These rates for workmen's train use were higher than anywhere else in Europe. German rail historians estimate that only 10,000 workers traveled on the subsidized suburban railways and 23,000 on the urban railways to Berlin with its population of 2.5 million people.[28]

The statistics suggest that despite the reluctance of British railways to cater to the workmen, they were moving in the same direction as the Belgian

26. Ernest Mahaim, *Les Abonnements d'ouvriers sur les lignes de chemins de fer belges et leurs effets sociaux* (Brussels: Misch & Thron, 1910), 38.
27. *Documents parlementaires*, Travaux publics, 1905–1906, Statistics A 32.
28. Paolo Capuzzo, "Between Politics and Technology: Transport as a Factor of Mass Suburbanization in Europe 1890–1920," in *Suburbanizing the Masses: Public Transport and Urban Development in Historical Perspective*, ed. Colin Divall and Winstan Bond (Ashgate: Aldershot, Hampshire, 2003), 26.

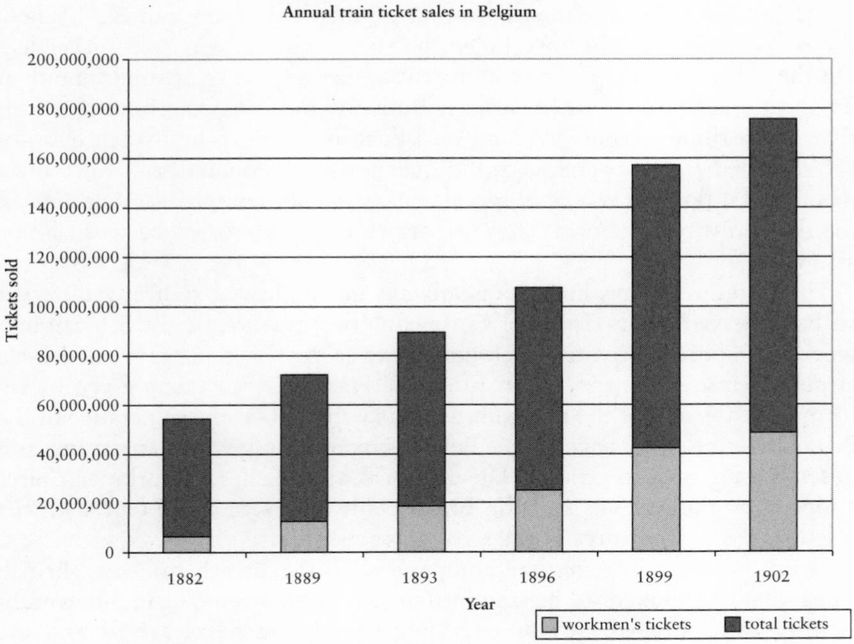

Annual sales of workmen's and total train tickets in Belgium, 1882–1902. Data from *Compte rendu des opérations de chemins de fer* (Brussels: Goemaere, 1911), 144–145.

railways. Workmen's tickets made up an ever larger percentage of total tickets in both countries, growing at a faster rate than all other ticket sales. In Belgium, that growth was more gradual in comparison to the steeper British increase. Otherwise, the differences between a private system pressured by reformers and a national railway increasingly monitored by a ministry and Parliament are not as evident as contemporaries believed.[29]

"The Railways Exist for the Public, not the Public for the Railways": The State and Private Companies

The Belgian workmen's fares fit in with the general conception of the public role of the national railway. In 1905, the minister of the railways, Jules Liebaert, told Parliament that organizing the workmen's trains was like

29. London County Council, "Workmen's Trains. Further Report of the Public Health and Housing Committee," April 1893, London Metropolitan Archives.

preparing for the daily embarkation of an army of 175,000 men.[30] Where the Belgian army might have failed, he stated, the railway had succeeded. On the other side of the Channel in 1904, George Neele, a superintendent on the London and North Western Railway, observed the infrequent arrival of workmen's trains coming into Euston station. The British had not yet solved their "perplexing traffic question," he concluded.[31] Reformers wondered if the two sets of observations reflected the very different wills in the two railway systems as they set out to carry workmen between home and work.

The two pioneering European railways had followed radically different paths of development. To other European governments, the British rail network exemplified private development while the Belgian trains had been largely a state enterprise. That difference was the first reason given by reformers at the end of the nineteenth century to explain the reluctance of the British and the enthusiasm of the Belgians in adopting workmen's trains and in serving the poor in general. The divergent approaches to workmen's fares adopted by the Belgian and the British railways were consistent with the organizational structures of the two railway systems.

From the beginning, private companies ran the British railways. British legislators had looked to the standard modes of eighteenth- and nineteenth-century transport—the roads over which stagecoaches traveled and the canals for shipping—as a model. In both cases, private vehicles competed for passengers. In private bills, the British parliament granted competing private railway companies the right to construct their own lines and to operate their own trains. As they expanded, however, the economics of the British railways did not fit classical liberal expectations. Passengers charged that the great railway corporations had established monopoly control over commerce and communication in their own regions of Britain, ignoring the needs of their customers.

In response to the mounting public outcry against the railway monopolies, the British parliament tentatively and gradually began to regulate the railways through a series of private bills. Regulation, however, seemed an imperfect substitute for pure competition; in the words of the historian E. Cleveland-Stevens, "controlling evil rather than promoting good."[32] William Gladstone, the future Liberal prime minister, launched an "open war" on those monopolies in 1844 as chair of a parliamentary select committee.[33] Based on the recommendations of his select committee, Parliament established a special railway department at the Board of Trade and required the railways to ac-

30. Jules Liebaert, 5 December 1905, *Annales parlementaires,* Chambre, 1905–1906, 114.
31. George P. Neele, *Railway Reminiscences* (London: McCorquodale & Co., 1904), 310.
32. Ibid., 260. Edward Cleveland-Stevens, *English Railways, Their Development and Their Relation to the State* (London: Routledge, 1915), 62.
33. Cited by Philip Sydney Bagwell, "The Railway Interest: Its Organisation and Influence, 1839–1914," *Journal of Transport History* 7 (1965–1966): 45.

commodate poorer travelers with the so-called parliamentary trains. Newly elected to Parliament, the Liberal John Bright opposed Gladstone's bill, insinuating that behind it lay an expectation that the state would eventually take over the railways, which was, he charged, "altogether a new principle in this country." Bright continued, arguing that "there was a wholesome absence of interference in this country in all those matters, which experience showed might wisely be left to private individuals, stimulated by the love of gain, the desire to administer to the wants and comforts of their fellow-men."[34] After that debate, rather than fighting in public, negotiations took place in the committee rooms of Parliament where lawyers advocated the railway companies' interests through private bills designed to grant individuals or companies special exemptions from common law or special powers.

The amalgamation of a number of railways in the 1850s increased British fears of what critics denounced as a powerful railway monopoly. Beyond the Traffic Act of 1854 and the Regulation of Railways Act of 1868 that defined the service obligations of the railways and provided some government oversight, however, Parliament hesitated to interfere directly with the operations of the railways. In the 1870s, public anxiety about the amalgamations within the railway industry intensified in Britain. Chambers of commerce complained that competition between lines—the accepted check on monopoly—was diminishing. In response, Parliament established the Railway Commission that was charged with administering laws governing the railways. In its first nine years, the Commission passed judgment on 110 cases. The railways commissioners, however, were constrained by their own belief that "all interference must be regarded as an exception from the ordinary rules which regulate commercial enterprise."[35] Without the power to compel compliance with its findings, the Commission disappointed reformers, who noted the strong presence of railway interests within Parliament. Although 157 railway directors sat in the House of Commons and 49 in the House of Lords in 1867, the transportation historian Theodore Barker argued that rivalry between the competing companies kept the rail directors from speaking.[36] Behind the scenes, especially after the formation of the United Railway Companies' Committee (later the Railway Companies' Association) in 1867, they did cooperate to squelch most legislation that might interfere with the direction of the railways.

The second national railway to develop in Europe, the Belgian railway, was conceived from the beginning as a national project, a state enterprise

34. John Bright, quoted in Cleveland-Stevens, *English Railways,* 117.
35. Quoted in Cleveland-Stevens, *English Railways,* 156.
36. Theodore C. Barker and Christopher I. Savage, *An Economic History of Transport in Britain* (London: Hutchinson & Co., 1959), 89. P. M. Williams provides some nuance to this general picture by categorizing the directors according to the railways they owned. P. M. Williams, "Public Opinion and the Railway Rates Question in 1886," *The English Historical Review* 67 (1952): 53–53.

that would promote Belgian commercial and industrial interests. The inauguration of the first Belgian rail line just four years after Belgium achieved its independence from the Netherlands in 1830 captured the imagination of the young nation. In its first decade as an independent nation, political leaders in Belgium proclaimed that a state-owned railway connecting Belgium to France and Germany and leading to the Channel crossing was critical to international trade. It would ensure the prosperity of the small but economically precocious new nation. King Leopold I noted in a letter to Lord Palmerston: "If our communications are too much limited and curtailed, we shall perish like a plant without water."[37] As the first major achievement of the new government, the railway crowned Belgian independence.

The engineers who guided the Belgian railway project through to realization, Pierre Simons and Gustave De Ridder, had traveled to Britain to study the new British rail network. They emulated the British technology in planning the first Belgian rail network, but did not copy the economic model of private competing railway companies. By 1843, the Belgian government had constructed the major arteries of the network, linking most Belgian cities and industrial centers, and extending to France, Germany, and Britain.[38] The Liberal Belgian government resisted pressure to award private concessions for new lines. Under the legislation passed by Parliament in May 1834, responsibility for construction was placed on the national treasury that sold government bonds. Tolls and fares would cover maintenance, wages, administration, and the amortization of the debt. Profits would go to the government; losses would be passed on to the taxpayers.

A second phase of Belgian railway construction, between 1843 and 1870, was dominated by private initiative, especially British promoters and investors. Parliament vigorously debated the benefits of national versus private ownership of the railways. In the end, the government ceded the rights over what it considered secondary lines to private entrepreneurs. During this period, some fifty private companies laid about 2,500 kilometers of track.[39] However, questions raised by the costly competition of state and private

---

37. Wolfgang Schivelbusch, *The Railway Journey: The Industrialization of Time and Space in the 19th Century* (Berkeley: University of California Press, 1986). Leopold I, quoted in Jean Stengers, "Leopold Ier et le Chemin de fer d'anvers au Rhin," in *Melanges offerts à G. Jacquemyns* (Brussels: Université libre de Bruxelles, 1968), 585.

38. Isabelle Cassiers, "La création et la gestion des chemins de fer (1850–1914): Une fonction importante de l'Etat libral," *Contradictions* 23–24 (1980): 160. Bart Van der Herten and Michelangelo Van Meerten, "De Spoorlijn Antwerpen-Gent, 1841–1897. De Wisselwerking tussen Prive-initiatief en Overheidsinterventie in de Belgische Spoorwegen," in *Belgisch Tijdschrift voor Filologie en Geschiedenis* 72, no. 4 (1994): 861–912.

39. Michel Laffut, "Belgium," in *Railways and the Economic Development of Western Europe*, ed. Patrick O'Brien (London: MacMillan Press, 1983), 203–226.

service led the state to reassert control, building new lines itself and gradually purchasing back the private concessions.

In 1875, the demand for a denser network of secondary lines led to proposals for a new network of regional rail lines. Rather than having the government engage in the new rail venture directly or conceding lines to private entrepreneurs, legislation in 1884 established a private society to run the regional railways, the Société Nationale des Chemins de Fer Vicinaux/Nationale Maatscappij van Buurtspoorwegen (National Society of Regional Railways SNCV/NHVB). By 1890, 888 additional kilometers of track had been laid.[40] These regional trains contributed significantly to the mainline workmen's trains as feeders. The organizational structure of the semi-private company would also serve as a model for a government initiative to provide workmen's housing.

Most historians of the Belgian railways, like the Belgian administrators themselves, explain state ownership not as an ideological choice but as wise pragmatism.[41] Politicians in the newly independent country wanted to keep the railways out of the hands of foreign capital, especially the British. The Liberal minister Charles Rogier justified public ownership by citing the greed of private interests. Liberals and Catholics alike pointed to the need for flexibility in setting rail fares to stimulate Belgian commerce and industry. Even deputies who usually opposed state intervention in areas such as housing that could be served by private enterprise defended the state ownership of the railways. Speakers in Parliament acknowledged that Britain, "the country with which we are always compared," had given free reign to private enterprise in the railway and recognized that many other European countries were following the British example.[42] Still, they argued Belgium should not abandon its grand national experiment.

In Britain, the reformer James Hole observed: "Few social questions have been more warmly contested than this:—whether the State should own the railways of a country, if not own them, to what extent it should control them." Like other critics of the private British railways, Hole persistently drew British attention to the Belgian railway system because "the Belgian Government has not tried to make a large profit for the State, but rather to develop commerce and industry by cheap transit." Hole compared the

40. Cassiers, "La création et la gestion des chemins de fer," 160; V. J. Devys, *Les chemins de fer de l'état belge* (Paris: Librairie nouvelle de droit et de jurisprudence, 1910); C. De Burlet, *Les chemins de fer vicinaux en Belgique* (Brussels: Schaumans, 1908).

41. Georges de Leener, *Les chemins de fer en Belgique* (Brussels: Maurice Lamertin, 1927), 10. See also "Rapport présenté à M. le Ministre des travaux publics par M. Gendebien inspecteur-général à l'administration des chemins de fer, postes et télégraphes," in *Annales des travaux publics* (1865): 575.

42. Minister Van Hoorebeke, quoted in Joseph Pauly, *Le chemin de fer et le parlement 1835–1860* (Brussels: H. Wauthoz-Legrand, 1935), 125.

state-owned Belgian lines that charged lower fares with the private British railways operating as monopolies that had "been allowed to do pretty much as they like."[43]

The Belgian reformer Ernest Mahaim agreed, explaining that the British could not expect to match the success of the Belgian experiment in workmen's trains as long as the railways serving London remained in private hands. The low fares and convenient service that set the Belgian trains apart from Britain, he argued, "must be understood as a natural consequence of State management, which aims less at a profit than at furthering the public good."[44] State-owned railways served the public interest, while private railways sought profits for their shareholders.

British railway directors complained in the *Railway News* about "harassing railway bills," noting that the railways actually had gone beyond what was required "by Act of Parliament, and have provided, at great inconvenience to the working of their system, and a minimum of profit, services of trains which have enabled the working classes to live at a distance from their work, which would otherwise be impossible." In providing workmen's train service, they added, "the traffic to be dealt with is thus, it will be seen, a particularly difficult one, and railway officials deserve the highest credit for the manner in which it is managed."[45] Railway trade publications and debates in Parliament were replete with examples of protestations by the railways and hand-wringing by reformers and regulators in Britain.

An editorial published in the *Times* in March 1907 summarizing the history of British railway regulations took the side of the railways, portrayed as the beleaguered victims of governmental regulation who "have done everything in their power to comply with the spirit as well as the letter of the Act [of 1883]," the workmen's trains legislation. Instead of requiring the railways to run workmen's trains at a loss, the editorial concluded, rates should be adjusted to restore "a businesslike basis" to the railways.[46] There was no echo of that conflict in Belgium where government and industry cooperated. Rather than arguing shareholders' profits versus public service, the government-operated Belgian railway strove to increase rail service, including workmen's trains, in the interest of promoting the national economy.

---

43. James Hole, *National Railways: An Argument for State Purchase* (London: Caswell, 1893), 373 and 260.
44. Ernest Mahaim, "The Belgian Experience of State Railways" (London: R. Clay & Sons, 1912).
45. "Harassing Railway Bills," *The Railway News* (21 June 1890): 1231.
46. "Workmen's Fares and Cheap Trains," *Times* (18 March 1907), in Clippings File, Archives, London Transport, London.

"The Equality and the Liberty Guaranteed by the Constitution": Fares and Classes

In his 1885 parliamentary testimony on the economics of pricing railway tickets, the Belgian inspector general pointed to the British railways, which were only interested in customers who could pay the highest ticket prices, as an example not to be followed.[47] The Belgians, he argued, should instead maximize profits by increasing ridership. That would be accomplished by offering more frequent train service and reducing fares. In support of this argument, Jamar, the minister of public works, cited an article by the British economist Samuel Smiles that praised those railways that had "the courage and wisdom to adopt the system of low fares." Smiles condemned "the stupid and indolent [British] policy of raising fares generally in the hopes of increasing dividends even though the usual result is to increase only the irritation and unhappiness of their customers."[48] Even if the British ignored their countryman, the Belgians heeded his counsel.

The first Belgian minister of public works, Jean Baptiste Nothomb, had testified before Parliament that the national railway should be priced to serve all classes. Charles Rogier, the government minister responsible for the establishment of the national railway, concurred: "Before the introduction of the route in iron, despite the equality and the liberty guaranteed by the Constitution, workers and peasants remained slaves in their villages without the ability to travel to follow their interests and to pursue their needs." But thanks to the railway, "It can be said that all Belgians are equal in this regard. All Belgians can travel.... There is a true material equality that is more advantageous and more real than the political equality guaranteed by the Constitution."[49] Jamar cited Rogier's declaration to justify the introduction of subsidized workmen's fares; both recognized the potential of the national railway to effect social change through the manipulation of the fare structure.

Effecting social change was not the concern of the British railways; they were interested in profit. British rail fares were almost double the Belgian fares in 1880. First-class fares were 7.56 francs in Belgium and 14.37 francs in Britain; third class, 3.78 in Belgium and 6.25 francs in Britain.[50] The general managers of the British railways explained that British fares were determined by their calculation of what the traffic would bear, or as a critic

47. M. Gendebien, in *Annales des travaux publics, 1865,* 570.

48. Jamar, 10 December 1869, "Chemins de fer de l'état, tarifs pour le transport des voyageurs. Exposé des résultats de la réforme introduite le 1er mai 1866," *Documents parlementaires,* Recueil des pièces imprimées par ordre de la chambre des représentants, Session de 1869–71.

49. Quoted in Pauly, *Le chemin de fer et le parlement 1835–1860,* 27.

50. Felix Loisel, *Annuaire spécial des chemins de fer* (Brussels: Bruylant Christophe & Cie, 1892), 256–57.

suggested sarcastically, the British railways followed a policy of not charging what the traffic would not bear. An inspector for the British Board of Trade reflected, "The object of company management is within certain limits and under certain circumstances to keep the charges at the figures which yield the highest dividends."[51]

The British railways generally preferred to improve services rather than lowering fares as a means of attracting riders and increasing revenue. They made first-class travel more comfortable, though improvements gradually spread to other classes of train travel. Train speeds also increased as did frequency of service when the British railways invested in new tracks at the end of the nineteenth century, often running lines that competed against other companies.

Even in Belgium, the promotion of train travel for all did not guarantee equality of travel conditions. In fact, equality of access necessarily implied the differentiation of travel by class in the nineteenth century. If the trains were to carry such a range of passengers, then the railway felt obliged to afford the passengers separation. Not only trains but also stations segregated waiting rooms according to class. The first Belgian trains provided riders with a choice of four classes differentiated by the comfort of the compartments and the price of tickets.

British trains also separated passengers by class. At first, because Parliament had granted third-class trains that stopped at all stations remission of passenger duties, all third-class riders were forced to board these slower trains. From the beginning, as distinct from the Belgian railway, the British railway catered to passengers in the first and second classes. The Duke of Wellington complained on behalf of the railways that the expansion of cheap third-class fares would offer only "a premium to the lower orders to go uselessly wandering about the country."[52] Critics noted that the third class was practically forced on the British companies. An 1845 report for the British House of Commons charged that most third-class carriages did not offer protection against wind, rain, and cold; illumination; seatbacks; or even windows.[53] Third-class passengers were carried like freight. Meanwhile, riders in first class enjoyed spacious seats in private compartments with individual heaters and lamps.

As regulations governing cheap trains were relaxed in the 1860s and as competition between the lines increased, the companies started to build composite carriages with compartments for each of the three classes. British railway managers continued to believe that the segregation allowed

---

51. Captain H. W. Taylor, quoted in John R. Kellett, *The Impact of Railways on Victorian Cities* (London: Routledge & Kegan Paul, 1969), 87.
52. The Duke of Wellington, as cited by James Hole, *National Railways: An Argument for State Purchase* (London: Caswell & Co. 1893), 151.
53. Lee, *Passenger Class Distinctions,* 21.

passengers to choose travel accommodations by the price they were willing to pay and the comfort they expected, but also by the type of passengers with whom they wished to be associated. Satirists suggested that those passengers who worried about their status often rode in first class when their pocketbooks suggested second class. Cartoonists depicted first-class passengers as aloof and self-absorbed. Even though there was not a significant difference in the comfort of second and third classes by the end of the century, many riders clung to the second class as a way of avoiding the poorer travelers of the lowest class. For a short time several British railways provided "ladies only" carriages for first- and second-class passengers. Since "women," not "ladies," traveled in third class, they were not offered a separate compartment.

The Belgian railways, too, hesitated to improve the third-class carriages, realizing that the level of comfort determined the class of train service people chose. Despite laments in the Belgian press about the rain, dust, and smoke that fell on passengers in the open carriages, it was not until 1838 that roofs were provided on many of the Belgian third-class coaches or windows closed by more than curtains. The Belgians may have been more willing to carry third-class riders, but they afforded them no more comfort than the British. Debating conditions of third-class travel in Parliament, the Catholic advocate of workers' rights Abbé Daens protested that passengers in third class and on the workmen's trains were herded as beasts, thirty to forty per car. Defending the segregation of railway carriages, the Catholic deputy Charles Woeste responded that immoral behavior of passengers in the third class warranted their separation from the respectable riders in the first two classes.[54] Similarly, British railway managers claimed that the "mischievous people" in the third-class carriages destroyed the carriages, cutting linings and breaking glass, forcing the companies to run stripped-down cars. Neither saw the need to provide more sumptuous accommodation to the poorest travelers.

What rail historian Edwin Course labels Victorian "apartheid" certainly resulted in additional expenses for both British and Belgian railways as they had to provide distinct refreshment rooms, waiting rooms, and booking offices.[55] When asked to offer season tickets to third-class travelers, the manager of the Great Eastern replied that he could not allow working men to ride with the passengers on ordinary trains. The laboring classes used offensive language, he complained. The few proponents of mixing classes on the trains countered that it would help society to level up. Although that argument prevailed among housing reformers, it convinced few of the men who set railway policy. The railways preferred to separate the classes on the railways.

---

54. Charles Woeste, 2 March 1904, *Annales parlementaires,* Chambre (1903–1904), 811.
55. Edwin Course, *London Railways* (London: B. T. Batsford, 1962).

The fare policy of the British railways evolved through the course of the nineteenth century. By the turn of the twentieth century, their pricing of passenger travel was not all that different from Belgian patterns developed in the mid-nineteenth century with first-class passengers charged double that of the third-class ticketholders. Ridership also changed, reflecting the evolving fare structure. In 1848, 40 percent of British rail passengers rode in first class as compared with 5 percent of Belgians; 17 percent of the British riders and 83 percent of the Belgians rode in third class. By 1875, these numbers had converged with 9 percent in first class and 77 percent in third class in Britain as compared with 4 percent in first class and 83 percent in third class in Belgium.[56] In 1899, a proposal was even entertained by the Great Eastern Railway to improve third-class suburban carriages by substituting cloth-covered seats for the wooden seats.

"With a Knapsack on Their Backs": Commuting by Trams, Regional Rail, and Dog Cart

The electrification of tramway networks at the turn of the twentieth century added another mode of transport for workers into European cities. Slower than trains, trams moved passengers within cities. Many of the first tramlines connected railway stations to destinations in the center of the city, running along public streets. Later lines extended outward to the suburbs, often adding service to areas not already served by horse-drawn trams. Throughout much of Germany and Austria, the use of trams was high, although the steep cost of tickets limited their use by workers. Amsterdam was the only European city in which the tramway was operated exclusively by the municipality. It offered worker fares that required 4.3 percent of a worker's income.[57] Trams in London, sanctioned by acts of Parliament and operated by private companies, contributed to commuting by workers at the turn of the century. According to an 1894 report to the London County Council, the trams were so heavily used that they filled up at the first stops and then just ran straight through the rest of their route.[58] The Council took over concessions on 148 of the 349 miles of tramway in London in the 1890s. It implemented the policies it had always wanted to enforce with

56. Jules Malou, *Tarif des voyageurs: Etude statistique d'une experimentation* (Brussels: Guyot, 1869); *Compte rendu des opérations de chemins de fer* (Brussels: Goemaere, 1894).
57. Paolo Capuzzo, "Between Politics and Technology: Transport as a Factor of Mass Suburbanization in Europe, 1890–1939," in *Suburbanizing the Masses: Public Transport and Urban Development in Historical Perspective,* ed. Colin Dival and Winstan Bond (Hants, England: Aldershot, 2003), 30; John P. McKay, *Tramways and Trolleys: The Rise of Urban Mass Transit in Europe* (Princeton: Princeton University Press, 1976).
58. A. G. Clarke, "Trams, Buses and Steam Boats in London" (1895), London Transport Library, London.

the railways, building an extensive network that consistently offered cheap fares. In 1905 in London, 260,000 of the 820,000 commuting workmen relied on the municipal trams, half the number who traveled on the workmen's trains.[59] Metropolitan Electric Tramways, running along main roads, extended into the suburbs of north London; other companies, the London County Council, and suburban councils ran trams in central London, to the east, and to the southeast. Workmen's tickets on the Tooting tram route increased from 581,626 in 1902–1903 to 8,426,140 in 1912–1913 (an increase of 93 percent).[60] The London buses made no special provisions for the working classes, so their service was generally limited to the middle-class commuters.

Brussels tram service, like that of London, was fragmented. Nine private entrepreneurs competed in Brussels to lay tracks and to attract suburban commuters. These privately run trams did not offer workmen's fares and seemed to follow, rather than to stimulate, development. After contentious debates between Catholic government ministers and Belgian municipalities, legislation deeded regulatory power over private tram lines to the national government.[61] Members of the Brussels Council, complaining that the lack of municipal trams limited suburban development, looked enviously to London's municipal control of the trams, just as British rail reformers cited the example of the national Belgian railway and its lower fares.

Unique to Belgium, the regional rail lines, operated by the SNCV/NMVB carried a significant number of workers. Many working-class commuters relied on these smaller rail lines to get to the main trunk lines, especially in the Brabant province around Brussels. "Thanks to the regional rail, especially in the farthest reaches of the countryside, in the smallest villages, along the routes and the fields," Mahaim wrote, "the opportunity is increasingly available to everyone to seek work and bread far away while conserving their habitual residence."[62] These regional trains that offered workmen's fares solved the problem of getting to and from the railway station for many workers in Belgium who, like the London commuters, complained of the long treks to the stations.

Remembering his early days traveling on workmen's trains, one Belgian commuter recalled the streams of "workmen, often accompanied by their wives and children, who were on the road before daybreak, with a knapsack on their backs" heading for the station, several kilometers in the distance.[63] Except in the summer, they trekked back and forth in the darkness.

---

59. Ibid.
60. Tarn, *Five Per Cent Philanthropy,* 121.
61. *Annales parlementaires* (21 June 1872), 318; Jean Bary, *Les Cités-jardins: Villas et cottages* (Hasselt, 1910).
62. Mahaim, *Les abonnements,* 133.
63. "De Onpartydige," Dendermonde, 22 August 1980, cited by A. Stroobants, *150 Jaar Spoorwegen te Dendermonde 1837–1987* (Dendermonde: Stadsbestuur Dendermonde, 1987).

The introduction of bicycles—in 1908, there were more than three hundred thousand licensed bicycles in Belgium—facilitated travel. Some residents of Tournais, according to Mahaim, even rode in dog carts, but foot travel from the cottages to the stations predominated.

"A Profound Social Revolution": Transporting Workers beyond the City

Minister Jamar proclaimed in his report to the Belgian parliament in 1869 that posterity would view the building of railways throughout Europe as one of the greatest accomplishments of the nineteenth century. Political leaders might argue over the organizational details and fare structures of the railways, he acknowledged, but all would agree on "the immense services that they have given to civilization." Over the course of the nineteenth century, track networks stretched farther and train travel became less expensive and faster. "Traveling has become a necessity" for all social classes, Jamar explained, as he introduced workmen's trains to Belgium.[64]

When railways opened to destinations not previously accessible to rooted individuals, the new pace of travel appeared to shorten the space between distant points. Distances separating industrial cities from the countryside shrank as homes and workplaces were linked by the new mode of transportation. In the words of sociologist Wolfgang Schivelbusch, locations collided.[65] Commuters sped through fields and villages barely aware of the intervening countryside as they pursued their destination. Ernest Mahaim concluded that the subsidized workmen's fares were eliminating the regional as well as local differences that distinguished Belgians from each other. He pointed to the laborers who had been displaced from their Flemish farms and now traveled daily to mines and industrial centers in Brussels and Wallonia.[66] The experience of urban life during the day made them cosmopolitan, while their rural homes planted them firmly in a stable, traditional culture. Similarly, British reformers celebrated the suburban comforts afforded the families of commuting urban workers who abandoned the urban chaos each evening as twilight descended on the city.

The Belgian Socialist Emile Vandervelde reminded the readers of his study of rural exodus that in contrast to the British schemes that were designed to move workers out of the city, the Belgian trains were organized to root

64. A. Jamar, 10 December 1869, "Exposé des résultats de la réforme introduite le 1er mai 1866," Documents parlementaires. Recueil des pièces imprimées par ordre de la chambre des représentants, Session de 1869–70, 31, 205.
65. Schivelbusch, *The Railway Journey.*
66. Mahaim, *Les abonnements,* 205.

laborers on their land, to counter the hunger that compelled rural laborers to leave their villages. The Belgian trains preserved the status quo, Mahaim acknowledged, while the British trains introduced new demographic patterns. In London, the rail lines that had displaced residents were opening new areas to commuters. The British workmen's trains would succeed only if cheap housing was available beyond the city and the workers could be induced to move their families to these new suburban estates.

The Times noted in 1861: "Much has already been done to tempt these people to purer air and better habits. Thousands of cottages are springing up yearly in the suburbs."[67] Yet relatively few workers moved to the London suburbs before the 1880s. In contrast to the Belgian ridership, the number of commuting laborers did not increase steadily in the first years of the workmen's train experiment in London. The tenants whose lodgings lay in the path of the railroad or street improvements could not afford the additional burden of daily train travel. And even if workmen's fares were held to a few pence a day, casual laborers could not move away from their ever-changing local labor market. More regularly employed workers, too, hesitated to uproot their families from urban neighborhoods. In the suburbs, they would not have families and relatives on whom they could count for assistance during bad times. The new suburbs lacked cheap sources for daily provisions. So the London laborer did not leave the city.

In contrast, it could be argued that the workmen's trains in Belgium accomplished their more limited aim. Despite declining employment in agriculture, the number of residents in the countryside remained stable in Belgium through the First World War. In times of industrial crisis, workers returned to their small parcel of land, cultivating crops instead of striking against the industrialists and mine owners. The workmen's trains also homogenized salaries by creating a national labor market. It worked both ways. Workers could travel in search of higher wages, but employers also had an army of peasants as well as workers on whom to draw, keeping wages low and fairly uniform. Unemployed urban workers did not pose as great a threat in Belgium as elsewhere; they returned to the land.

67. *Times,* 2 March 1861, cited by H. J. Dyos, *Exploring the Urban Past: Essays in Urban History,* ed. David Cannandine and David Reeder (Cambridge: Cambridge University Press, 1982), 105.

4 "*Le Cottage*"

Pastoral Villages and Tidy Suburbs

> I am quite sure that the remedy for the great disease of overcrowding is...a question simply of time and space, and nothing else. If you can accommodate, by raising the height of your buildings, a larger population on a given area, well and good. But if you cannot do that, then you must go outside the narrow area at the centre of your congested district, and you must trust to modern inventions, and modern improvements in locomotion for abolishing time.
>
> —Arthur Balfour *cited by Charles Booth,* 1901, 2

In 1901, Charles Booth, the renowned author of the multivolume survey of poverty in the British capital, *Life and Labour in London,* addressed the Browning Hall Conference on housing in London, which was convened by the clergyman and reformer Francis Stead. The assembled reformers agreed with Booth that "locomotion" was key to relieving the overcrowding of London and "that a complete system of transportation radiating from congested centers, which shall be cheap, rapid, and owned by the London County Council, is a primary step towards dealing with the Housing problem in London." The working class needed to be convinced to move out to the suburbs. At the second Browning Hall Conference, Booth elaborated on his earlier remarks in a paper entitled: "Improved Means of Locomotion as a Cure for the Housing Difficulties of London." He cited the Conservative minister Lord Balfour's argument in the House of Commons in May 1900, positing two choices to the housing reformers: to build up in high-rise blocks or to "trust to modern inventions and modern improvements in locomotion for abolishing time."[1]

Both Booth and Balfour thought the solution was to give workers cheap and convenient mobility. Then workers would eagerly move out of the center of London. Their outward movement would result in "happiness, comfort and health"—a pursuit common to all classes, according to Booth.[2] With adequate transportation, Booth predicted, "London will spread in all directions." Workers would move to new suburbs complete with town halls and commercial centers where the worker's wife "will look for her shopping."[3]

Rather than allowing the private railways to segregate residential development by class as they had done by limiting the sale of workmen's tickets to a few stations, Booth proposed that the London County Council run "a large and really complete scheme of railways underground and overhead, as well as a net-work of tram lines on the surface."[4] Booth's proposals for municipal control of public transport echoed continental reformers. Laissez-faire liberalism did not serve the interests of the public, especially when public utilities were run as natural monopolies. Otto Beck, mayor of Mannheim, Germany, had proposed municipal control of suburban rail lines so that workers, who would otherwise migrate permanently to live near the industrial port, did not desert the countryside. He did not want "the interests of the general public . . . to take a back seat to the private profits of some big capitalist enterprise," like the South German railway.[5]

Booth believed it would be easier to justify municipal control of locomotion than municipal construction of housing. "It is quite possible to imagine all organized methods of locomotion (like all roads) as State or municipal monopolies, without any serious shock to the individualist basis of life," he asserted, "but, short of the wildest scheme of socialism, it is quite impossible to conceive of arranging the entire housing of the Nation on that plan."[6] Unless trains competed for rights of way on the tracks, "scientific locomotion" required monopoly control, so why not grant the authority to the municipality?

The editors of the *Housing Journal,* published by the Workmen's National Housing Council, condemned Booth for his naive faith that government

---

1. Arthur Balfour, quoted in Charles Booth, *Improved Means of Locomotion as a First Step towards the Cure of Housing Difficulties of London* (London: Macmillan, 1901), 2.
2. Booth, *Improved Means of Locomotion,* 4, 2, and 10.
3. Ibid., 17.
4. Ibid., 16.
5. "Die Voortbahnen der Stadt Mannheim," as cited by Dieter Schott, "Suburbanizing the Masses for Profit or Welfare: Conflict and Cooperation Between Private and Municipal Interests in German Cities, 1890–1914," in *Suburbanizing the Masses Public Transport and Urban Development in Historical Perspective,* ed. Colin Divall and Winstan Bond (Aldershot: Ashgate, 2003), 99.
6. Booth, *Improved Means of Locomotion,* 19.

control of locomotion to existing suburban housing would solve the problems of both workers and of the city. Why, they asked, was Booth willing to call for municipal ownership of the trams while he continued to worship at the shrine of private enterprise in housing? Instead, they called for national control of the railways and for municipal control of housing.[7]

A worker whose house in central London was demolished to make way for a railway terminal inquired simply: "Why don't they build us a great village or town out Epping way . . . and then let the railways bring us backwards and forwards for a trifle? They take our homes; let them give us something in return."[8] Rather than squeezing displaced laborers and their families into adjacent and overcrowded neighborhoods, why not construct housing outside of the city for the evicted workers, enlisting the railways that had evicted them to transport them back to the city to work. The Conservative housing reformer Robert Salisbury agreed, suggesting that the British emulate their continental neighbors and find homes for the workers in the suburbs outside the congested urban centers.[9] The *Housing Journal* urged local governments to acquire land and build "enough good cottages to satisfy the demand."[10]

Looking beyond the city for a solution to urban overcrowding, the British garden city planner Raymond Unwin explained that "something could be done to relieve the pressure on the outside—where it originates."[11] Affordable, rapid transport and the construction of workers' housing beyond the city would encourage regularly employed urban workers to follow the middle class to the rural stretches beyond the old walking city. "That the question of transportation has an influence on that of housing is one of those truisms, one of the axioms that no one debates," Charles Didier, the Belgian editor of *Le Cottage* announced to planners in 1903.[12] Trains had extended the distance that could be traveled between home and work. "The most important thing that the state, cities, individuals or groups can do to ensure that everyone, whether employee or worker, enjoys a healthy and gay house surrounded by a little garden can be summed up in one simple formula: Make transportation available," he added the next year.[13]

Workmen's trains would remove the workers and their families from the urban congestion that bred disease and disorder to cottages set in traditional

7. *Housing Journal* (October 1901) and (August 1900).
8. *Working Man* 2 (1866): 136, cited by H. J. Dyos, "Railways and Housing in Victorian London," *Journal of Transport History* 2 (1955): 113.
9. Robert Salisbury, "Labourers' and Artisans' Dwellings," *National Review* 9 (November 1883): 301–316.
10. *Housing Journal* 1 (August 1900).
11. Raymond Unwin, *Housing Journal* 12 (July 1901).
12. *Le Cottage* (July 1903).
13. *Le Cottage* (January 1904).

rural villages that would nurture and civilize them. The resulting division of work and home was not planned. Slow to recognize the revolutionary impact of commuting, of the distancing of work from home, most reformers were equally loathe to acknowledge the related development—social segregation. As workers commuted outward into the greenery surrounding the capitals, the middle class moved further afield. Workmen's trains and housing reforms in Brussels and London radically altered settlement patterns around the two capitals. On the one hand, train travel brought destinations closer together. On the other, the integrated housing and transportation reforms made residential isolation the norm in the two capitals by the First World War.

"So Many Box Dwellers": Rejecting Urban Tenements

Charles Buls, the Liberal mayor of Brussels, chastised nineteenth-century planners for ignoring the "suffering of the small and the humble whom they crush under the ruin of their buildings."[14] It was clear to most European reformers by the 1880s that the rash of demolitions carried out by nineteenth-century urban planners in the name of hygiene had actually exacerbated the overcrowding of the cities. When hovels gave way to massive commercial buildings, laborers and their families were squeezed into ever more restricted areas of the Belgian capital. "Men, women and children swelter in a stewing agglomeration of demoralizing promiscuity," a Liberal sitting on the Brussels Council observed.[15] Residents chased out of homes in the Marolles district of Brussels by the construction of the mammoth Palais de Justice had found refuge along the rue Delcourt in St.-Gilles/St.-Gillis, only to be threatened a decade later with eviction a second time by another set of urban improvement projects. The Brussels Council continued to demolish unsanitary buildings, dislodging over fifteen thousand tenants between 1900 and 1908. During that period, the population of the Belgian capital grew from 183,686 to 196,882 residents.[16]

Reformers acknowledged that few of the tenants of workers' housing constructed by philanthropists, industrialists, and municipalities at the center of the capitals to house the displaced actually came from razed buildings.[17] Charles De Quéker, the director of public assistance for Brussels and secretary of the Brussels Housing Committee reported that after the demolition of

14. Charles Buls, *Esthétique des villes* (1894; reprint, Brussels: St.-Lukasdossier, 1981), 37.
15. Ville de Bruxelles, *Bulletin Communal 1911*, vol. 1, Compte rendu des séances (Brussels: Guyot, 1911), 581.
16. Camille Lemonnier, "Habitations ouvrières," *Bulletin Communal de Bruxelles* (1911): 580.
17. Michel De Beule, "Du droit au logement au droit de cité," *La Fonderie* 3 (November 1987): 43–46. See also Archives de la Ville de Bruxelles, Fonds Maisons ouvrières, Boîte 2. Procès verbaux du Comité de Patronage (5 February 1891), Archives de la Ville/Stadsarchief, Brussels.

housing deemed unsanitary in the central St. Roch district, only 19 of the 175 evicted families (11%) had chosen to move to new housing outside of their neighborhoods.[18] Sixty-two percent had crowded into lodging within five hundred meters of the housing from which they had been evicted. The evicted tenants could not afford the rents charged in either the private or the municipal dwellings constructed for them by the reformers. Besides, these massive dwellings looming over city streets seemed incompatible with the individuality that the reformers aspired to inculcate in their working-class subjects. Rather than separating families, tenement blocks forced the masses to dwell one on top of the other, overcrowding them vertically rather than laterally. At the turn of the century, reformers condemned apartment buildings "in the shape of tall blocks containing great heaps of humanity" that trapped their inhabitants inside, "so many box dwellers," for days at a time.[19] Block dwellings loomed as breeding grounds for revolution.

In his 1904 report to the International Congress on Low-Cost Housing, Raymond Unwin confirmed the shared argument against large-scale housing developments. Not only were the blocks of flats "ugly," he explained, but it was impossible to "give any expression to the sense of homeliness" in tenements that "consist of the repetition of tiny cell-like units."[20] Flat-dwelling mothers could not oversee their children playing in the urban streets below. And residents of flats, surrounded by the smells of their neighbors' cooking and the sounds of their squabbling, enjoyed little privacy, other reformers added. By 1906, London authorities had virtually abandoned the construction of congregate urban housing. "Block dwellings common enough in some places . . . never appealed to the English," the British author and lecturer on housing and transportation reforms, Ernest Dewsnup, declared.[21] Other British reformers offhandedly suggested that large blocks of flats belonged on the Continent rather than in Britain.[22] The Belgians were not so sure. Several Brussels reformers thought that perhaps multistory urban dwellings had their place in Paris, not Brussels.[23]

---

18. Charles De Quéker, Ville de Bruxelles, Comité de patronage des habitations ouvrières et des institutions de prévoyance, Rapport sur l'exercice de 1896 (Brussels: Imprimerie des Institutions de prévoyance, 1897), 6–7.
19. W. Thompson, *The Housing Handbook* (London: National Housing Reform Council, 1903), 5.
20. Raymond Unwin, "Rapport, Vie Question," *Congrès International des habitations à bon marché* (1905), 31.
21. Ernest Dewsnup, *The Housing Problem in London* (Manchester: Manchester University Press, 1907).
22. J. N. Tarn, "French Flats for the English in Nineteenth-century London," in *Multi-Storey Living: The British Working-Class Housing,* ed. A. Sutcliffe (London: Croom Helm, 1974).
23. Edouard Van der Linden, *Etude sur l'amélioration des habitations ouvrières et sur l'organisation du domicile de secours* (Brussels: Librairie Polytechnique Decq & Duhent, 1875), 26–27; H. Langerock, *De arbeiderswoningen in Belgie* (Ghent: Boekhandel J. Vuylsteke, 1894), 10.

Boundary Street Estate, August 1906. Blocks built in the East End of London by the London County Council. Reproduced with permission from London Metropolitan Archives 80/2749.

Brussels mayor Charles Buls summed up the prevailing Belgian sentiment when he declared: "We do not like the 'huge barracks' divided into apartments. Like Dante, we want to ascend our own stairway." He mused: "Like the Anglo-Saxon, whose cousins we are, we love our home, the family fireside."[24] Perhaps, Buls speculated, that explained why the few multistory blocks that had been built in the center of Brussels were occupied by foreigners, not Belgians. The love of privacy, of the home away from the prying curious eye of a neighbor, was as much a part of the Belgian as the British national character, he asserted.

Most Belgian housing reformers observing the construction of philanthropic blocks in London in the mid-nineteenth century concluded it was an experiment not to be imitated. The Belgian reformers argued that if the practical British were now advocating housing workers in individual cottages,

24. Charles Buls, *Esthétiques des villes* (1894) (Brussels: Sint-Lukasdossier, 1981), 28.

then perhaps the Belgians should follow the example of their now-chastened "Anglo-Saxon cousins."[25] Like the British housing reformers, they took the cottage, not the barracks, as their inspiration. Even the Belgian Socialists shared the pervading dream of providing a healthy, cozy cottage as opposed to an urban "lodging that is sad, dirty, without air, where nothing keeps the worker at home and so he goes to the cabaret, becomes a drunk and only returns to his home to throw himself on his heap of linen."[26]

Flats in the city constricted their lodgers, "cubes of masonry, rental machines constructed by the devil," lacking a soul, the editor of the Belgian journal *Le Cottage* complained in his call for an urban exodus and return to the countryside.[27] In their place, he imagined "a small lodging, simple but practical and dignified, set in a large garden, far from the fever of the city."[28] For the Belgians, with fewer philanthropic blocks to reject, that meant encouraging workers to remain in the countryside, constructing small units of worker housing within the city where necessary, and even smaller units of suburban housing where possible.

The middle-class reformers who relished their own comfortable domestic shelter from the industrial world assumed that elite workers and their families would readily adjust to new domestic environments where they could live in peaceful contentment. Belgian delegates explained to the 1900 International Congress on Low-Cost Housing that away from the cities, workers "might find themselves secluded from the action and distractions that animated life in the center, but they would also be removed from the contagion of subversive ideas that spread so easily within tenements."[29]

The reformers planned to dismantle the robust working-class communities of Bethnal Green in London and the Marolles district in Brussels, replacing the mutual obligations of the improvident with the self-sufficient individualism of the cottage. Looking beyond the central city itself, reformers dreamed of laborers' families housed in suburban and rural cottages, enjoying the cultivation of their gardens in their leisure time and the higher wages of the city in their working hours. The private nuclear self-sufficient family would replace the public sociability and intimacy of working-class neighborhoods. In suburbs and the countryside, respectable family life would flourish in cottages, for workers as it did for the middle class.

---

25. See, e.g., Charles Lagasse, *Quelques mots sur l'habitation ouvrière* (Brussels: Société belge de librairie, 1889); Buls, *Esthétiques des villes,* 28.
26. Louis Bertrand, *Le socialisme communal* (Brussels: Messageries de la Presse Belge, 1890), 21.
27. Charles Didier, "Notre programme," *Le Cottage* (June 1903).
28. *Le Cottage* (August 1903).
29. Eugène Neve and H. Royer de Dour, *Congrès international d'habitations à bon marché tenu à Paris les 18, 19, 20, et 21 juin 1900.* Compte rendu et documents. (Paris: Secrétariat de la Société française des habitations à bon marché, 1900), 15.

"Surrounded by a Corner of Greenery": Cottages for Workers

The distrust of the dense urban housing that congested European cities at the end of the nineteenth century directed reformers toward greenery in their search to secure morally uplifting housing for urban laborers. British and Belgian reformers shared a dream with the French, Danish, Dutch, and Germans of a future when "the face of the whole land may be made merry with colonies of cottages and with smiling gardens and orchards, verdant meadows and waving corn, happy village workshops, and beautiful buildings."[30] They envisioned cottages congregated around a village center set in the countryside. Belgian reformers contrasted the "'workers' barracks, less healthy than prisons" with the "small well-aired houses lodging one family surrounded by a corner of greenery."[31] The privacy ensured by greenery would prevent the spread of epidemics, the scourge of urban life. But more than that, cottages would enhance home-life for the families of respectable workers. In the evenings, workers' families would tend the gardens of half-timbered cottages set along winding roads that romantically followed the contours of the land. This suburban life would afford the workers as it did the middle class a retreat from the tumult of the city. Boredom beyond the crowded public streets of the urban capital was easily compensated for by the private reveries of the quiet hearth.

Housing reformers on both sides of the Channel drew inspiration from the British garden cities designed by Ebenezer Howard, who expected to transform society by radically changing the physical environment in which people lived.[32] In planning the first garden city of Letchworth, the firm of Barry Parker and Raymond Unwin had set out to promote the social welfare of the working classes with low-density dwellings that bore no resemblance to urban tenements. Unwin invoked "the great charm of the old English village, and of many continental villages," with their grass and trees and simple thatched structures.[33] Rather than taking detached middle-class villas as his model for the working-class dwellings, the Socialist Unwin looked to the working-class family itself, with its focus on the hearth, as his inspiration. The practical dwellings were joined together in rows, affording substantial

30. Robert Williams, *London Rookeries and Collier's Slums: A Plea for More Breathing Room* (London: W. Reeves, 1893), 12.

31. *Moniteur des Comités de patronage et des sociétés d'habitations ouvrières* (25 October 1900).

32. Ebenezer Howard, *Garden Cities of To-morrow* (Cambridge, Mass.: MIT Press, 1965), 48.

33. Raymond Unwin, "Rapport VIe question," *Congrès international d'habitations à bon marché* (1905) (Liège: Imprimerie industrielle et commerciale, 1906), 33.

Letchworth cottages, a garden city. Photo by author (2002).

sunlight to the individual interiors. The site plans offered communal open areas and recreation spaces.[34]

Henrietta Barnett, a leader of the Charity Organisation Society, constructed a housing estate on a tree-covered hill on the edge of Hampstead Heath. Drawing on her own experiences living in Whitechapel with her husband, Canon Samuel Barnett, she wanted the wealthy and the poor to mix happily together in the midst of nature. "Cities must grow, but it is the gift of science that the growth may be so directed that the citizen may have both

34. Mervyn Miller, *Letchworth: The First Garden City* (London: Phillimore, 2002).

the inspiration of a garden and the stimulus of a living community," Barnett explained. She contrasted the "stunted... ugly, half-washed, ill-nourished" children she had observed in her charity work on the streets of London with her vision of those same children transplanted "into a garden, father working, mother watching, children helping, the land yielding with that generosity which under any climate seems to follow spade labour and personal interest."[35]

Already integrated into nature, good housekeeping would make the cottage a true home. This physical representation of idealized domesticity envisioned by the reformers just needed a wife tending its hearth. In their imaginations, the working-class mother, like her bourgeois model, hovered at the center of the home, surrounded by her children and welcoming her husband each evening as he returned from his commute. These cottages would transform urban workers into model citizens for the British reformers such as Barnett.

Delegates returned from the 1907 International Congress on Low-Cost Housing meeting in London full of admiration for the garden cities they had visited that sited workmen's cottages near middle-class villas. The Belgian reformer E. Harmant reported that the British viewed the creation of the garden city as the resolution of the question of workmen's housing.[36] The Belgian magazine *Ma Maison. Mijn Huis* (my house) passed on to its readers descriptions of the "delicious cottages that were healthy and restful, surrounded by flowers and greenery," homes that encouraged "the relaxation of the family together after the father returned from his day's work."[37] Patronage committees in Belgium sponsored contests for housing plans destined for workers who had bought a small piece of land and applied for financial assistance under the 1889 law. Judges ranked the plans based on their practicality, cost, and beauty. Architecture was being democratized, they suggested.

In 1903, Charles Didier, the Belgian editor of *Le Cottage,* called on his readers to join in the building of the first garden city in Belgium: Lahorville.[38] Modeled on Howard's garden city, Lahorville would provide concerts, meetings, and festivals, rather than the more typical working-class music halls and pubs, in a rural setting. It was never built. The Belgian architect Vuylsteke also proposed the construction of a garden city in the Brussels suburb of Laeken that would provide individual cottages. It, too, never progressed beyond the planning stage. Belgian reformers attributed

---

35. Henrietta Barnett, "Science and City Suburbs," in *Science and Public Affairs* (London: Allen, 1906).

36. E. Harmant, *La Question des habitations à bon marché au congrès de Londres en Août 1907* (Brussels: Librairie Albert Dewit, 1908), 23.

37. *Ma Maison. Mijn Huis. Bulletin périodique illustré publié sous le patronage de diverses associations d'employés communaux* (January 1906).

38. *Le Cottage* 5 (October 1903).

the failure to the absence of philanthropic backers and the refusal of municipalities to go up against the property speculators.

In Britain, Fred Knee of the National Workingmen's Association admonished the garden city advocates: "I can only hope you will hurry up and get your scheme through so that its futility may be the more quickly demonstrated, and the people be induced to set to work at their own housing."[39] Knee and the other working-class writers noted that garden city rents prohibited occupation by anyone without regular, well-paid employment. Too, the paternalism of the garden city developers grated on trade unionists.

Yet, the garden city planners clearly influenced the design of workers' housing beyond the city center on both sides of the Channel. In his planning of Brussels and its environs, Mayor Buls consciously mirrored many of the design features of the garden cities.[40] Rather than being laid out in mathematical grids, he argued, streets should resemble the veins and arteries of a living being. In London, the band of young architects hired to design Council housing estates for workers at the outer edge of the county had been trained by the garden city planners whose optimism originally propelled reformers beyond the city in their quest for a solution to the urban housing crisis. Belgian architects also borrowed cottage plans from British garden city planners, adapting their designs to blend with traditional features of Belgian peasant dwellings. Belgian builders scaled back some of the features the British reformers copied from their own middle-class villas. Home-owning workers, whether in their rural Belgian cottages or in their British suburban semi-detached houses, like the bourgeoisie, would learn from their environment to become independent individuals, unlike the masses of workers haunting the cities.

Reformers expected private and semi-private housing societies to build cottages for the workers in the suburbs outside of Brussels and London that would facilitate "the exodus of working families to localities where the air and light could be widely available."[41] Co-partnership tenants' societies such as Benjamin Jones's Tenant Co-operators Limited constructed garden villages such as Upton Park, just outside of central London. By 1913, there

39. Fred Knee to Thomas Adams, 19 September 1902, First Garden City Heritage Museum file, "Collection of Source Material," cited by Standish Meacham, *Regaining Paradise: Englishness and the Early Garden City Movement* (New Haven: Yale University Press, 1999), 63.
40. Buls, *Esthétique des villes*. See also Marcel Smets, *Charles Buls: Les principes de l'art urbain* (Liège: Pierre Mardaga, 1995).
41. Professor Putzeys, quoted in Henry Delvaux de Fenffe, Conseil provincial de Liège, Séance d'ouverture du 6 juillet 1909, *Les habitations ouvrières* (Liège: Thone, 1909), 194–195. See also Alfred Marshall, "The Housing of the London Poor," *Contemporary Review* 45 (1884): 224; C. B. P. Bosanquet, E. Chadwick, Professor Fawcett, G. Godwin, C. Wren Hoskyns, E. Lankester, J. S. Mill, Lord Shaftesbury, Sir J. Kay-Shuttleworth, Alderman Waterlow, "Report: Committee on Dwellings for the Labouring Classes," *Journal of the Society of Arts* 13 (May 12, 1865): 651.

Le Cottage "Little Nest," a model working-class house.
From *Le Cottage* (January 1905).

were about sixty estates containing 11,479 houses whose tenants received stock in the development.[42] The housing societies of Brussels, such as the Société anonyme des habitations ouvrières dans l'agglomération bruxellois (Limited Society for Workers' Housing in the Brussels Region), assisted workers who moved to the inner ring of faubourgs: St.-Gilles/St. Gillis, Anderlecht, Molenbeek, and Schaerbeek/Schaarbeek. Other Brussels societies built clusters of cottages in Forêt/Vorst and Laeken, suburban communes where land was more affordable. Most of the private housing constructed on the periphery of Brussels with funds from the government savings bank, the Caisse générale d'épargne et de retraite (CGER), consisted of individual units, not the larger multifamily projects that were being constructed at the same time in London. As a result, workers were dispersed, usually on the

42. Co-partnership Tenants' Housing Council, *Garden Suburbs, Villages, and Homes* (London: Co-partnership Housing Council, 1912).

edge of the built-up region of the city, rather than grouped in homogeneous suburban districts as in London. That intentionally allowed for mixing, rather than segregating, social classes.

Around Brussels, the ring of communes of Anderlecht, Etterbeek, Ixelles/Elsene, Laeken, Molenbeek, St.-Gilles/St.-Gillis, Saint-Josse/St. Joost, and Schaerbeek/Schaarbeek gained 81,535 new residents between 1870 and 1880.[43] The growth followed the axis of roads out of Brussels, as the urban agglomeration swallowed up rural villages. At one point, in suburban Uccle, for example, new residents moving out of the city were met by migrants coming in from the adjacent rural areas. Including its ring of suburban communes, the Brussels agglomeration mushroomed from 288,400 residents in 1866 to 458,700 residents in 1890, a growth of 59 percent.

London's ring of suburbs grew at the same pace, from 414,226 residents in 1861 to 1,405,852 in 1891.[44] Building for the working class had almost ceased in the center of London. Cottages were springing up throughout working-class suburbs to the East, such as Tottenham, Edmonton, West Ham, and Walthamstow, the Working class Housing Committee of the London County Council explained, because "of the facilities that have been given by the railway companies and the cheap rates for traveling."[45] In these suburbs, workers' families were housed in terraces containing four, eight, or more units, intersected by passages opening onto small, walled courtyards at the back. The front doors opened directly onto straight streets.

The author of some of the most important housing legislation of the nineteenth century, Lord Torrens, ridiculed the reformers' vision of working-class suburban estates as a "mystic myth" of "beautiful little cottages, the doors and windows covered with honeysuckle and roses."[46] The slums were reproducing themselves around London, ever farther removed from the center. The Travelling Tax Abolition Committee complained that "alterations and 'improvements' in the Metropolis" had driven so many laborers to migrate to certain suburbs that poor relief from the new municipality was necessary to alleviate distress.[47] In suburbs such as Edmonton that

43. Sint Lukas Archief, *Straten en Stenen. Brussel: Stadsgroei, 1780–1790* (Brussels: St. Lukas Archief, 1982); F. Dussart, "Quelques réflexions sur l'urbanisation des campagnes et ses répercussions sur l'habitat rural de la Belgique," in *Mélanges Tulippe* (Brussels: Duculot, 1967); Guillaume Jacquemyns, "Introduction," *Une commune de l'agglomération bruxelloise, Uccle* (Brussels: Université libre de Bruxelles, 1958).

44. Paul Meuriot, *Des agglomérations urbaines dans l'Europe contemporaine* (Paris: Belin Frères, 1898), 160.

45. Samuel G. Burgess, 10 July 1903, Royal Commission on London Traffic, Report of the Royal Commission appointed to inquire into and report upon the means of locomotion and transport in London (London: 1905–1906).

46. Lord Torrens, quoted in Anthony S. Wohl, *The Eternal Slum: Housing and Social Policy in Victorian London* (Montreal: McGill-Queen's University Press, 1977), 293.

47. F. W. Buxton, "Workmen's Trains and the Passenger Duty," *Gazette of the Travelling Tax Abolition Committee* 12 (11 June 1883): 208–209.

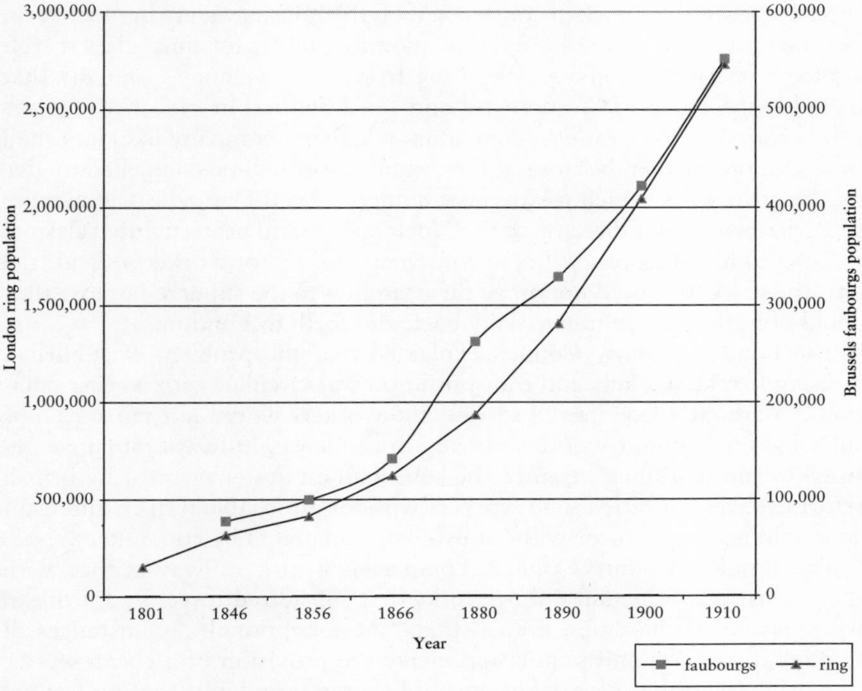

Suburban population growth, London and Brussels, 1801–1910. Data from Royal Commission on London Traffic, *Report of the Royal Commission appointed to inquire into and report upon the means of locomotion and transport in London* (London: HMSO, 1905–1906), 126; *Les Recensements de 1910* (Brussels: E. Guyot, 1912), 21.

were already congested with workmen's housing, the population grew from 10,930 in 1861, to 23,463 in 1881, to 98,409 in 1911.[48]

Unless workmen's train service was improved to all districts, the philanthropic Artizans, Labourers and General Dwellings Company (Dwellings Company) charged, it would be "quite impossible to relieve the overcrowding of the working classes in London by the removal of the best of them—not necessarily those receiving the highest wages—but those who appreciate a home with all its associations and elevating influences."[49] In their application for reduced fares from the Hornsey and Wood Green stations, the Dwellings Company testified in 1884 that working families wanted to rent their

48. John Nelson Tarn, *Five Per Cent Philanthropy: An Account of Housing in Urban Areas between 1840 and 1914* (Cambridge: Cambridge University Press, 1973), 120.
49. The Artizans, Labourers and General Dwellings Company's application for reduced fares to Hornsey and Wood Green (Noel Park Estate Houses), Workmens' Trains and Fares, 1884, RAIL 236 353 6, National Archives.

suburban cottages they had constructed on the housing estate in Noel Park, but the railway companies offered no monthly tickets for third-class travelers from nearby stations. A delegation from the Dwellings Company that included the Duke of Westminster and Lord Shaftesbury testified: "It depends entirely on the railway companies whether a company like ours shall progress, or whether, because of the distance, we shall be compelled to give up the great work which we are now doing."[50] Lord Lymington, a member of Parliament and a director of the Noel Park Estate protested that despite their best philanthropic efforts to construct housing for workers outside the city, the workers would not move their families to the suburbs because they could not afford to commute daily back and forth to London.[51]

The London County Council explained that the problem of suburban housing for the workers and transportation was circular, with no easy solution.[52] Without adequate rail service, the workers would not move to new suburbs. But without workers already in residence, railway companies refused to run workmen's trains. The suburban estates envisioned by British reformers were of little use to workers without affordable transit, and transit would not pay returns without dwellings inhabited by commuters.

The London County Council, comparing British railway service with the extensive continental rail networks that subsidized travel by European workers out of the cities, argued that "the exceptional circumstances of London, as to size and population, make the provision of a cheap service of workmen's trains essential in the public interest and in the interest of the workmen themselves."[53] If the railways would accommodate the workers, they would migrate to the suburbs, relieving the overcrowding of the cities. Samuel G. Burgess, housing manager for the London County Council testified in 1903 that while one-third of the tenants of their central London blocks moved house each year, they did not migrate to the suburbs: "They go to where their work is situated, which proves that the traveling facilities are no good to them at the present time," he explained.[54] The laborers who assisted bricklayers, carpenters, printers, and plasterers had to be at work by six in the morning, before workmen's service ran. Earlier trains would allow these laborers to join the elite workers who labored shorter hours and had already migrated to the London County Council estates in the

50. Ernest Noel to the editor of the *Times*, 26 May 1885, reprinted in *Gazette of the Travelling Tax Abolition Committee* 12 (11 June 1885): 321.
51. Harry Barnes, *The Slum: Its Story and Solution* (London: P.S. King & Son, 1931), 214.
52. Alfred Smith, *The Housing Question* (London: Swan Sonnenschein, 1900), 46; William Thompson, *The Housing Handbook* (London: National Housing Reform Council, 1903), 236.
53. Edgar Harper, Select Committee on the Working and Administration of the Cheap Trains Act 1883, Workmen's Trains, General, CL/HSG/1/78, London Metropolitan Archives, London.
54. Samuel G. Burgess, 10 July 1903, Royal Commission on London Traffic, Report of the Royal Commission appointed to inquire into and report upon the means of locomotion and transport in London (London, 1905–1906), 217.

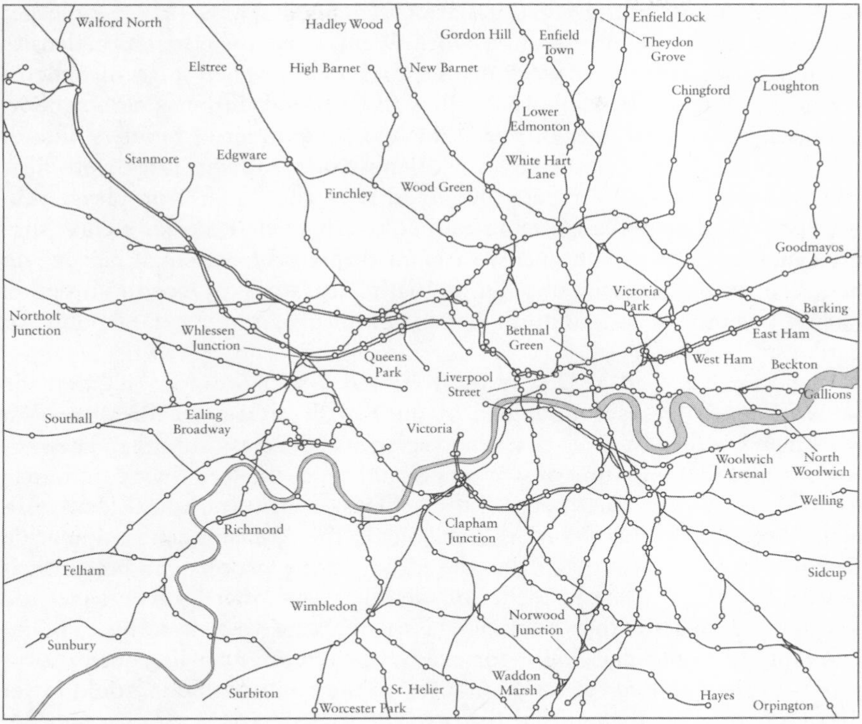

Mainline railways into London. Data from Royal Commission on London Traffic. Report of the Royal Commission appointed to inquire into and report upon the means of locomotion and transport in London (London: 1905–1906.)

suburbs. As in Belgium where workmen's trains made it possible for laborers and their families to own their own home, some assisted by the 1889 housing legislation, the shifting employment would not force them to move from one residence to another, following temporary jobs in the industrial economy.

Based on evidence from the reports of the National Association for the Extension of Workmen's Trains in Britain, the Belgian Socialist Emile Vandervelde observed: "All of one side of London, well served by cheap transportation, is overrun with inhabitants and residences, while, on the other side, excellent land remains unoccupied because there is no cheap train service there."[55] In London suburbs without workmen's train service, the middle

55. Emile Vandervelde, *L'exode rural et le retour aux champs* (Brussels: A. Vromant, 1901), 150.

class predominated and the population remained sparse—2.5 people per acre in the decade before the First World War—while the population density of suburbs with extensive workmen's train service swelled to 37.8 residents per acre.[56] Rarely were suburban villas to be found in the same neighborhood with the vast estates of jerry-built boxes. Speculative builders did not construct cottages for artisans or workers where railway fares were high and stations few and far between. A critic of the "go-as-you-please railway policy" that prevailed in Britain complained that working-class suburbs such as "Tottenham and West Ham spring up from small places into huge centres of industrial population, with vast estates of jerry-built boxes, having bogs for foundation, ditches for pathways, and stagnant pools for gardens."[57]

Critics such as George Dew of the National Association for the Extension of Workmen's Trains complained of the British railways' refusal to offer workmen's trains on lines that also served middle-class suburbs. The railways feared that an influx of workers would cause the wealthier commuters to move away from their lines. "I think that is a great mistake," Dew testified, "because I think the more you mingle the working class population with the middle class the better the ideals of the people, the better their morals become."[58] The residents of the villas with their gravel drives did not agree with Dew that working-class neighbors were desirable. The inhabitants of Tunbridge Wells, for example, petitioned Parliament in 1874 protesting a proposed reduction in fares on the grounds that it would lower the class of people living in the district.[59]

While the villages and faubourgs surrounding Brussels grew during this period, the same patterns of residential segregation did not develop. Instead, Belgian planners inserted small grouping of cottages and semi-detached houses for workers that resembled the existing housing stock. The Belgian clusters of workmen's housing conformed to and confirmed existing residential patterns, unlike the London housing estates that transformed social relations as well as the built environment. Controlled by the government, the national Belgian railway that carried the middle-class and working-class commuters adapted more readily to the evolving commuting needs of the workmen dispersed around the periphery of the city. What the Belgians lacked were builders willing to speculate on suburban construction of affordable working-class housing. Charles Buls complained about the lack of

56. Mr. Harper, Royal Commission on London Traffic, Report of the Royal Commission appointed to inquire into and report upon the means of locomotion and transport in London. London 2 (1905–1906): 183.
57. Clement Edwards, *Railway Nationalization* (London: Methuen & Co., 1897), 96.
58. George Dew, Select Committee on Workmen's Trains, British Parliamentary Papers (1904), vii.
59. Edwin Course, *London Railways* (London: B. T. Batsford, 1962), 205.

planning outside of the capital and the mundane appearance of the outer faubourgs of Brussels, invoking "l'aspect champêtre" (the rural appearance), the appealing greenery of the British suburbs.[60] The suburbs around Brussels, he complained, unlike the London garden suburbs that he had visited, "formed a banal zone" without parks or monuments around the still vibrant center, the capital.[61] Buls wanted Brussels, like London, to build suburban housing outside of the capital to encourage further migration.

"Cottages Cheap not Nasty": London County Council Housing Estates

In 1898, fully aware that they had not been meeting the needs of the poor families displaced by the clearance schemes, the Progressive majority on the London County Council sought a new solution to the housing crisis. The question facing reformers was how to build suburban "cottages cheap not nasty."[62] Acknowledging the high cost of land inside London, in 1898, the London County Council took advantage of the powers granted by the 1890 Housing Act and resolved to build housing for workers outside of the county of London. They followed the "outward tendency of the population" to construct four suburban housing estates. These clustered developments of workmen's cottages resembled middle-class suburban housing, but on a smaller scale.[63]

The London County Council purchased land in Wandsworth, just inside the county line, to build the 38.5-acre Totterdown Fields Estate. In January 1901, planners laid out the development on a grid with streets running between Upper Tooting Road and Church Lane. To make the houses more affordable, the frontage of the plots was kept narrow. In their overall design, the planners minimized the typical bylaw street effect by dividing multiple housing units into irregular lengths to create variety. From the exterior, it was not obvious where one house began and the other ended. Architectural details further blurred the separation of the units. Only the number of doorways, often hidden in archways or paired to face each other, indicated the high density of the housing development. The Council planners also provided open spaces between the housing groups. Four shops faced each other at a central intersection.

---

60. Buls, *Esthétique des villes,* 28.
61. Ibid., 46.
62. M. Kaufman, *The Housing of the Working Classes and of the Poor* (East Ardsley: EP Publishing, 1975).
63. Henry Jephson, *The Making of Modern London: 21 Years of the London County Council. Progressive Rule 1889–1917* (London: Bowers, 1910), 243.

Green grocer, Totterdown Estates, 1910. Reproduced with permission from London Metropolitan Archives 78/7380.

The first building phase at Totterdown Fields was completed by June 1903. Each of the homes had its own small back garden and a plot at the front. Designed to resemble country houses, the cottages also had porches. Attention to detail clearly mattered to the architects in this high-density development; bay windows overlooked the streets and gables broke up the monotony of the small houses. Contemporary observers lauded the London County Council architects for their ingenuity in the pleasing and varied design of the simple cottages that differed so markedly from previous municipal building for the working class.

The thousand Totterdown cottages were easily filled. At the terminus of a tram line, the estate was also located a mile from stations on two rail lines.[64] Of the first seventy-five tenants, about half worked in central London. Council planners had recognized the importance of affordable economic transportation for commuting; they calculated expenses for the family of the typical commuting laborer. The average resident earned a wage of thirty-two

64. Tram traffic developed so rapidly that riders reported fierce battles to board the tram cars as they passed by the estate. After reports of rough handling of girls and women, the Council added women-only cars.

shillings. Compared to the rent of a five-room house in London, workers in these cottages saved as much as two shillings and six pence a week, including workmen's tram fares. After 1909, the Council began building smaller houses of three or four rooms and a scullery for families who could not afford the larger houses. Totterdown Fields Estates continued to expand until 1911.

The Council planned its next estate outside the County of London, near Croydon, south of Streatham. The 28.5 acres purchased in 1901 cost six hundred pounds an acre, about half of what the Council had paid at Tooting for Totterdown Fields inside the county. The layout of the streets for the Norbury Estate resembled Totterdown Fields. Between 1906 and 1910, the Council built 498 two-storied cottages, some with bathrooms, on a 17.5-acre plot. The brick paving and low walls lent a rural feeling to the Norbury Estate. Critics, however, ridiculed the fanaticism of the Council's unsuccessful attempt to manufacture bricks from local London clay.

Since Norbury lay outside the county, municipal trams did not connect the housing estate directly to the city. The electric line that opened to Croydon in 1901 stopped at the county boundary, a mile's walk from the Council tram terminus at Streatham Library where electric car service began in 1904. Even after service was extended to the county boundary in 1909, passengers still had to walk between the two systems. From the Norbury train station, a quarter of a mile away from the estate, only a limited number of workmen's trains were available to London Bridge and Victoria. In 1911, third-class season tickets were finally offered at a cost of about three shillings a week, affordable only for regularly employed workers and artisans. Not surprisingly, the Norbury workers who commuted to London protested against the expense of living on the London County Council estate.

Although a number of prominent architects contributed to the design of the cottage groups, the plans of the individual Norbury cottages came under attack. Alderman Fleming Williams complained that "the homes of the people were so planned as to give no pleasure to the inmates."[65] They were decidedly drab. Similarly, the editors of the *Housing Journal* condemned the tendency of the Council architects to reduce the size of rooms in the "rabbit hutches."[66] The workers themselves criticized the lack of a parlor that could be set aside for social and family special use. Middle-class architects thought parlors, a common feature of working-class housing, an inefficient waste of space, and did not include them in their plans. Working-class tenants then saved the living rooms for Sunday parlors, squeezing all of their everyday family activities into the scullery. Defending Norbury's design, John Burns admitted that "he had no sympathy with the working man having wax-fruit,

65. Alderman Fleming Williams, *Housing Journal* (July 1903).
66. *Housing Journal* (June 1903).

Norbury Estates, Corner of Newlands Rd., September 1908.
Reproduced with permission from London Metropolitan Archives 581C.

dusty antimacassars and the family bible" in a room reserved for special occasions.[67] Other reformers criticized the overall design of the Norbury Estate for having compromised to meet Croydon bylaws.

While critics of the Progressives' schemes had originally labeled the suburban estates "utopian," the garden city planner Ebenezer Howard pointedly noted the differences that distinguished the municipal housing estates from his ideal.[68] The Council estates' density of over twenty-five houses per acre contrasted with the eight to twelve houses per acre characteristic of garden cities. The Council did not seem to be trying to combine the best features of urban development and rural life, as in garden cities, Howard complained, but instead simply planted urban workers in the countryside. In contrast to the privately developed garden cities such as Letchworth, the London County Council suburban estates had to conform to bylaws, and so they were laid out as an extension of the city of London, not designed as self-contained cities with their own commercial and administrative center. Nevertheless, the grouped spacing of cottages surrounded by flowers and

67. John Burns, *Housing Journal* (June 1903).
68. *Housing Journal* 2 (September 1900).

trees on the Council estates reminded contemporaries that reformers on the Council shared inspirational roots with the philanthropic developers of the garden cities.

The Progressives on the Council sought to put into practice their complete vision of a workers' garden city at the White Hart Lane Estate. The Council purchased the land for the development in the northern suburb of Tottenham outside the county in 1901, expecting to accommodate thirty-three thousand people in two-story cottages and in flats over shops. The eight different house plans designed for White Hart Lane used bay windows and gables to distinguish one house from the next and to break up the monotony. Once again, however, the architects found themselves limited by the grid pattern of the streets necessitated by local bylaws. The density of 30.5 houses per acre necessitated by funding requirements also constrained them.

Three months after the completion of the first construction phase, only twenty-three of the nine hundred houses planned at White Hart Lane had found tenants. Critics complained that the district was already saturated with working-class developments. As the Council housing manager realized on touring neighboring private developments, including the large Noel Park Estate built by the Artizans, Labourers and General Dwellings Company, the houses offered by the Council at rents of nine shillings nine pence a week did not outshine the ones already available in the cheap housing market.[69] Too, without schools and shops, tenants were reluctant to move to the new estate, even though White Hart Lane was well-served by the Great Eastern Railway, by the Great Northern, and by Metropolitan Electric Tramways (MET) and Council trams. The empty houses discouraged the Council from proceeding with its planned second construction phase.

In 1899, the banker Sir Samuel Montagu had offered the Council twenty-five acres of land at Edmonton for rehousing the poorest tenants displaced by clearance schemes in Whitechapel. When that proved difficult, Sir Montagu promised ten thousand pounds toward the cost of further development of White Hart Lane. Montagu's gift allowed the Council to lay out the streets of a new Tower Gardens section of the estate around a small village green. In the center of this western section of the estate, the architects placed the Tower Gardens, with grass for tennis and bowling surrounded by raised terraces and flower gardens. The Council also decreased the density of this section of the estate to twenty-five houses per acre. As in the other Council estates, cottages had three, four, or five rooms. Within the constraints dictated by economy, the architects provided bay windows and other details to distinguish the individual cottages from one another. The gift allowed the builders to provide more generous cupboards and larger bathrooms.

69. R. Thorne, "The White Hart Lane Estate: An LCC Venture in Suburban Development," *London Journal* 12 (1986): 84.

White Hart Lane Estate, De Quincey (July 2002). Photo by author.

In the midst of the early flurry of municipal suburban construction, the *Workmen's Housing Journal* queried candidates running for election to the London County Council about their priorities for workmen's housing, hoping to find candidates who favored construction. They asked candidates if they would seek new building sites inside or outside of London. Would they keep rents as low as possible and rooms as large as possible? Would they manage the estates themselves or lease buildings to private developers? And would they extend the tram lines, using the profits to subsidize housing estates?[70]

The election of a Moderate majority to the Council in 1907, however, dashed the *Journal*'s hopes for expanding the municipal building program. The Finance Committee of the new Moderate-controlled Council pushed for a reexamination of the housing schemes, searching for an alternative financing plan before proceeding with the plans for developing 103 additional cottages that they had inherited from the Progressives. Given the difficulty in renting existing cottages, the Moderates proposed selling off some of the land, rather than building additional housing on the suburban periphery.[71] Fred Knee of the Workmen's National Housing Council fought the sale. The editor of the *Workmen's Housing Journal* bitterly remarked: "they will

70. *Housing Journal* (1903).
71. *Housing Journal* (October 1910).

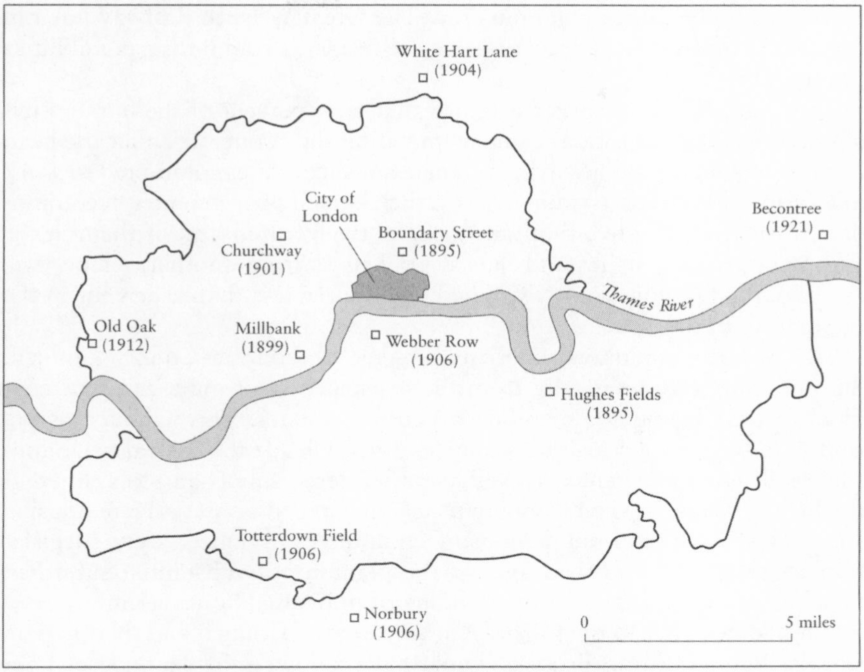

London housing estates. Data from *Home Sweet Home: Housing Designed by the London County Council and Greater London Council Architects, 1888–1975* (London: Academy Editions, 1976), 12–13.

play their own game—that of the landlord and the propertied class."[72] He regretted the passing of an opportunity for further innovation in municipal housing. The Moderates also decided to intermix social classes in London housing rather than continue to build separate workmen's estates. Inspired in part by Henrietta Barnett's Hampstead garden suburb, the Moderates resolved to use part of the land on the White Hart Lane Estate to house the middle classes. Aspiring to make the estate a true "Garden Suburb," they appealed for an exemption from local bylaws requiring that streets be laid out in a grid. Parliament, however, refused to allow the Council to build middle-class dwellings.

The Council had bought land in Acton in 1905, but given the conservative politics on the Council, it did not begin building the Old Oak Estate until 1912. Once completed, the Old Oak Estate in Acton was lauded as the Council's highest architectural achievement for its innovative grouping of

72. *Housing Journal* (July 1908).

houses around an open common area. The Great Western Railway line ran diagonally through the estate, offering the residents commuting possibilities to London.

The Council's 1910 survey revealed that 74.4 percent of the families living on the first three estates came from within the county and that the head of 81.3 percent of families living on their housing estates commuted to work in London.[73] Between 1902 and 1913, the Council provided new accommodation for over fifty-five thousand people, twelve thousand of them in the 3,400 suburban cottages and flats.[74] Looked at from another perspective, in 1910, the London County Council still housed less than 2 percent of the population of the city.[75]

The Brussels communal councils, unlike the London County Council, did not shift so dramatically from the construction of inner-city tenement blocks to the laying out of suburban cottage estates. Throughout this period, building of workmen's housing continued inside the central pentagon-shaped Brussels city center as well as on scattered suburban plots. In what the Belgians cited as their "pragmatism," they relied on the private housing societies and the semi-public housing committees organized by the legislation of 1889. That worked against the planning of substantial suburban housing estates and favored the building of individual housing units.

If it had been left to the Liberals on the Brussels Council and their mayor, Charles Buls, however, Brussels would have followed the example of London and built suburban estates. "Brussels cannot escape the general law," Buls argued. "In no other capital of the world are they trying to build inexpensive housing in the center of the city, but you want to make us the exception. Brussels has become the true city of the Brussels metropolitan area, and its situation should not be compared with anywhere except the City of London."[76] Buls recognized the bureaucratic difficulties posed by the administrative separation of the faubourgs from the central Brussels commune and the economic difficulties posed by the lack of public assistance beyond the capital for the poor, but based on his discussions with officials in London, he believed that workers' housing should be built where land was less expensive. If workers could somehow be encouraged to move out from the city to the suburbs, in Brussels as in London, they would enjoy single-family suburban houses and be able to access their employment in Brussels by public transportation. At one point, Buls proposed offering the workers who migrated out to the suburbs a coupon guaranteeing inexpensive transport

73. London County Council, *Housing of the Working Classes in London* (London: Oldhams, 1913), 104.
74. A. Jackson, *Semi-Detached London* (London: George Allen & Unwin, 1977), 33.
75. Pat Thane, *Foundations of the Welfare State* (London: Longman, 1982), 97.
76. Rapport présenté par M. le Bourgmestre, "Habitations à bon marché," *Bullétin Communal Bruxelles* (1899): 264.

as well as the assurance of public assistance provided by Brussels. Other European cities availed themselves of such solutions, he noted: "Look how easily the problem is resolved in London, Berlin, Vienna and even Paris, as a result of the methods we have indicated: the availability on the periphery of the city of spacious, inexpensive grounds and inexpensive public transportation."[77] Despite Buls's persistent backing, that never happened.

"All Move up One Place and All Move out One Place": Working-Class Suburbs

Advertisements for the London County Council estates depicted happy, robust children romping in gardens around stucco cottages.[78] Surrounded by parks but lacking pubs, with public libraries and quiet tree-lined streets, but without carnivals and street football games, and with clearly demarcated boundaries between public and private spaces, the Council expected that "respectable" London workers would live like the bourgeoisie.

Just as the British imagined themselves a nation of quiet, content, garden-tending home dwellers, Belgian politicians wary of industrial urbanization looked to thatched cottages to confirm their rural self-image. Rather than advocating migration to the suburbs for the workers, Brussels reformers championed the healthy life of the countryside. Advertisements in *Ma Maison/Mijn Huis* proclaimed: "Live in the Countryside. That is the dream of all urban citizens."[79] In contrast to the British, Belgian housing reformers encouraged individual laborers to build their own houses in the countryside with the assistance of the government savings bank, the CGER, and the housing committees. Owning their home, rooted to the land, laborers would reap the benefits of a national labor market by commuting on workmen's trains, the Belgian reformers believed.

A model "inexpensive self-standing house" built by the CGER for the Exposition Universelle de Bruxelles in 1910 boasted ivy-covered balconies, bow windows, and a white brick facade to contrast with the overhanging red roof. Visitors noted the resemblance of the model to the cottages

77. Charles Buls, *Bulletin Communal de Bruxelles* (1899): 274, quoted in Smets, *Charles Buls*, 91.
78. London County Council, *Workmen's Trains and Trams, with Particular of the Council's Dwellings for Workmen* (2 February 1914), London Metropolitan Archives. The pamphlets and time schedules are filed under Workmen's Trains as well as Housing at the Greater London Record Office, Minutes of the London County Council.
79. *Ma Maison/Mijn Huis*. See also "Notre programme," *Le Cottage* (June 1903); *Les logements de la classe peu aisée dans le ressort du comité de patronage des habitations ouvrières et des Institutions de prévoyance pour les Communes d'Anderlecht, Laeken, Molenbeek et Saint-Gilles. Enquêtes & Rapports* (Brussels: Imprimerie des institutions de prévoyance, 1892); Comités de patronage, *Rapport pour l'année 1891* (Brussels: P. Weissenbruch, 1893).

Affordable housing at the Universal Exposition of Brussels 1910, Caisse Générale d'epargne et de Retraite, *Une habitation à bon marché* (Brussels: CGER, 1910), 2.

designed for the British garden cities. Inside this "ménage modeste" (modest household), the architects expected family life to "pivot" around a kitchen, although individuals could retreat to the privacy of three separate bedrooms upstairs.[80] Although the spacious cottage, inspired by middle-class ideals of family life, was clearly beyond the budget of any laborers, planners held it up as an ideal.

Reformers at the turn of the century planned to revitalize rural life by "repeopling it" as they improved urban capitals by razing the slums and redesigning monumental spaces. If the garden city brought the country to the city, then, reformers expected, the suburbs would extend the city into the country.[81] One of the most astute contemporary observers of European transportation, Charles L'Evesque, suggested that the workmen's trains would in all likelihood result in the complete deconcentration of cities—hence the ruralization of cities and the urbanization of the countryside.[82]

80. Caisse générale d'épargne et de retraite, *Une habitation a bon marché* (Brussels: CGER, 1910).
81. Stephen Kern, *The Culture of Time and Space, 1880–1913* (Cambridge, Mass.: Harvard University Press, 1983), 191.
82. Charles L'Evesque, *La mobilisation du travail et le transport des ouvriers par chemin de fer* (Paris: Guillaumin, 1905). Fredereick H. Aalen goes so far as to suggest that with Ebenezer

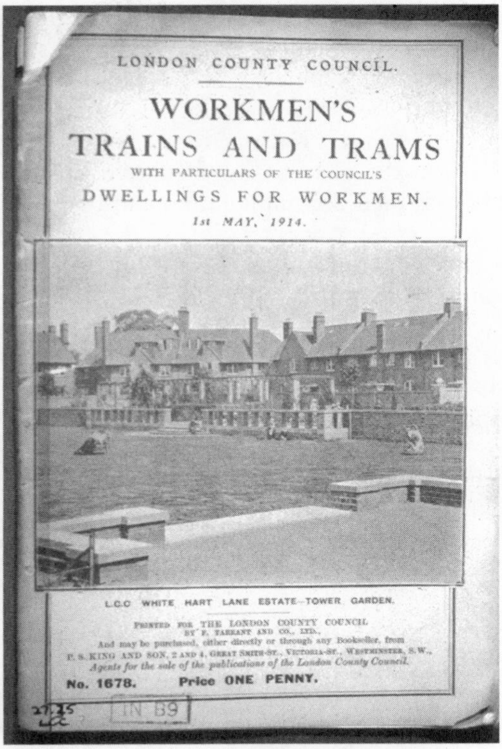

LONDON COUNTY COUNCIL.

WORKMEN'S TRAINS AND TRAMS

WITH PARTICULARS OF THE COUNCIL'S

DWELLINGS FOR WORKMEN.

1st MAY, 1914.

L.C.C WHITE HART LANE ESTATE–TOWER GARDEN.

PRINTED FOR THE LONDON COUNTY COUNCIL BY P. TARRANT AND CO., LTD.,

And may be purchased, either directly or through any Bookseller, from P. S. KING AND SON, 2 AND 4, GREAT SMITH-ST., VICTORIA-ST., WESTMINSTER, S.W.,

Agents for the sale of the publications of the London County Council.

No. 1678. Price ONE PENNY.

Workmen's train to White Hart Lane.
Reproduced with permission
from London Metropolitan Archives.

British and Belgian reformers touted the benefits of a separation between work and residence for commuting workers. The expectation that the planning of the new suburbs would open opportunities for social as well as geographic mobility prevailed on both sides of the Channel. The demolition of urban slums and the construction of suburban housing linked by workmen's trains to the city would allow regularly employed workers and their families to emulate middle-class life away from the nefarious influence of casually employed, unskilled laborers and the unemployed who remained behind.

Howard's vision of the "spontaneous movement of the people from our crowded cities to the bosom of our kindly mother earth," the reformers moved from the realm of social to environmental activism. Their attention had shifted to the effects of the sun, air, greenery, and light and to halting the deleterious effects of pollution. Frederick Aalen, "English Origins," in *The Garden City: Past, Present and Future,* ed. Stephen V. Ward (London: E & F Spon, 1992), 29

Residing outside the city, beyond the reach of disease and revolt, the rooted workers would take on the qualities of model citizens as they cultivated their kitchen gardens in the evenings.

Alfred Smith, chair of the London County Council, believed that even if one-quarter of London workers remained in the city to live within walking distance of their work, the rest could be induced to move farther out to the suburbs "where rational accommodation can be provided at a reasonable cost."[83] The housing reformers were also convinced that benefits would eventually reach those who remained behind. William Thompson, author of the *Housing Handbook,* reasoned, "If half the workers could be induced to leave the congested districts of London, exorbitant rents would fall, overcrowding would be diminished and the health of the people enormously improved with little or no cost to the rates."[84] Raymond Unwin joined the optimistic chorus of the planners celebrating the trickle-down effect of the new housing. "It would be a case of 'all move up one place and all move out one place,'" he proclaimed.[85] Even the Belgian housing administrator Charles De Quéker, who had condemned Liberal plans to force Brussels workers to move out of the city, concurred. The migration of skilled workers and artisans to the suburbs would leave vacant housing for unskilled workers in the center of the city, thus relieving the overcrowding.[86]

Unskilled workers refused to leave London and Brussels because, as one Brussels councillor suggested, in contrast to the bourgeois who had eagerly sought refuge in the suburban greenery, "the worker remains attached to the neighborhood of the city where he was born."[87] A study of one of the impasses in the center of Brussels in 1897 found that of the thirty-two workers and their families who refused to move, six were peddlers whose work took them all over the city and fourteen worked within a six-minute walk of their housing.[88] If the husband could not find work, the wife could take in washing or charring for families she knew in the area, and these families could rely on the informal care networks functioning in their urban neighborhoods or on welfare not available in the suburbs.[89] Little poor relief could be found in the new suburbs, and families could not secure credit

83. Alfred Smith, *The Housing Question* (London: Swan Sonnenschein, 1900), 59.
84. William Thompson, quoted in James A. Yelling, *Slums and Slum Clearance in Victorian London* (London: Allen & Unwin, 1986), 65.
85. Raymond Unwin, *Housing Journal* 12 (July 1901).
86. Charles De Quéker, *La bienfaisance publique & privée* (Brussels: Imprimerie des institutions de prévoyance, 1894).
87. *Moniteur des Comités de patronage et des sociétés d'habitations ouvrières* 17, no. 414 (10 April 1911), 1.
88. Charles De Quéker, *Des maisons ouvrières à appartements en ville* (Brussels: Imprimerie des institutions de prévoyance, 1904), 5.
89. Camille Lemonnier, "Logements ouvriers—Emplacements," *Bullétin Communal de Bruxelles* (20 July 1906): 21; Halle, *Bullétin Communal de Bruxelles 1899* (24 April 1899): 581.

in new shops where they were not known. Besides, they did not relish a long commute on top of a physically demanding workday. A factory worker from London testified that unlike the skilled workers and clerks, "I always live near the factory where I work, and so do all my mates, no matter how small, dirty, and dear the houses may be.... Walking exercises at five in the morning don't suit men who are hard at work with their bodies all day. As to railways and omnibuses, they cost money, and we don't understand them, except on holidays when we have got our best clothes on."[90] Trapped by urban redevelopment and beyond the reach of suburban development, "the unemployable and the wastrels" would not be aided by the schemes of the philanthropists or the urban reformers.[91]

The Liberal mayor of Brussels in 1910 acknowledged, after years of encouraging workers to move out of the central pentagon, that the poorest workers and their families preferred to live near their work, especially when it was casual.[92] Buls speculated that younger, more mobile workers were following new jobs to the outer suburbs while older and less-skilled workers remained within the central pentagon where public assistance was available. The Brussels Socialists feigned little surprise that the Brussels housing societies could not entice workers to abandon their urban tenements for the larger houses they had built beyond the congested urban center. A hatmaker's wife told the Socialist leader Emile Vandervelde that she had no intention of going to the countryside to live like a peasant.[93] In an argument rarely voiced in London, the Belgian Socialists derided the "rustic utopia" of the reformers and championed the cause of the workers who wanted to remain in the city. The workers had as much right to remain in the capital as the king or the new commercial establishments, they proclaimed.[94] One parliamentary deputy compared the Belgian bourgeois attempt to drive the proletariat from the cities into the suburbs with the American treatment of the Indians.[95]

The London philanthropist Helen Bosanquet, nevertheless, observed with her customary matter-of-fact optimism: "Large segments of the population [are] on the move, so that any district may get the class of resident for which it provides suitable accommodation. If it cherishes its slums it will have left to it that mixture of the incapable, the unfortunate, the reckless and dissolute which goes to make up the residuum, while the stronger and

90. Jack Simmons, *The Victorian Railway* (New York: Thames & Hudson, 1980), 368.
91. Mansion House Council on the Dwellings of the Poor, "The Present Position of the Housing Problem in and Around London," (1908); *Le Foyer Schaerbeekois. XXVè anniversaire* (Brussels: Denis, 1925).
92. L. Verniers, "Les Impasses Bruxelloises," *Le Folklore Brabançon* 14 (August 1934): 30–109.
93. Vandervelde, *L'exode rural*, 290.
94. De Quéker, "Les maisons ouvrières à appartements en ville," 4.
95. Dausi, Commune de Schaerbeek, *Construction d'habitations à bon marché par la commune* (Brussels: Becquart-Arien, 1898).

more fortunate and those who aspire to better conditions will seek them elsewhere."[96] Those who could migrate would, while the rest, in her opinion, suffered the fate they deserved.

On both sides of the Channel—contrary to the intentions of the reformers—the increased mobility intensified the social segregation and isolation of laborers. Commuting not only distanced the respectable workers from the marginally employed but also allowed the middle class to isolate itself from the workers and their families. Ever the critic, the writer C. F. G. Masterman observed that whenever middle-class suburban commuters saw "cable trams [coming] down their thoroughfares closely packed with men outside and in, smoking short pipes or reading pink papers hurtling past their very front gardens, with blanched faces they gather up their household goods and flee away."[97] Other essayists and reformers in London noted the staunch opposition of "golf players on Blackheath" to the influx of artisans and workers, resulting in a kind of leapfrog progression, every move outward from London by the lower classes occasioning a subsequent migration farther up hill or into the countryside by the middle and upper classes.[98]

The builders of private suburban estates around London did not see the segregation of the social classes as a bad thing. It seemed obvious to them that constructing houses of one kind in a district encouraged a particular class to migrate there, while other economic groups built their houses elsewhere. An agent of the Associated Garden Estates, Ltd., testified to Parliament that by making cheap plots near the train station available, the company did not intend to promote social intermingling but just the opposite. "Although the Company aims at introducing all classes into the community, it is not intended to indiscriminately mix all classes and sizes of houses together; different portions of the estate lend themselves to different types and sizes of houses," he explained.[99] The artisans and regularly employed workers would inhabit small semi-detached houses on the streets bordering the rail station, while the middle class lived at the end of gravel drives up the hill.

In our society, everyone has the right to live wherever he can afford, Charles Didier, the Belgian editor of *Le Cottage* agreed. He cited the example of the cottage estates around London where "little conservatives" resided contentedly in "adorable little houses as an example to be emulated by Belgian workers. In an article published in the Belgian Housing Societies' *Moniteur des Comités* (Committee Monitor) entitled "Must we keep

---

96. Helen Bosanquet, "Housing Conditions in London," *The Economic Journal* 27, no. 107 (September 1917): 343.
97. Charles F. G. Masterman, *From the Abyss of Its Inhabitants by One of Them* (1902; reprint, New York: Garland Publishing, 1980), 48.
98. Browning Hall Conference, Report of the Subcommittee in Housing and Locomotion in London 1902–1907 (London, 1907).
99. Jackson, *Semi-Detached London*, 39.

workers housing in the center of our major cities?" Didier challenged the "tired cliché" that it was unchristian to separate classes by forcing the poor out to the suburbs. Was it Christian to force the poor man to walk by grand villas day in and day out on his path from his modest flat to the workplace? Did it promote class harmony to subject him to "the daily spectacle of your excess well-being?" he asked his middle-class readers.[100]

Other reformers on both sides of the Channel claimed that interspersing worker housing within middle-class neighborhoods, as the Belgians were doing, better suited a democratic society. The developer of Hampstead, Henrietta Barnett, denounced "the division of social classes resulting obviously in each class's ignorance of the ways of the world foments suspicion and distrust."[101] Living together, the poor would learn from their neighbors who could provide an example of moral living. Deprived of middle-class supervision, workers' families might fall into the bad habits of the rookeries and the impasses they had left behind in the city centers. And left to their own, the middle class would ignore the needs of the poor and complacently retire to their villas in the city. Neither served the cause of the nation.

The suburban development and stabilization of rural villages facilitated by the transportation networks of Britain and Belgium allowed reformers to transform the metropolis on both sides of the Channel. With the respectable workers and their families safely housed in residential districts outside the city, British and Belgian reformers could reconfigure the built environment at the center of their capitals. After the free-for-all growth of cities during the first two-thirds of the nineteenth century, Belgian and British planners reclaimed the center of their capitals for commerce, government, and entertainment at the turn of the twentieth century.

The dynamic mayor of Brussels, Charles Buls, oversaw the transformation of the Belgian capital, defining land use patterns that have endured even as Brussels established itself as the capital of Europe. Brussels councillors in the first decade of the twentieth century lauded the efforts of the city administration to improve the sanitation of the city by cutting large boulevards through districts previously infested by impasses. Only 196 of the 357 impasses lined with worker housing remained in 1906.[102] Across the Channel, Raymond Unwin shared Buls's belief that "urbanism must be the expression of a community."[103] Unwin maintained that municipal governments had a

100. C. D. [Charles Didier], "Faut-il maintenir les logements ouvriers au centre des grandes villes?" *Moniteur des Comités de patronage et des sociétés d'habitations ouvrières* 67 (25 October 1896).
101. Henrietta Barnett, "Science and City Suburbs," in *Science and Public Affairs*, ed. J. E. Hand (London: Allen, 1906), 50.
102. Camille Lemonnier, *Bulletin communal* (20 July 1906), 17.
103. Raymond Unwin, *Town Planning in Practice* (London, 1911), 9, as quoted in Marcel Smets, *L'avènement de la cité-jardin en Belgique: Histoire de l'habitat social en Belgique de 1830 à 1930* (Brussels: Pierre Mardaga, 1976), 85.

responsibility to plan for the common life of the city, but he feared the uniformity of a centrally dictated plan would create a monotonous city. Paris was not an example to be followed. Instead, the British Housing and Town Planning Act of 1909 addressed working-class housing as part of town planning. John Burns, the president of the Local Government Board, introduced the 1909 Act, explaining that the object was "to provide a domestic condition for the people in which their physical health, their morals, their character and their whole social condition can be improved." The bill promoted "the home healthy, the house beautiful, the town pleasant, the city dignified, and the suburb salubrious."[104]

Catholic reformers in Belgium complained that only the wealthy, in their large apartments on the wide boulevards designed by planners, could afford to live in the city. Senator Jules Lammens lamented: "The moral result of the Babylonian transformation of our large cities is the more and more entrenched demarcation between the propertied and the proletariat, between rich and the poor." He feared the disastrous social consequences of the planners' axiom: "the city to the rich and the bourgeois, the faubourgs to the poor and the workers"[105] Councilors in Brussels remembered that the Belgian capital had always enjoyed a mixing of social classes.[106] The planners separating homes from work would destroy that balance.

At the 1907 London meeting of the International Congress of Low-Cost Housing, Charles De Quéker courageously challenged the prevailing British and Belgian wisdom that workers should live outside of the cities. "We must not try to transport the worker out of his milieu, far from his friends, his customs, his workshops, etc., far from hospitals, relief agencies, and (but this is never said), from his favorite cabarets," he declared.[107] Few other middle-class observers in either Brussels or London saw the networks of assistance that sustained workers or recognized urban neighborhood sociability as beneficial.[108] They certainly did not defend the presence of drinking spots.

---

104. John Burns, quoted in London County Council, *Housing of the Working Classes in London* (London: Oldhams, 1913), 14–15.

105. Jules Lammens, quoted in Annick Stelandre, "Contribution à l'histoire des habitations ouvrières 1889–1919," Mémoire présenté en vue de l'obtention du grade de licenciée en philosophie et lettres group histoire, 1982–1983, Université libre de Bruxelles, 28.

106. Fonds "Maisons Ouvrières," Boîte 2, Procès verbaux du Comité officiel de Patronage des Habitations à Bon Marché et des Institutions de Prévoyance, Archives de la Ville de Bruxelles/Stadsarchief, Brussels.

107. Charles De Quéker, "Congrès international des habitations à bon marché" (London, August 1907).

108. Ellen Ross, "'Not the Sort That Would Sit on the Doorstep': Respectability in Pre-World War I London Neighborhoods," *International Labor and Working Class History* 27 (1985): 39–59; Elizabeth A. M. Roberts, "Women's Strategies," in *Labour and Love: Women's Experience of Home and Family 1850–1940, ed.* Jane Lewis (Oxford: Oxford University Press, 1986); Standish Meacham, *A Life Apart: The English Working Class, 1890–1914* (Cambridge,

In 1882, the Liberal undersecretary of state for home affairs, Lord Rosebery, had worried that the London Metropolitan Public Gardens Association would raze every building standing in central London, returning the city to an immense swathe of greenery.[109] Instead of making the city into one huge garden, however, the planners replaced the rookeries with monumental buildings and transplanted the residences into the greenery outside of the city. The outward migration of first the bourgeoisie and then the respectable workers allowed urban planners to restructure their capitals.

The national magnificence of the stately monuments and broad avenues at the center of the redesigned urban spaces of the capital cities of Brussels and London contrasted purposely with the privacy of the individual spaces of the outer residential regions. Consequently, the British writer and craftsman William Morris's suggestion that "one meets in the cities, but lives in the countryside," would be as true for the Bruxellois as for the Londoner, Vandervelde observed.[110]

Mass.: Harvard University Press, 1977); Gareth Stedman Jones, *Outcast London* (Oxford: Clarendon Press, 1971).

109. Stephen V. Ward, *The Garden City: Past, Present and Future* (London: E & F Spon, 1992), 39.

110. William Morris, quoted in Vandervelde, *L'Exode rural,* 318.

5 *"Charged by the Workingmen, Pelted and Charged Again"*

The Politics of Reform

I have thought of workmen until I have had workmen on the brain.

—Gooday, *Select Committee on Workmen's Trains: British Parliamentary Papers (1904), vii*

Most Belgian and British reformers had come to the conclusion in decades preceding the First World War that the migration of skilled workers to the London suburbs and the rooting of Brussels laborers in the Belgian countryside would substantially alleviate the misery of their overcrowded capital cities. Convinced that workers and their families would thrive outside the modern city, urban reformers applauded the Belgian transportation policy that subsidized workmen's trains, and they urged British railways to follow their neighbor's example. Many, but not all, of the reformers called on the governments to help house the workers in the greenery beyond the city. They were convinced that these elite workers and their families, citizens under the expanded franchise of the late nineteenth century—1867 in Britain and 1893 in Belgium—could then be expected to vote responsibly.

London reformers, explaining in 1908 that "the housing problem is at the root of many social evils, and many social evils are at the root of the housing problem," looked to the cities themselves to make fuller use of the powers delegated to them by Parliament to regulate and construct lodging for the poor.[1] However, the proponents of the status quo of laissez-faire individualism had the political odds stacked in their favor in Belgium as well

1. Mansion House Council on the Dwellings of the Poor, "The Present Position of the Housing Problem in and Around London," 1908.

as Britain, even as a housing crisis loomed over both capitals in the decade before the First World War.

British Conservative Robert Salisbury prophesied in the 1880s that as long as the housing question remained outside of politics, the cause of reform would move forward, but, he warned, "once it is mixed up with questions which bring powerful sections of the community into conflict, practical remedies will be postponed for a very long time."[2] By the turn of the century, housing, the so-called reformers' reform, had been politicized, especially at a local level.

Housing and transportation reforms were mutually dependent, the reformers on both sides of the Channel recognized. Without convenient transportation, few workmen wanted to move away from their work in the center of the city; without affordable housing they could not leave the impasses and tenements. Housing reformers could not take advantage of cheaper land outside of the central cities if workers could not get to the suburbs and rural villages. On the other hand, cheaper rail fares without government intervention to construct or subsidize housing played into the hands of the suburban landowner and the jerry builder.[3] Left to their own devices, the private British railways would concentrate the working-class population into districts where speculators could build inadequate houses and charge high rents. The Belgian workmen's trains had already shrunk the distance to rural villages throughout the country. "Given nominal fares, with rapid, frequent, continuous, and widely accessible means of locomotion, mere distance becomes practically annihilated," the British housing reformer William Thompson explained.[4]

Gradually but steadily in the last three decades of the nineteenth century, the national Belgian railway had added trains to accommodate increasing numbers of workers who traveled from their rural and suburban homes to industrial and construction sites. In Britain, to the great frustration of the reformers, the private railways continued to stall, questioning the profits to be gained by improving workmen's train service to the burgeoning suburban settlements. The British railway companies serving London did not see the ever-expanding workmen's train service on the national Belgian railways as an example to be emulated. They resisted any change that threatened their profits or their independence.

In its 1897 report, the London County Council (LCC) complained that "after eight years' operation of the Cheap Trains Act, which was expressly intended as a remedy [to relieve the overcrowding]...the metropolitan

2. Robert Salisbury, "Labourers' and Artisans' Dwellings," *National Review* 9 (November 1883): 301.
3. *Housing Journal* 2 (September 1900).
4. William Thompson, *The Housing Handbook* (London: National Housing Reform Council, 1903), 221.

railway companies have, as a whole, failed to carry out the intentions of the legislature, and have not fully acted up to their statutory obligations."[5] It took a concerted campaign by British reformers and workmen themselves to compel the British railways to follow the Belgian example.

Workmen's Trains in Edmonton: "A Fierce Struggle"

Tired of fighting for seats on overcrowded, overpriced, and inconveniently scheduled trains, a group of commuting workers from the northern suburb of Edmonton grumbled: "Surely we are the most long suffering people in the world or the biggest fools."[6] The workers had lobbied for years without success as members of the National Workmen's Trains Association to secure a sufficient number of trains between six and eight in the morning for stations within a twenty-mile radius of London at reasonable, uniform rates.

During the frigid winter of 1898–1899, Edmonton commuters signed petitions, assembled, and finally stormed barriers at their Great Eastern line station to secure later morning transport for workers. Women, whose shopkeeping jobs often did not begin until after 9 a.m., were among the most affected by the Great Eastern Railway's insistence that workers who could not squeeze onto the 6:17 or the 6:21 a.m. trains should travel by even earlier trains.

On Monday morning, 29 January 1899, when the Great Eastern refused to issue tickets to all the commuting workers in line for the last workmen's morning train from Lower Edmonton to London, the commuters rushed the barrier. Despite the contingent of police called by the company, the commuters knocked down the ticket collector and stormed the train. Once in London, they again pushed past the police barriers to exit at Liverpool Street. On Tuesday, the Great Eastern closed the ticket office in Edmonton at 6:16 a.m. Four hundred people missed the last workmen's train that morning. Instead of paying the additional fourpence halfpenny (4½d.) to ride the more expensive half-fare train as railway officials advised, "after a fierce struggle" with the police and company guards, the crowd took the platform and boarded the next train for London. *The Enfield Chronicle* reported, "the struggle was a most exciting one—young girls fainting and women screaming in the awful pressure, while the platform was strewn with hats." When the train pulled into the Liverpool Street station, the Edmonton commuters refused to pay the fare, shoved the collectors aside,

5. Workmen's trains, General, CL/HSG/1/78, London Metropolitan Archives.
6. "The Workmen's Trains: How They Defied the Act of Parliament," *Enfield Chronicle*, 3 February 1899, 1. For an example of one among many grievances, see also Cockshoft, Great Northern Railway to Metropolitan Railway, 14 October 1881, RAIL 236 338 15, National Archives.

and "proceeded on their way to their daily work." Upon returning home to Edmonton, the reinforced police forces limited their protests to "hooting and shouting."[7]

The next Saturday evening, the commuters held a mass meeting at the Edmonton Town Hall. One after another, workers protested that the railway had been dealing unfairly with them, holding back tickets for the later trains in order to sell more for the earlier ones. Thomas Lough, a Liberal Member of Parliament (MP) for Islington, addressed the enthusiastic gathering. Lough proclaimed that more was at stake than just overcrowding on Edmonton trains. Workmen's fares needed to be lowered and service increased along all the lines or the few stations with low fares and frequent trains would become congested, he explained. The speakers who followed complained that "the owners of a private enterprise have been quietly allowed to frustrate the object of an Act of Parliament for sixteen years, to the great injury of the public." Declaring that "public health must not be sacrificed for private greed" and that "the last two workmen's trains from Edmonton at 6:17 and 6:21 are overcrowded to a dangerous and alarming extent—20 persons in compartments made to hold 10 being a common occurrence," the assembled workers demanded additional workmen's trains be run before 7:21 a.m.[8] The protesters left the meeting vowing to collect evidence on the needs of commuters by going door to door. Lough appealed to workers throughout London to join the Edmonton protest. Together, London commuters would storm the barriers.

In a series of articles, the *Enfield Chronicle* reminded its readers that "the agitation on this question has for years been incessant." The editors cited petitions from the Workmen's Trains Association complaining that 126 of every 300 commuters were forced to travel to London at least an hour earlier than they needed and then forced to loiter around the station. They pointed to the failure of Parliament to pass a Cheap Trains Bill. "After the owners of a private enterprise have been quietly allowed to frustrate the object of an Act of parliament for sixteen years, to the great injury of the public, something will now be done to bring the noses to the grindstone."[9]

The Great Eastern Railway reacted to the agitation by tightening control of its workmen's trains. The railway issued different colored tickets for the various trains, limiting capacity to 750 riders per train. Two hundred tickets on the 6:21 a.m. train were to be reserved for women. The railway also decided to sell tickets ahead, to avoid the early morning crush at the gate. Tickets were to be sold on Saturday beginning at noon for the week and then

7. *Enfield Chronicle*, 27 January 1899.
8. "The Workmen's Trains Question," *Enfield Chronicle*, 3 February 1899; *Weekly Herald*, 3 February 1899.
9. "The Workmen's Trains," *Enfield Chronicle*, 3 February 1899.

again each day between 2 and 6 p.m. for the next morning's travel. The result was that all the tickets for the 6:21 train sold out by 3 p.m. on Saturday and the 6:15 tickets by early that evening.

The first morning after the new ticket system went into effect, large numbers of men and women who arrived to buy their tickets for the 6:21 were left behind. Many commuters, unable to afford regular half-fare tickets, picked up their lunch pails and walked to work in London. When the tickets for the trains went on sale the next Saturday, five hundred people, mostly women and children, gathered at 11:30 a.m. The ticket windows opened at noon, resulting in a "wild, mad rush to secure the spoil."[10] By 12:10, the last ticket for the 6:21 train had been sold. Police reinforcements in Edmonton on both the high- and low-level platforms contained disturbances. When the Edmonton train pulled into Liverpool Street on Monday morning, a substantial police force was waiting on the platform. The London constables attempted to escort the workers quietly out of the station that Monday.

The next day, more police met the trains at Liverpool Station. Crowds of spectators joined the commuting Edmonton workers leaving the trains and together they rushed the police barriers. Reinforcements of one hundred constables tried to drive the men and women from the station. When the surging crowd encountered a truck parked across its path, the workers mounted a brief stand against the police. The police drove the crowd up an incline toward the street. One young man was seized by the police, and the crowd, now numbering two thousand, attempted to rescue him. They failed. According to reports, a number of women were crushed by the stampeding crowd in the melee.

The skirmishes between police and commuters continued the next day, with the addition of the launching of lunch pails as weapons. A local poet depicted "the Battle of Enfield":

> "Half a loaf, half a ham,
> Sandwich-men onward!
> Into the railway yard
> Edmonton thundered;
> Up by the workmen's train,
> More than six hundred!
>
> Lunches to right of them,
> Tea-cans to left of them,
> Hard-boiled eggs right on 'em,
> Constables wondered!

---

10. Ibid.

Arrival of a workmen's train at Liverpool Street. Reproduced from G. A. Sekon, *Locomotion in Victorian London* (London: Oxford University Press, 1938). Reproduced with permission from Oxford University Press.

Charged by the working men,
Pelted, and charged again!
Up came the City train;
Off went the victors then,
Carried to town, but no,
Not the six hundred.—[11]

The Workmen's Committee convened a mass meeting on 10 February at the Edmonton Town Hall. The three men who had been arrested sat on the platform, celebrated as martyrs to the cause of commuting workmen.[12] The workmen dispatched a deputation to the Edmonton Council, seeking their support. In response, the clerk of the Edmonton Council asked the Enfield and Tottenham Councils to send representatives to consider a united appeal to the railway commissioners. The Edmonton Council also decided to help cover the legal costs of the men arrested in the disturbances. The London Reform Union lent its support to the Edmonton workers.

11. *Enfield Chronicle*, 17 February 1899.
12. "The Workmen's Trains Question," *Weekly Herald*, 7 February 1899.

The Edmonton commuters then approached members of both sides in the House of Commons, reminding them of the tremendous growth of the region—in 1871 Edmonton and Southgate together had about 10,000 residents, and in 1899 about 40,000 people lived in Edmonton alone. Colonel Bowles, the local MP, told them to fight their own battle, adding that he had already met with the railway company. He did subsequently promise to take their concerns up with the Board of Directors of the Great Eastern. However, he warned the deputation that the president of the Board of Trade, unmoved by accounts of the riots, had already dismissed their grievances with: "Let the men get up earlier."[13] In his speech to Parliament, Bowles said that he thought the workers wanted a bit too much and advised the builders of large estates to contribute a recompense to the railway companies.

When Bowles's speech was read to the gathering of workers, it was met with hissing and jeers of "rats."[14] The workers resolved to elect men to Parliament who were not supporters of monopolies. The speakers denounced the railway monopolies and proposed giving the London County Council control over all railways within twenty miles of Charing Cross. A. J. Wrampling, the first Socialist to serve on the Edmonton Council, called on the workmen to organize and to agitate. He complained that for five years the Workmen's Trains Committee had been asking for relief from the overcrowding of the cars on which "the people are packed like fowls in a crate," but nothing had been done.[15] The Great Eastern did not appear to take the month-long agitation seriously. They dismissed the meetings and the lobbying as the result of Socialist agitation.

The Workmen's Trains Committee meanwhile distributed questionnaires from house to house in Edmonton. When the delegates of the committee met on 17 March, they reported that of the 125 women who had returned questionnaires, only 5 needed to go as early as the current trains ran, and 117 needed to be at work between 8 and 9:30. Of the 1,220 men who responded, 250 liked the current arrangements, 870 preferred later trains, and 100 gave no information.[16] In April, the committee was still pressing forward with its canvass.

The London Reform Union also submitted an appeal on behalf of women commuters against the Great Eastern Railway Company. The London County Council, the Association for the Extension of Workmen's Trains, and the Edmonton Workmen's Trains Committee supported the Union's case. Women whose shopkeeping jobs did not typically begin until after nine were among the most affected by the Great Eastern Railway's insistence that

13. *Enfield Chronicle*, 10 February 1899.
14. *Enfield Chronicle*, 24 February 1899.
15. *Enfield Chronicle*, 10 February 1899.
16. *Enfield Chronicle*, 17 March 1899.

workers who could not fit onto the 6:17 or the 6:21 trains should travel on earlier trains. They were compelled, petitioners complained, to loiter on the streets of London before they could gain admittance to workshops in which they were employed. Alpheus Morton, MP, brought the question to the House of Commons. He cited Mssrs. Spicers' envelope factory that opened at 8:30 a.m. and employed a considerable number of women who rode trains arriving between 6:30 and 7 in the morning.

William Birt of the Great Eastern bluntly responded to the requests for special service for women: "I beg to inform you that my directors are of opinion that the workmen's train and fare arrangements on this railway are at the present time sufficient to meet all the reasonable requirements of workmen and work women, and they regret their inability to add to them."[17] The London Tilbury and Southend Railway answered that they ran until 6:55 after which cheap fares were accepted. A few railways did accede. Some companies subsequently allowed working women to travel by later trains, and a few companies added special compartments for females.

In response to the complaint that women and children were forced by the early trains to loiter around the station, All Hallows Church near the Tower of London was opened to shelter the commuters. The women and children were forbidden to engage in conversation, to eat, or to read newspapers while they waited in the church for their places of employment to open. Nevertheless, they did come seeking shelter. The *Enfield Chronicle* reported that "The Rector has also been gratified by the reverent demeanour of those who have availed themselves of the warmth, light, and comfort the opening of the Church affords, while the short service held at seven o'clock each morning has been heartily appreciated."[18]

The disagreements between the railways and the commuters continued to simmer, especially along the Great Eastern lines. The Edmonton Workmen's Trains Committee called a public meeting in 1901 to protest the Great Eastern's plans to eliminate one of the three-pence trains it had added after the riots. Members of Parliament Henry Ferryman Bowles and Thomas Lough, as well as delegates from the Workmen's Trains Committee, addressed the gathering. In 1902, the Edmonton Workmen's Trains Association applied to have the three-pence experimental trains, added after the riots, stop at intermediate stations, including Angel Road, Bethnal Green, and Hacknay Downs. They also reminded the directors of the Great Eastern of the agreement of April 1899 from the Railway and Canal Commissioners to run later trains to accommodate workers whose employment did not necessitate

17. Correspondence between the Board of Trade and the railway companies having termini in the metropolis on the question of an alleged necessity for the provision of later cheap trains for work women, 1895. RAIL 1053 210, National Archives.
18. *Enfield Chronicle,* 10 February 1899.

their early presence in London. The directors replied that stops would make the trains late into London, but promised to consider the question. The Great Eastern replied that it was physically impossible to add more trains; the workers should distribute themselves more efficiently in the morning. Two additional trains were eventually added, but the number of workmen's trains running to Edmonton remained an issue of contention for years as the population of workers in the Enfield-Edmonton area continued to grow as laborers from Shoreditch were attracted by the newly constructed, cheap working-class housing.

"Cheaper Facilities for the Conveyance of the Working Classes": The Campaign for Workmen's Trains

The London County Council spearheaded the lobbying effort of middle-class reformers to improve workmen's train service between London and the suburbs in cooperation with the London Reform Union and the National Association for the Extension of Workmen's Trains. The London Reform Union, whose goal was to move the working class "a step nearer to the ideal of a separate house and garden for every family," drew its membership from middle-class reformers. In contrast, the National Association for the Extension of Workmen's Trains was organized by workers in 1896 and associated with trade unions, trades, councils, and working men's clubs.[19] Its chair, George Dew, sat on the London County Council Workmen's Housing Committee, presiding over the Council's Workmen's Trains Sub-Committee, a useful connection for the National Assembly. The Council also worked with the Metropolitan Association for Procuring Cheap and Regular Railway Accommodation for the Working Classes, established in 1868.

Only one Belgian group lobbied for better service, the Société des voyageurs (society of travelers). They were much less active than their British counterparts because there was little need for sustained pressure to alleviate overcrowding on the trains. There was also remarkably little discussion in Belgium of the workmen's trains, either inside or beyond Parliament. Typically, a parliamentary deputy presented petitions from constituents who had been forced to take earlier trains to avoid overcrowding, but these complaints were resolved expeditiously.[20] That was not the case in Britain.

In December 1889, the London County Council instructed its Housing of the Working Classes Committee to inquire into the adequacy of the

---

19. London Reform Union Leaflet no. 50, British Library, London.
20. Julien Liebaert, 5 May 1904, *Annales parlementaires: Chambre* (1903–1904), 1574; Julien Liebaert, 20 December 1904, *Annales parlementaires: Chambre* (1904–1905), 362; Paul Hymans, 28 February 1906, *Annales parlementaires: Chambre* (1904–1905), 808.

workmen's train service connecting London to its suburbs. It cited the costs of clearing land and erecting workers' dwellings within London as justification for its interest in running more workmen's trains to the suburbs. The Committee asked the Board of Trade, charged by Parliament with overseeing the railways, to convene a "friendly and unofficial conference" with the railway companies. The Council optimistically expected "to keep them [the railways] as friends" by acknowledging the difficulties the companies faced in making concessions. They did confer in 1893, but few concessions were offered.

The Public Health and Housing Committee of the London County Council realized the need to support its demands for additional workmen's trains and uniform fares with statistics. It dispatched inspectors to count commuters entering stations and boarding workmen's trains and to conduct interviews. The first Council report, issued in 1891, condemned most of the railways for their rules and regulations that restricted workers' access to trains and recommended that workmen's train service be extended to additional stations located farther out on most of the rail lines serving London. The report quoted workers who complained about the high cost of tickets, the inadequately publicized schedules, and the overcrowding of the trains.

Based on the interviews it conducted and the reams of statistics it collected, the Council recommended that workmen's train service be extended to additional stations located farther out along most of the lines serving London. It reminded readers of the well-established correlation between urban density and mortality to buttress its arguments for an extension of service outward. The Council singled out Willesden Junction as an area desperately in need of workmen's service. A police constable from Ealing testified that he had to wake workmen as early as 3:30 a.m. so they could walk the three miles to Shepherd's Bush, the closest station selling workmen's tickets. The Council pointed to "the urgent necessity which exists for further encouraging the migration of the working classes into the suburbs" as its justification for issuing a second report on workmen's trains in 1893.[21] The Council distributed its extensively documented reports to the Board of Trade that was charged by Parliament with overseeing the railways. The Council wanted workmen's trains to run until 8 a.m., workmen's tickets to be valid for any afternoon return, and fares to be uniform by zone.

The Council surveyed rail service again in 1894. Comparing rail service to the major European cities, the Council report demonstrated that the infrequent London trains were overpriced relative to the Continent. The statistical officer for the Council noted that the mean rate per kilometer for travel with workmen's tickets was 0.320 pence in London as compared

21. London County Council Report, Public Health and Housing Committee on Workmen's Trains for Districts South of the Thames (1892), 40.

to 0.127 pence in Brussels.[22] Although they won some minor concessions from the railways, the Board was not willing to exert pressure on the private companies. So, the Council continued to collect statistics and to issue reports. In 1897, the Council's statistical officer prepared an extensive report on the inadequacy of workmen's train service south of London, an area where few workmen had settled, and in 1898, the statistical officer prepared the same data for the north. In presenting the workers' complaints about the inadequacy of service and the overcrowding on the workmen's trains, the London County Council provided the statistical data to back up their anecdotal testimony. It surveyed the travel requirements of the membership of 167 trade societies, finding that the 195,000 workers who traveled daily in 1897 crowded into 99 trains with seating accommodation for only 43,000 passengers.[23]

The managers of the railways coalesced to stave off the Council's challenge; their rejections of the Council's requests were worded identically, all drafted by the counsel for the Council of the Railway Companies.[24] Henry Oakley of the Great Northern, on behalf of all the railway managers, insisted that power to determine fare structures belonged to the railways, not to the government. If it was "thought desirable in the public interest to ask further for cheaper facilities for the conveyance of the working classes beyond those which the companies are themselves able or willing to afford," then the employers or the community should be asked to bear the cost, not the shareholders, they argued.[25] The railways protested that they lost money on the workmen's trains; the Great Eastern explained to the Royal Commission on London Traffic that the cost per train mile in suburban districts was three shillings and seven pence while workers' train receipts per train mile brought in only three shillings and three pence. The railway managers also reminded the Board of Trade that they had to run the workmen's trains empty out of London on the return journey. They suggested that the railway companies serving London had already done their share in attempts to "settle the housing problem."[26]

In 1899, the London County Council, together with the London Reform Union and the National Association for the Extension of Workmen's Trains, appealed to the Great Northern Railway not only to meet but to anticipate

22. Public Health and Housing Committee, "Third and Concluding Report of the Public Health and Housing Committee giving the results of a comparison of the cost of workmen's and other privilege tickets on the London railways with those of the principal metropolitan cities on the continent." LCC\MIN\7336 E 16, London Metropolitan Archives.

23. Harold J. Dyos, "Workmen's Fares in South London, 1860–1914," *Journal of Transport History* 1 (1953): 12.

24. Minutes of the Board of the Great Eastern Rail, 8 January 1902, RAIL 2 27/26, National Archives.

25. Letter to the *Times,* 21 March 1906, RAIL 410 367, National Archives.

26. John Francis Sykes Gooday, *Royal Commission on London Traffic,* vol. 2, 669.

demand by running workmen's trains to sparsely populated suburbs so that workers would move outward.[27] The Great Northern countered that few workers lived in the districts in question, showing photographs of middle-class commuters boarding their trains as evidence. Why run workmen's trains where there were no workers in residence? The Royal Commission on London Traffic concluded in favor of the Great Northern: the intention of the Cheap Trains Act passed in 1883 was not to force the railways to open up new districts but to serve existing suburban populations.

By 1898, the Council had become frustrated not only with the railway companies but with the Board of Trade "for failing to exercise its regulatory role."[28] The Board of Trade seemed to the Council to hold "peculiar views" of the regulatory terms "sufficient" and "reasonable" in the Cheap Trains Act.[29] The laws also required that the workers themselves appeal their own cases for increased service, even though workers had neither the legal training nor the funds to take on the powerful lawyers employed by the railways before the Board of Trade. When pressed on the cost of bringing a case, Frederick Harrison, general manager of the London and North Western railway, did not think that an expenditure of six hundred pounds by a worker was exorbitant—London laborers earned an average of twenty shillings or one pound a week. Harrison agreed that it might be intimidating for a dissatisfied worker to come on his own to the Commission, but suggested that since most of the workers were satisfied, that was a moot issue.[30]

The Council therefore asked for authority to initiate inquiries into the needs of the working classes and to petition the Board of Trade on their behalf. Although it received that right in 1899, the Council's statistical officer found himself buried under requests for evidence by groups petitioning for increased train service for workers. Several local committees wrote to the Council requesting their intervention in battles for extra trains to London. When he protested that he could not meet all of the requests for statistical support, the Council refused to gather additional data for the London Reform Union since their court cases for improved service often went down to defeat.[31]

---

27. "London Reform Union and Great Northern and North London Railway Companies and National Association for the Extension of Workmen's Trains and Great Northern Railway Company in the Court of the Railway and Canal Commission in the Matter of the Cheap Trains Act, 1883," 21 July 1899, Leicester University Library, Leicester.
28. Suggested Draft Report of the Housing of the Working Classes Committee on Workmen's Trains, 2 February 1898, CL/HSG/1/78, London Metropolitan Archives.
29. Report of the Housing of the Working Classes Committee, 22 February 1898, LCC\MIN\7368, London Metropolitan Archives.
30. Sir F. Harrison, Select Committee on Workmen's Trains: British Parliamentary Papers, House of Commons (1905), viii.
31. George Gomme to Housing of the Working Classes Committee, LCC\MIN\7368, London Metropolitan Archives; 30 November 1898, LCC\MIN\7259, London Metropolitan Archives;

In November and December 1901, Colonel Horatio Yorke, an inspector of the Board of Trade, heard an inquiry into the service of the Northern London Railway. Workers and their families were alleged to be moving out of newly opened housing in the districts served by the railway as a result of the inadequate train service. Workers had persistently protested the high price and infrequent service of workmen's trains, sending petitions with hundreds of signatures to the railway, but they failed to convince the Commission. In January 1908, a deputation of workers living in Barnet presented a petition signed by 409 persons to the Great Northern Railway requesting that workmen's tickets be issued on all trains up to 7:45 in the morning. Their request was refused. The railway convinced the judge that "such reduction [in fares] would necessarily have to be extended to the whole of the suburban district," and the judge would not force such a change in the railway's fare policy.[32]

The Council tried again in 1911, charging that even the "workmen's railway," the Great Eastern, was purposefully limiting the development of certain suburban districts. In the ensuing struggle, the question of the obligation of the railways to anticipate development finally came to a head. The counsel for the Great Eastern made it clear that the railway did not want workers and their families to settle in new areas that seemed ripe for middle-class development. It feared that the first- and second-class ridership would drop if the railway offered workmen's tickets from their suburban stations. Workmen explained that they preferred to live farther out like the middle class, away from the cramped workers' cottages built around the stations. These cottages "were not fit for a dog to live in," they complained, and there were no shops in the neighborhoods.[33] The judgment in the 1911 Great Eastern case reaffirmed the government position that unless there was an existing demand, railways could not be compelled to run trains. The districts would be opened up first, then served by the trains.

The number of appeals supported by the Council declined steadily in the first decade of the twentieth century. In part, the Council had begun making astute decisions on the cases it believed it could win, refusing to represent plaintiffs in obviously lost causes. The Council took on a case against the Great Western only because the statistical officer suggested that, based on his evidence, "the companies can't resist us."[34] Looking back, reformers

22 February 1899, LCC\MIN\7259, London Metropolitan Archives; Gomme, 26 July 1899, LCC\MIN\7368, London Metropolitan Archives; Board of Trade to the London County Council, 18 January 1899, LCC\MIN\7259, London Metropolitan Archives and Workmen's Fares 1888 to 1910, RAIL 410 367, National Archives.

32. Great Northern Railway, RAIL 236/724/9, National Archives; RAIL 529 103 North London Railway, National Archives.

33. *London County Council v. Great Eastern Railway,* Minutes of Proceedings, 1911, London Metropolitan Archives, London.

34. George Gomme to Housing of the Working Classes Committee, 16 May 1900, LCC\MIN\7368, London Metropolitan Archives. See also Harper's testimony to the Workmen's

credited the Council with pressuring the railways to increase service for workmen. In general the Council itself was pleased with the outcome of its efforts, citing "very great improvements in the workmen's train services."[35] They acceded, however, that while they had secured some changes, the demand for additional facilities had increased even more rapidly.

Parliaments and Select Committees: "To Exhaust All the Opportunities the Present Legislation Affords"

The commuting workers and their political supporters found themselves on opposite sides of the workmen's train argument on the different sides of the Channel. While British reformers lobbied for more train service, some Belgian reformers questioned the rationale behind the workmen's train scheme. The Belgian railway, they charged, was responding to industrial demand as defined by the employers. In contrast to the antagonism that characterized the relationship between the British railways and the government, the Belgian government defined public and industrial interests as one and the same. In Belgium, production required a mobile national workforce. Whether that mobility also benefited the workers was the subject of discussion among the political parties.

The Belgian Socialists, in particular, claimed that government and industry cooperated all too eagerly. Together with the populist Catholic deputy the Abbé Adolphe Daens, who championed workers, they offered the only resistance to the trains. For example, when the mines of Mariemont-Bascoup near Charleroi needed more Flemish workers, the government added train service on the condition that the industry would guarantee a minimum of three hundred daily commuters.[36] In response, the Catholics and the Liberals in the government repeatedly joined forces to expand workmen's train service.

The issue of workmen's trains came to a head in the Belgian Parliament in 1905. While the heavily used Brussels North Station was being enlarged, rail traffic was limited to full-paying passengers. Workmen's trains were routed to the less convenient Tours et Taxis station. The Socialists and the Abbé Daens took up the workers' complaints about the less convenient train connections from the Tours et Taxis station that resulted in work days beginning

Train Subcommittee concerning its case against the South Eastern and Chatham Railway in 1903, LCC\MIN\7387, London Metropolitan Archives; Report of the Housing of the Working Classes Committee to the London County Council, 1 August 1899, LCC\MIN\7368, London Metropolitan Archives.

35. LCC\MIN\7387 38, London Metropolitan Archives.

36. Yves Quairiaux, "Abonnements ouvriers et problème de main-oeuvre," *Le centre mémoire du rail, 1839–1989* (La Louvière: Ecomusée regional du Centre, 1989).

at two in the morning and ending at eleven in the evening. Without their direct connections from North Station, the workers waited for their trains in the rain and snow, the Socialists added.[37] The Catholic minister of Rail, Post, and Telegraph, Julien Liebaert, replied that the growth in rail passenger volume had forced the measure. Economic trends, like physical laws, were immovable, he explained, adding that the Belgian government, especially under the Catholics, had done more than any other country for worker housing and transport. In Belgium, he shrugged, everyone always attacked governmental administration; complaining was simply part of the Belgian national character.[38]

No sooner had the North Station incident been settled than a change in workers' train schedules triggered riots in the village of Jette where the police had to disperse rock-throwing commuters. Minister Liebaert downplayed the severity of the riots in his report to Parliament and angrily accused the Socialists of trying to win the workers' favor by championing their cause in Parliament. The Socialists in turn charged the minister with hostility toward cities and workers. The parliamentary discussion over the Jette riots opened the first full-scale Belgian debate over the workers' fares and trains. Liebaert justified the government subsidy of workers' trains by reminding delegates that it was universally agreed that contact with the cities was dangerous for workers. The workmen's trains allowed workers to rejoin their families in the countryside in the evening, he reiterated, and that was good. On the other side, the Socialists pointed to the long hours endured by commuting workers in contrast with the benefits accrued by the employers who could draw from a national labor force.[39] The workmen's trains served the interests of industry, not the workers. The Socialists did not go so far as to advocate an end to workmen's trains, however.

In the 1890s, British reformers launched a concentrated push for national legislation to improve the workmen's train service into London. In 1891, Sir Blundell Maple introduced the first Cheap Trains (London) Bill. Mr. Woods, Captain Norris, and C. E. Schwann introduced similar bills in subsequent years. The National Association for the Extension of Workmen's Trains and the London County Council attempted to rally support for each of the various versions of the Cheap Trains (London) bills in Parliament. Despite all of the lobbying efforts by the reformers, in 1899, the Cheap Trains (London) Bill lost on the second reading in Parliament.

In 1901, the Local Government and Statistical Department of the London County Council advised the Housing of the Working Classes Committee

37. Edouard Anseele, 28 November 1905, *Annales parlementaires: Chambre* (1905–1906), 54.
38. Julien Liebaert, 28 November 1905, *Annales parlementaires: Chambre* (1905–1906), 49 and 55.
39. 5 December 1905, *Annales parlementaires: Chambre* (1905–1906).

that it no longer judged conditions to be conducive to fighting for amendment of the Cheap Trains Act. Rather, it believed that it was "desirable to exhaust all the opportunities the present legislation affords."[40] Parliament responded to the efforts of the London County Council and other reformers in 1903 by establishing a Select Committee on Workmen's Trains. Sir Francis Hopwood testified before the Select Committee for the Board of Trade that the Board had never strictly enforced the provisions of the Cheap Trains Act. To justify their hands-off approach, he explained that if the Board had undertaken investigations into inadequacies and had levied penalties, that "would practically mean our undertaking the administration of railways." Instead the Board had preferred to rely "upon the voluntary action of the railway companies stimulated as it will be from time to time" by "judicious pressure."[41] Rather than applying a uniform standard, the Board had considered each railway separately, taking their finances into consideration in the enforcement of regulations.

The statistical officer of the London County Council, Edgar Harper, argued that fares for workmen's trains should be determined by what workers could afford to pay, not by what each railway preferred to charge. Harper also asked why women, particularly those employed in bookbinding, many of whom lived on the outer fringes of London, could not take later trains to work. Mr. Galloway, a member of the Select Committee, responded that although he worried that a few of the women waiting for their place of employment to open might get up to mischief, he was more concerned that for the hour or two in question, "they would be much more usefully employed at home in looking after their own domestic affairs."[42] The Select Committee on Workmen's Trains did press the manager of the Great Eastern Railroad to describe the conditions on the trains that the women rode. Was it true, they asked, that women had to sit on men's laps on overcrowded trains? The manager denied the charge, but did little to allay their general concerns. When members of the Select Committee asked whether working women were meant to be included in the provisions for workmen's trains, they were told: "What would be a good definition for workmen, would not, in my judgment, be a good definition for workwomen." Although generally laws included women within the category of men, Harry Samuel contended that the 1883 Cheap Trains Act was intended to serve only "corduroy" men, or rougher workers. In debate, it became clear to the members of the Select Committee that in practice "women do get the cheap train tickets just

40. Local Government and Statistical Department to the Housing of the Working Classes Committee, 1 May 1901, LCC\MIN\7378 38, London Metropolitan Archives.

41. Sir Francis Hopwood, Select Committee on Workmen's Trains, British Parliamentary Papers (1905): (27 June 1905): xii.

42. Mr. Galloway, Select Committee on Workmen's Train, British Parliamentary Papers (1904): (6 July 1904): 50.

as much as men." That was problematic not only because Select Committee members did not think women should be encouraged to travel to work aboard trains, but women arrived in London long before their places of employment opened.[43]

George Dew of the National Association for the Extension of Workmen's Trains testified before the Select Committee that the 1883 Act had failed to guarantee adequate workmen's train service. No minimum level of service had ever been set and railway companies had not been forced to anticipate demand, making it impossible to open up the suburbs to working-class development. A number of workers also appeared before the Select Committee requesting daily as opposed to weekly tickets, especially for casual laborers who never knew where they would be working the next day. John Francis Sykes Gooday, general manager of the Great Eastern Railway, dismissed all of the reform proposals. Why, he asked, should the railway carry workmen at a loss? Besides, later workmen's trains would interfere with other service, he explained. Finally he lost patience: "I have thought of workmen until I have had workmen on the brain."[44] The British railway managers did not want to be bothered with service that had not proved to be profitable. William Forbes, general manager of the London, Brighton and South Coast Railway testified that if he advocated introducing workmen's fares into a district in which workmen might someday live—a speculative proposition at best—he "should get 'sacked'" at the end of the year.[45] Above all, he had shareholders to consider.

The final report of the Select Committee on Workmen's Trains presented in 1905 acknowledged the lack of effective regulation. "What has been done by the railway companies in the provision of workmen's trains is little more than enlightened management on the part of the companies would have dictated," they suggested. "The existence of the act...has had little effect in determining the most important factor in the service, viz. the fares to be charged by such trains."[46] Based on three years of testimony, the Select Committee recommended changes that they knew might "go beyond what the companies may be willing to grant." Nevertheless, they declared: "We have no hesitation in coming to the conclusion that this is a question of such vital importance to the public that the limits of voluntary action should be exceeded and the State should require the companies to do more than they

43. Colonel Bowles, Samuel Henry, and Mr. Lough, Select Committee on Workmen's Trains, British Parliamentary Papers (1903): (29 July 1903): 8.

44. Gooday, Select Committee on Workmen's Trains, British Parliamentary Papers (1904): (20 July 1904): 92.

45. William Forbes, Select Committee on Workmen's Trains, British Parliamentary Papers (1904): (18 July 1904): 77.

46. Select Committee on Workmen's Trains, British Parliamentary Papers (1905): (27 June 1905): xii.

would be willing to do if governed by commercial considerations alone."[47] That conclusion laid out a bold new direction for the British legislation and regulation—one that promised to bring the British closer to the Belgians in their rationale for organizing workmen's trains.

The Select Committee called for the addition of several new workmen's trains to be run after 8 a.m., although the decision of which companies were to be required to add the later trains was left to a tribunal. The Committee cited the example of the cheap fares charged to workers on the Continent as one to be emulated. Where working women traveled in sufficient numbers, they were to be provided separate carriages. Defining the area to be served by trains as extending twenty miles from London termini, the Committee acknowledged the threat of overcrowding in London and concluded that workmen's travel needed to be added to reach districts spread throughout greater London at fares set at less than the difference between London and suburban rents. That was a consideration shared by Belgian lawmakers.

Not content to let things stand, the government appointed a Royal Commission in 1905 to inquire into and report on the Means of Locomotion and Transport in London. The commission held 112 meetings and examined 134 witnesses. Its recommendations reached well beyond those of the Select Committee. Edgar Harper of the London County Council testified extensively on the overcrowding of the city that would be relieved if the railways anticipated demand and offered cheaper fares to new suburban districts. It would be better "for the whole community" for the workman and his family to live outside, he concluded.[48] The Royal Commission members asked whether the Council would be willing to share the financial risks of such service with the railways.

The Commission refused to consider London as "a city under conditions special to itself . . . in respect to facilities for locomotion" and decided that London transportation should be "judged by the standard of other cities." Because of London's size, its demands for workmen's train service were greater than those of the smaller continental cities, but it was clearly lagging behind other cities in the provision of transportation for the workers who commuted daily to its center. Five members of the Commission visited America to inspect the means of locomotion in New York, Philadelphia, and Boston. Others visited Vienna, Budapest, and Berlin. They also entertained evidence from foreign experts and collected their statistics. The report concluded that "if the standard of movement cannot be raised to the level attained elsewhere, London must fall behind in competition with other

47. Select Committee on Workmen's Trains, British Parliamentary Papers, House of Commons (1905) 270: (27 June 1895): xv.
48. E. Harper, Royal Commission Appointed to inquire into and report upon the Means of Locomotion and Transport in London (London: HMSO, 1905), 2:169.

cities, and the life and growth of the Metropolis will be slowly strangled by the choking of the great arteries of traffic."[49]

The Commission recommended the appointment of a permanent governmental authority to develop a comprehensive plan integrating housing and transportation development to relieve the overcrowding of London. "Means must be provided for taking the population into and out of London, not in one or two directions, but in many directions, at rapid speed, frequent intervals and cheap rates."[50] While they did not intend to force railways to run unprofitable trains, they did recognize the advantage of extending railway service to thinly populated areas, assisted by local authorities. Failure to improve locomotion, they warned, would have dire economic and social consequences for the British capital.

"On Such Questions, There Should Be No Parties": Municipal and National Housing Politics

In his *Bitter Cry of Outcast London,* Andrew Mearns despaired: "Without State interference nothing effectual can be accomplished upon any large scale." Laissez-faire liberalism had successfully cleared the capital of the public health hazards, but not housed the displaced urban workers. "And IT is a fact. These wretched people must live somewhere."[51] Despite an understanding of the housing problem as a question of the relationship between high rent and low wages, few reformers proposed that the government intervene in the labor market or redistribute income through taxation so that workers could afford to pay rent. Most Belgian and British reformers looked to schemes to make housing more affordable. Some saw a role for the government in accomplishing that.

For several decades, a minority of British and Belgian reformers had promoted government intervention to alleviate the crisis in public health. Just as individual initiative could not be expected to address drainage or water supply, they explained, housing reform could be more effectively treated as a social issue. But the British philosopher B. Kirkham Gray observed that the argument for government intervention ran up against the widespread conviction that property belonged in private hands and that the market should prevail, especially because housing proved to be relatively expensive to fix as compared to public health reforms.[52]

49. Ibid., 1:6.
50. Ibid., 1:16.
51. Andrew Mearns, *The Bitter Cry of Outcast London: An Inquiry into the Condition of the Abject Poor* (London: James Clarke, 1883), 18.
52. B. Kirkham Gray, *Philanthropy and the State* (London: P.S. King & Son, 1908), 135.

In Belgium, Charles Woeste, leader of the Catholic party, condemned state intervention as smacking first of the French Revolution and then of the Manchester School, both foreign.[53] "Truly Belgian" politicians would resist the incursion of government and continue to look to generous charitable actions to supplement the market, Woeste argued, setting an example by lending his personal support to a number of charitable institutions.[54] If the state intervened to house the workers, then why not also feed their families? he asked. Where would the line be drawn?

A growing chorus of Catholics dissented. In the name of paternal activism, they criticized Woeste's application of a laissez-faire approach to housing workers. If the state could construct schools and prisons to improve the moral condition of workers, it should also be able to build housing. "There is nothing that is more 'practical' than to do nothing and to just let it happen," a delegate told Woeste.[55] Pragmatism, not ideological conviction, finally allowed the national and municipal governments to assume roles that would be viewed as inevitable in the twentieth century. The Catholic minister of finance, Paul de Smet de Naeyer, responded to the shift, asking incredulously whether out of fear of the Socialists, the Catholics would themselves end up advocating socialist theories.[56] The 1889 law gave workers the opportunity to buy a house. Give the programs time to work, he counseled.

Belgian Liberals, who steadfastly opposed any government interference with housing, also condemned paternalist Catholic reformers for tilting too far away from the market. In Brussels, the citadel of Belgian liberalism, Charles Buls argued that the municipality had no more right to supply housing than clothes or food.[57] In a classic restatement of liberal principles, the Liberal majority on the Brussels Council asserted that in a society founded on the liberty of the individual, public authority existed only as an exception

---

53. The Manchester School, economic policies espoused by Richard Cobden and John Bright, advocated free trade.

54. Charles Woeste, Congrès des oeuvres sociales. Liège, 26–29 September, 1886 (Liège: Imprimerie et Lithographie De Marteau, 1886), 174; Charles Woeste, "Les Catholiques belges et les intérêts ouvriers," *Revue générale* 65 (April 1897): 481–501; Charles Woeste, *Annales parlementaires: Chambre* (2 July 1889), 1519.

55. Prince Eugène de Caraman Chimay, "Rapport sur la question des habitations ouvrières" (présentés à l'assemblée générale de la fédération des sociétés ouvrières catholiques belges, 3–4 December 1878; *Moniteur des Comités de Patronage pour les Habitations Ouvrières et pour les Institutions de Prévoyance* 3, no. 39 (25 August 1895).

56. De Smet de Naeyer from Ghent served as Minister of Finance, 1894 to 1907, and as Chef du Cabinet from 1896 to 1907. He was named director of the Société générale de Belgique, 1908–1913. In addition to his involvement with railways throughout Europe, he served on the CGER. Jean-Luc De Paepe and Christiane Raindorf-Gerard, *Le parlement belge, 1831–1894. Données biographiques* (Brussels: Académie Royale de Belgique, 1996).

57. Habitations ouvrières et à bon marché 1887–1914, Archives de la Ville de Bruxelles, Fonds Charles Buls, III 20 A-D; Charles Buls, "Habitations à bon marché," *Bulletin Communal de Bruxelles* (1899): 259.

agreed to by the citizens to accomplish certain discreet common tasks—tasks that did not include the provision of individual housing. Buls expected that after he had cleared away the impasses, private entrepreneurs would construct worker housing outside the city, a view he shared with neither the Catholics nor the Socialists.

Hector Denis, the lone Socialist appointed to the 1886 Belgian Royal Commission that had launched the 1889 housing law, proposed the establishment of a Société national des habitations bon marchés (National Society for Affordable Housing) to be funded and controlled by governmental authorities.[58] This national solution represented for the Belgian Socialists "a happy middle ground in which the central authority, all the while respecting the autonomy of the communes, contributes its advisory intervention to realize progress in the service of hygiene that the communes, acting alone, could not achieve."[59] For the Socialists, the question was not if the government should intervene, but at what level: national or municipal. The housing reformer from Liège, Ernest Mahaim, who supported the National Society, compared Glasgow where bankers and entrepreneurs embraced municipal socialism with Brussels where Socialists alone advocated municipal control of public works. The substantial majority of housing reformers in Brussels, however, stuck to their conviction that if allowed time to play itself out, the 1889 law would bring a solution to the housing problem in Belgium.

In 1883 in Britain, Lord Robert Salisbury, long an opponent of municipal activism, argued for the extension of government housing loans to the laboring poor, much like the Belgians had done. The Conservative Salisbury acknowledged in an article published in the *National Review* that it was low wages, not moral inadequacy, that forced thousands of families to dwell in single rooms. "Laissez-faire is an admirable doctrine; but it must be applied upon both sides," he explained, concluding: "This unhappy population has a special claim on any assistance Parliament can give."[60] The Liberal president of the Board of Trade, Joseph Chamberlain, responded with a widely cited article published in the *Fortnightly Review,* which countered that the burden of improving cleared land should be placed not on the municipalities as Salisbury advocated but on the land owners.

The intense public debate that followed drew in Lord Brabazon, a prominent conservative, and the Reverend Samuel A. Barnett, the founder of the settlement, Toynbee Hall. "Until our working classes are decently housed,

58. Hector Denis, "Société nationale d'habitations ouvrières," *L'Avenir Social* (1900): 487–491.

59. Hector Denis, *Habitations ouvrières: Comité officiel de patronage d'Etterbeek, Ixelles, Saint-Jossse-ten-noode, Schaerbeek, Uccle & Watermael-Boitsfort* (Schaerbeek: Bauvais, 1895).

60. Robert Salisbury, "Labourers' and Artisans' Dwellings," *National Review* 9 (November 1883): 306.

it is useless to look for any improvement in their moral, social or physical condition," Lord Brabazon declared.[61] He criticized Progressive proposals that assigned responsibility for housing the poor to local governments. Municipal intervention would prove more expensive than private action, he contended. Besides, the provident should not assume the burden of the improvident. It was the local authorities who had allowed the evil to fester in the first place with their misguided clearance schemes.

In an article entitled "Mischief of State Aid," Lord Shaftesbury concurred, arguing: "If the State is to be summoned not only to provide houses for the labouring classes, but also to supply such dwellings at nominal rents, it will, while doing something on behalf of their physical condition, utterly destroy their moral energies."[62] As the Charity Organisation Society had been arguing for decades, Shaftesbury maintained that municipal charity would demoralize the poor. He did allow that if all else failed, the state might intervene to do the work that would otherwise not be done. But, he asserted his faith that philanthropic ventures and the market could meet the housing needs of the poor.

On the London County Council the battle over municipal activism raged between the Progressives—who won majorities in the elections of 1889, 1892, 1898, 1901, and 1904—and the Moderates. The Progressives, many actively involved in their local Liberal and Radical Associations and aligned with London labor, supported municipal intervention in housing. They denigrated their Moderate opponents as self-interested spokesmen for private interests in housing, water, and transportation.[63] The Moderates, identifying themselves as the party of the rate payers, objected to programs that enlarged the role of municipal governments. In 1907, the Moderates, under the label Municipal Reformers, won a majority of seats on the Council and remained in control until the First World War.

The urban historian Anthony Sutcliffe suggests that only "rarely do we fully appreciate the extraordinary ambition of specifically urban modes of intervention in economic and social processes during a century in which the informed public was generally unsympathetic to administrative limitations of individual freedom."[64] The decision of the London County Council to intervene in housing and to campaign for workmen's trains appears all

61. Lord Brabazon, quoted in John Nelson Tarn, *Five Per Cent Philanthropy: An Account of Housing in Urban Areas between 1840 and 1914* (Cambridge: Cambridge University Press, 1973), 112.

62. Lord Shaftesbury, "The Mischief of State Aid," *Nineteenth Century* 14 (December 1883), quoted in Tarn, *Five Per Cent Philanthropy*, 112.

63. Henry Jephson, *The Sanitary Evolution of London* (London: T. Fisher, 1907), 274.

64. A. Sutcliffe, "The Growth of Public Interventions in the British Urban Environment during the Nineteenth Century: A Structural Approach," in *The Structure of Nineteenth-Century Cities*, ed. J. H. Johnson and C. G. Pooley (London: Croom Helm, 1982), 107.

the more extraordinary in juxtaposition with the reluctance of most Brussels housing reformers to follow their successful example. The differences on housing cannot be reduced to government intervention versus private enterprise, as in transportation. The divergent housing reform strategies adopted by the majority of the Brussels and London housing reformers reflect the complex and evolving relationship between municipal and national authority on both sides of the Channel in this period marked by the "politicization of social policy."[65] In both countries, social policy was set at a national rather than local level, Sutcliffe explains. In Britain, however, unlike Belgium, Parliament gave "the municipalities powers and duties ... to supplement the defects of private enterprise or to compete with its efforts," in the words of the 1908 Mansion House Report.[66]

The prewar Belgian government is usually described by historians as a weak overseer of the quintessential laissez-faire entrepreneurial society made up of a patchwork of strong municipal communities.[67] In fact, in the nineteenth century, before the rise of regional identities, Belgian reformers celebrated the national unity of the young country that allowed them to legislate on a national stage rather than to concentrate their attention at a municipal level. Since achieving independence in 1830, the centrifugal tendency in Belgium had been complicated, but not overtaken, by the particular interests of the 2,587 communes.

There was decidedly less enthusiasm for national government action in Britain. The Liberal Lord Rosebery, president of the London County Council, explained: "[T]he State was the last and the desperate remedy in this country for great evils which private enterprise could not deal with."[68] Before the establishment of the Council, the municipality was not an obvious alternative to the state in either capital.

Despite long histories of local autonomy, both Brussels and London had lacked a unitary government that could oversee housing or urban planning in the nineteenth century. The capital government's jurisdiction did not extend beyond the "pentagon" at the center of Brussels or the "City" of London. The indirectly elected Metropolitan Board of Works of London was supposed to coordinate sewerage, paving, and lighting for the myriad of London parishes, but it never enjoyed much popular support. In Brussels no common administration at all linked the central commune of Brussels with

65. Susan Pedersen, *Family, Dependence, and the Origins of the Welfare State: Britain and France 1914–1945* (Cambridge: Cambridge University Press, 1993), 47. Pedersen contends that during this same period, on questions of family policy, British reformers looked to the "high politics" of the national government for a solution.

66. Mansion House Council on the Dwellings of the Poor, "The Present Position of the Housing Problem in and Around London," 1908.

67. Ernest Mahaim, "La législation sociale en Belgique, 1869–1919."

68. Rosebery, quoted in F. H. Millington, *The Housing of the Poor* (London: Cassell, 1891), 46.

the eighteen surrounding communes or "faubourgs" that retained their status as autonomous villages. This chaotic structure of Brussels survived the period of reform untouched.

In London, the Reform League convened massive public demonstrations, sometimes attended by over one hundred thousand people, to hear rousing speakers demanding a municipal government for the British capital, but the London Government Bill introduced in the Commons in 1884 failed after the second reading. In 1888, Parliament passed the Local Government Act establishing the London County Council. In contrast to the tangled representational system of the Metropolitan Board of Works, the 118 London County Council members were directly elected and sat for three-year terms. Part of the rising tide of national reform, the London County Council drew strength from its mandate to create a municipal identity for London and to tackle the urgent social problems left untouched by national legislation.[69] The successful reform of municipal government for London can be explained by the larger national context. After a period of low investment in the municipal infrastructure in Britain, local governments assumed a new legitimacy in the 1850s and 1860s with the depoliticization of central taxation.[70]

That never happened in Belgium, where the national government relied increasingly on indirect taxation. Despite a century of attempts to annex the faubourgs to the central commune of Brussels, opposition from the national government as well as the jealousy of the suburban faubourgs blocked unification.[71] Charles Buls, the mayor of Brussels, confronted a homogeneous

---

69. Ken Young and Patricia Garside, *Metropolitan London* (London: Edward Arnold, 1982); Sir George Laurence Gomme, *The London County Council: Its Duties and Powers According to the Local Government Act of 1888* (London: Nutt, 1888); Henry Jephson, *The Making of Modern London: 21 Years of the London County Council: Progressive Rule 1889–1917* (London: Bowers, 1910); H. J. Dyos, "Greater and Greater London: Notes on Metropolis and Provinces in the Nineteenth and Twentieth Centuries," in *Britain and the Netherlands,* vol. 4, ed. John Selwyn Bromley and Ernst Kossmann (The Hague: Martinus Nijhoff, 1971); Susan S. Fainstein, Ian Gordon, and Michael Harloe, *Divided Cities: New York and London in the Contemporary World* (Oxford: Blackwell, 1992).

70. Nicolas Crafts, "Some Dimensions of the 'Quality of Life' during the British Industrial Revolution," *Economic History Review* 50, no. 4 (November 1997): 617–639; Simon Szreter, "Urbanization, Mortality, and the Standard of Living Debate: New Estimates of the Expectation of Life at Birth in Nineteenth-Century British Cities," *Economic History Review* 51, no. 1 (February 1998): 84–112; Martin Daunton, *Trusting Leviathan: The Politics of Taxation in Britain, 1799–1914* (Cambridge: Cambridge University Press, 2001).

71. Guillaume Jacquemyns, "Le problème de la 'Cuve' de Bruxelles de 1795 à 1854," *Revue de l'université de Bruxelles* (1932): 347–375; Xavier Carton de Wiart, "Le problème des grandes agglomérations," *La Revue générale* 70 (15 December 1937): 702–719; Pierre Gourou, "L'Agglomération Bruxelloise: Eléments d'une géographie urbaine," *Bulletin de la Société Royale belge de Géographie* 82, no. 1 (1958): 3–84; Louis Verniers, *Bruxelles et son agglomération: De 1830 à nos jours* (Brussels: Les Editions de la Librairie Encyclopédique, 1958). Belgian Socialists in particular called for the unification of the Brussels communes. Camille Huysmans, *Moniteur des Comités de patronage et des sociétés d'habitations ouvrières* 415 (25 April 1911).

Catholic government at the national level that thwarted his aspirations to unify the central city of Brussels with the faubourgs. Catholics in Parliament hailed the ubiquitous Belgian commune as the traditional cornerstone of liberty and decried the proposed centralization of power in the capital as a threat to the rest of the small nation. The nineteen Brussels communes came together only informally through sporadic meetings of the mayors at the City Hall in Brussels.

While British reformers celebrated the municipality as the representative of the common civic good, Belgians distrusted city governments as, at the worst, dens of competing self-interested politicians and, at the best, uncoordinated and ineffective. British municipal politics tended to focus pragmatically on particular local issues, whereas in Belgium they often reflected the ideological divisions of the national political arena. The reform-minded Progressives on the London County Council paid little heed to the national political fallout for Liberals in Parliament from their radical proposals for housing and transportation reforms. The Conservative prime minister and opponent of municipalism, Lord Salisbury confided: "I rather look to the new London County Council to play the drunken helot for our benefit."[72] During the years that the Progressives ruled the Council, the Conservatives controlled Parliament, except for the period 1892–1895. Conversely the years of Moderate control of the Council coincided with Liberal majorities in Parliament, except for the period 1906–1907.

Belgian national political agendas overwhelmed local affairs in all of the nineteen separate communal councils of Brussels. In 1911, in exasperation, Liberal Brussels mayor Adolphe Max prefaced his urgent call for action in response to a housing crisis with the admonition: "On such questions, there should be no parties."[73] But even a Brussels Council discussion of whether a proposed block of flats should stand two or four stories tall stirred debates on the dangers of collectivism (four stories), countered by Socialists' denunciations of capitalist oppression (two stories). When the Liberals voted down a plan for municipal construction, a Socialist councillor responded with the threat of proletarian revolution.[74] Wary of these relentless pitched ideological battles among the three political parties waged at the municipal level, Belgians hesitated to invest their local governments with increased power.

British reformers themselves explained their housing activism at the municipal level by national temperament and custom. The French housing reformer Arthur Raffalovich agreed with the British self-assessment: "It seems to me that the English and the North Americans are guided by a higher degree of a sort of public spirit that manifests itself in the coming together, the association of individual forces, the method of pragmatically attacking the

72. Lord Salisbury, quoted in Young and Garside, *Metropolitan London*, 62.
73. Adolphe Max, Conseil Communal, *Moniteur des Comités de Patronage*, 25 April 1911.
74. M. Rochette, 27 March 1899, *Bulletin Communal de Bruxelles* (1899): 487.

most difficult questions, and sometimes of resolving them."[75] The problem with that explanation is that the Belgians also claimed pragmatism as their motivation; their 1889 housing legislation fit common sense and the Belgian temperament, they explained.

The president of the Belgian Association for the Improvement of Worker Housing admitted that the task of achieving meaningful reform was like pushing the rock of Sisyphus up the hill, especially if one looked at the number of unhealthy houses in Brussels and realized that the reformers had been able to help only a few workers each year to find new houses and distributed beds and linens for a few more. But he added: "We have done what we could! With too small resources we have made very appreciable improvements.... We have helped and consoled the poor worker and shown him evidence of our interest and sympathy. In one word, each of us has done our duty."[76] Housing reform fit within the Belgian Catholics' definition of individual duty.

The Belgian housing law of 1889 rehoused one family at a time. "The elite of the laboring class, that is to say the workers who are frugal and who save, are comfortably lodged in their own homes," one reformer concluded.[77] The state had granted exemptions to building companies totaling 41,191,717 francs, and the Caisse générale d'épargne et de retraite (CGER; the semi-public savings and loan bank) had loaned 99 million francs for the construction or the acquisition of worker housing by the end of December 1911, making possible the construction of about 53,850 houses for workers. Less optimistic, the Belgian Conseil supérieur d'hygiène publique (Belgian Superior Council for Public Hygiene) wondered how anyone could expect to resolve the housing crisis "when each municipality is abandoned to its own initiative [and] when the national state is so disarmed that it cannot intervene to establish the rules and basic regulations to control the construction and maintenance of housing?"[78]

Countering the "Slum and Block-Dwelling Fog": Working Men and Political Action

The editors of the *Housing Journal,* published by the Workmen's National Housing Council, including Fred Knee, the first secretary of the London

75. Arthur Raffalovich, *Le logement de l'ouvrier et du pauvre, Etats Unis, Grande Bretagne, France, Allemagne, Belgique* (Paris: Librarie Guillaumin, 1887), 203.

76. Association pour l'amélioration des logements ouvriers, Assemblée générale annuelle de 1897, 7.

77. Henry Delvaux de Fenffe, *Les habitations ouvrières: Conseil provincial de Liège, Séance d'ouverture du 6 juillet 1909* (Liège: Thone, 1909).

78. Conseil supérieur d'hygiène publique (1887–1888), *Habitations ouvrières* (Brussels: F. Hayez, 1887), 47.

Labour Party, attacked middle-class reformers who muddled along "in the slum and block-dwelling fog," trying to improve the lives of the workers without ever seeking advice from the workers themselves.[79] These reformers planned the housing and arranged the transportation of workers to resemble their own on a smaller, cheaper scale, but they gave little thought to the interests of the working men. The editors pointed out, for example, that the Sanitary Institute of London never even invited the workmen's associations to their meetings. These "two great modern problems," housing and transportation, "would have to be settled first by the working men," the *Housing Journal* wrote.[80]

The Social Democratic Federation argued for a public works program, for fair rent tribunals, and for the enforcement of building and sanitation laws, all the while explaining that improvement demanded a change in the capitalist system. To rally workers to their revolutionary cause, the Federation held open-air mass meetings. Three members of the Social Democratic Foundation, compositors plagued by high rents themselves, organized the Workmen's National Housing Council in 1908. They struggled to secure municipal house construction, to pass legislation to bring down interest rates, and to establish fair rent tribunals.

In North London, the Tottenham Working Men's Housing League declared that workers would have to solve the housing question themselves. They defended workers engaged in battles with their landlords. Tenants' protection leagues brought together over one thousand people to protest disputes with landlords in Southwark. To pressure political groups to support housing reform, the London Trades Council held large demonstrations at Hyde Park and sent questionnaires on housing to all candidates for the London County Council. The Willesden Housing Council, the Marylebone Housing Council, the Bermondsey Tenants' Protection League, the Enfield Housing League, and the Woolwich and Plumstead Tenant Defence and Fair Rent League also pressured their borough councils to make active use of the 1890 Housing Act that gave municipalities the right to construct housing. Two thousand people met at Bethnal Green to protest the failure of landlords to extend provisions of the 1867 Reform Act, and one thousand marched in a torchlight procession in Hackney. British workers also engaged directly in battles with their own landlords, but the poorest tenants simply moved on when they could not pay higher rents. Vandalism, an active if indirect protest against housing conditions and landlords, also persisted in poor neighborhoods.

Despite this evidence of at least sporadic political action by workers' reform groups, the Social Democratic Federation condemned workers for not

79. *Housing Journal* 2 (September 1900).
80. *Housing Journal* 3 (October 1900).

rebelling against slum conditions. The Workmen's National Housing Council acknowledged, "whoever else takes the housing question seriously, the mass of those most affected by it—the working people—have not done so."[81]

In Belgium, the Socialist Party took up the protests of workers. Although most of the Socialist deputies came from middle-class backgrounds, the Belgian Socialists, who sat in Parliament and also served on communal councils, assiduously cultivated their local ties with laborers within their districts where they condemned middle-class reforms that, in the words of the Brussels Socialist Louis Bertrand: "gave two sous to those who needed one thousand francs."[82]

Until land and transit were wrested from the control of private individuals, Alf Watts of the Social Democratic Federation argued, any reforms would prove inadequate. Ultimately, George Dew argued for the nationalization of land as well as the railways to solve the sanitary and moral question of housing the workers. The surveyor Arthur Crampton declared in 1901: "The question used to be whether government should interfere at all in the matter of housing. The question now is what is the best form for that interference to take."[83] George Shipton of the London Trades Council agreed: "What the individual cannot do the state, the municipality must seek to accomplish . . . for it also possesses the necessary power and wealth."[84]

---

81. *Housing Journal* 7 (February 1901), cited by Anthony S. Wohl, *The Eternal Slum: Housing and Social Policy in Victorian London* (Montreal: McGill-Queen's University Press, 1977), 320.
82. Louis Bertrand, quoted in Annick Stélandre, "Contribution à l'histoire des habitations ouvrières 1889–1919," Mémoire présenté en vue de l'obtention du grade de licenciée en philosophie et lettres group histoire, 1982–1983, Université libre de Bruxelles.
83. Arthur Wesley Crampton, *The Housing Question* (London: Land Agents' Record, 1901).
84. Shipton, quoted in Stephen Merrett, *State Housing in Britain* (London: Routledge & Kegan Paul, 1979), 25.

6 *"With Morality Brimming Forth"*

Rooted Workers and Their Families

> In the evening, when one returns from the city, tumultuous and over-excited, it is delicious to find the countryside asleep, the silent serenity of the earth and sky, the calming splendor of the starry heavens.
>
> —Emile Vandervelde, *L'exode rural et le retour aux champs,* 317

The Belgian and the British middle class envisioned workers' homes beyond the city that gathered affectionate parents and their children around the hearth at the end of the workday. In the first issue of the Belgian journal *Le Cottage,* the editors described this "home": "a habitation that is airy and joyous, surrounded by greenery in the middle of a big garden, truly healthy and comfortable, with morality brimming forth, the foyer where one lives happily and in the midst of which one is loved."[1] They consciously adopted the English word *home* to describe their ideal. Like the English cottages built in the suburbs by the London County Council, Belgian cottages would be designed to incorporate "the simple dignity and beauty," which garden city architects Barry Parker and Raymond Unwin believed was "necessary, not only to the proper growth of the gentler and finer instincts of men, but to the producing of that indefinable something which makes the difference between a mere shelter and a home."[2] Already integrated into nature, good housekeeping would make the cottage a true home. At the center of the

1. "Notre programme," *Le Cottage* 1 (June 1903).
2. Barry Parker and Raymond Unwin, quoted in Susan Beattie, *A Revolution in Housing: LCC Housing Architects and Their Work, 1893–1914* (London: The Architectural Press, 1980), 89.

rural or suburban household, the reformers envisioned a wife tending its hearth.

The middle class, in their suburban retreats surrounded by gardens and shaded by trees, had come to resemble an idealized version of eighteenth-century peasants who tended their kitchen gardens before gathering around their hearth for the evening meal. Unlike the furtive urban workers who were marginally employed, both middle-class and peasant families depended on the husband's labor farther afield and on the mother's care of home and children. The families of the commuting workers would live like the idealized peasants. On both sides of the Channel, reformers intended to separate these regularly employed workers and their families in comfortable accommodations in the suburbs or the countryside away from the so-called residuum who remained behind in the urban slums.

"Reunited under the Paternal Roof": Observing Suburbs and Villages

In 1899, Charles Booth, who had studied the London poor, ventured into the new suburbs encircling London to observe the families of the working-class commuters. What he found in the Artizans, Labourers and General Dwellings Company housing estate at Queen's Park confirmed the expectations of reformers: The skilled workers and artisans who had been rehoused in the suburbs had adopted middle-class ways. "The estate provided the same sort of retreat from urban temptations that the middle class suburb did, not only public houses but cook shops and restaurants being excluded," Booth observed. "It is a district of home-life and of comfort."[3] Men were not distracted by the pub, work was separated from the home, and women could not turn to cook shops to shirk their domestic duties. Working families, like their bourgeois counterparts, had found privacy amidst greenery, far removed from the public lives of slum dwellers. These reformed families would thrive, he believed, and evolve into responsible working class citizens.

Few of the other British observers and fewer of the novelists who had so closely scrutinized the lives of the poor inside London in the 1880s followed the workers' families to the suburbs in the decade before the First World War. One group of British social scientists undertook a detailed study of the development of Outer London in the first decade of the twentieth century.[4] They focused on West Ham, a suburb with factories of its own—soap, rubber,

3. Charles Booth, quoted in Donald J. Olsen, *The Growth of Victorian London* (London: B. T. Botsford, 1978), 289.

4. Edward G. Howarth and Mona Wilson, *West Ham: A Study in Social and Industrial Problems* (London: J.M. Dent, 1907).

chemicals, bonemeal, paint, glue, and tarpulin—as well as good train connections to London. The population of West Ham had grown by 138,000 between 1881 and 1901. The investigators found deteriorating housing built by speculators. Rental rates in 1906 were almost double what they had been in 1888, and the jerry-built houses were ill adapted to the needs of the inhabitants, the authors complained. Given the haphazard development of the suburb, no land had been set aside for green spaces. The most prosperous residents did indeed commute regularly to London for work, but the casually employed sublet houses and sought work on foot. Often, their wives and daughters also worked to supplement their meager earnings. Their work was poorly paid and inconsistent. Given the location of the Victoria and Albert docks, casual labor predominated and a large number of people depended on irregular wages in this new workers' suburb. The Liberal journalist Charles Masterman's observations filled in the dreary picture supplied by the West Ham investigators: "We fight for places in the tardy tram which bear us to the north in the morning; we fight for similar places on our return from the long day's toil. Forced from our dwellings by swarms of sleepy children, at even we crowd into the public-houses, never able to get at arms' length from our fellow men."[5] This was not the idyllic life pictured by Booth.

A multitude of Belgian social scientists fanned out into the countryside to investigate the worker-peasant hybrid that had been created by their workmen's trains and the housing legislation of 1889. Ernest Mahaim, the internationally recognized expert on workers' housing, set out "to penetrate social life itself." He "undertook a series of personal investigations" to discover the effects of commuting on the health and the family life of "cultivateur-propriétaires" (cultivator-land owners) like the men who farmed in the summer in the village of Lorcé on a hill above the Amblève River and commuted in the winter.[6] To supplement his interviews and personal observations, Mahaim also addressed questionnaires to station chiefs to collect data on the seasonal variations in commuting, the average length of trips, the basins of supply and sites of demand, and the professional background of the commuters.

Mahaim's study of workmen's trains, *Les abonnements d'ouvriers sur les lignes de chemins de fer belges et leurs effets sociaux* (Workers' Fares on the Belgian Railways and their Social Effects), published in 1910 by the Institut

5. Charles Masterman, *From the Abyss of Its Inhabitants by One of Them* (1902; reprint, New York: Garland Publishing, 1980), 13.

6. Ernest Mahaim, *Les Abonnements d'ouvriers sur les Lignes de Chemins de fer belges et leurs effets sociaux* (Brussels: Misch & Thron, 1910), viii and 141. Mahaim had succeeded Emile de Lavalère as a professor at the Université de Liège. He went on after the First World War to direct the administration of unemployment assistance in Liège and to work for the Ministère de l'Industrie et du Travail, as well as the Institut Solvay and the Bureau International du Travail.

Solvay, depicted working men, happy to be providing for their families, but exhausted from their long day of travel and work. Dispersed during the day, "thanks to the workers' fares, family members all return each evening, reunited under the paternal roof," Mahaim observed.[7] The men passed their evenings amidst the domestic peace of a quiet family supper and, like their peasant forefathers, devoted their free time to the cultivation of a kitchen garden. The lives of the rural families portrayed by Mahaim closely resembled the ideals of the suburban havens planned, if not observed, by the British reformers. Families gardened and gathered, far from the disruptive chaos of industry and commerce.

Mahaim portrayed frugal, contented wives standing in their front doorways surveying their children at play during the day. He did not see the busy complexity of their households as these wives assumed many agricultural tasks that had previously been the responsibility of the now-commuting husbands and older children who were now commuting. The women were not idle, but they did not labor outside the home. Mahaim saw women lining up at the village train stations each Sunday to buy coupons for the next week's travel, but he assumed that exhausted husbands had sent their wives to purchase tickets for them. His detailed charts and graphs included no category for women workers, although he divided and specified practically everything else. He simply listed *ouvrier* (worker), undifferentiated by gender.

Mahaim recounted his conversations with the wives of commuters who were sound asleep in their chair in the next room. Sometimes, he found workers in the gardens in the evenings, their arms full of giant peppers and lettuces. He asked them why their families did not move, for example from Edegem to Antwerp where the husband was employed. The commuters' wives pointed to their garden and indicated the house that cost only fourteen francs a month in rent. In their villages they had neighbors and family, and that was important. Mahaim approved, concluding that taken together the workmen's trains and the 1889 Belgian housing legislation gave working men the freedom to pursue employment in cities while rooting their families in the countryside. In the countryside, the houses were more sanitary, and the workers' families breathed good air, he explained; families could grow vegetables and keep animals. And, as Mahaim reminded his readers, many of these commuters owned property, unlike other European workers.

In response to Mahaim's optimistic picture of commuting, the Catholic writer Demain published his own set of case studies of "typical families," demonstrating that trains were causing the erosion of the virtue of the "peasants . . . the most healthy and robust sector of the population."[8]

7. Mahaim, *Les abonnements,* 141.
8. H. Demain, *Les migrations ouvrières à travers la Belgique* (Louvain: Hugues Bomans, 1919), 205.

"At home (Etre chez soi)": To live "at home," reside in "your own" house, cultivate your own piece of ground, to be seigneur and master. Who is the man, who, at the hour when destinies were decided, has not dreamed and imagined realizing this ambition. From *Vers l'avenir* (Brussels: Société anonyme belge d'imprimérie, 1912), 40.

Demain described a metalworker who lived ten minutes from the train station in a small house built with a loan from the "Foyer Brainois," a housing society established by the 1889 legislation. He took the 5:10 train each morning, beginning work at 7 a.m., and returned at 7:30 in the evening. His oldest son served as an apprentice in the same factory as his father, while his daughter worked in the village. Working away from home, both children had forgotten the modesty taught in their village school and inculcated in them by their mother, Demain observed. The father frittered away his earnings on pigeons and drink in his ample free time; the mother gossiped with neighborhood women.

Belgian observers debated whether the commuting laborers remained peasants despite their work or had been transformed into urban workers by their travels, even though they lived in traditional villages. Based on a study of their budgets—workers were believed to spend and peasants to save—Demain concluded that the commuters had adopted the bad habits of urban workers. The commuters were unwilling to save money for a bad day as peasants would do. There also seemed to be an increase in beer drinking and a decrease in popular participation in village festivals.[9] Other Belgian observers noted that only rarely did commuters' families suffer "the habitual misery" of peasants as a result of the higher wages earned in the cities. They even ate meat several times a week; twelve butchers had established themselves in the Brussels suburb of Braine l'Alleud, for example. As another sign of wealth and spending foreign to peasants, observers described laboring commuters who worried about their appearance, wearing their Sunday best to walk through the village. Their wives shopped in Brussels. Otherwise, though, there were few luxuries in these hybrid budgets, and that pleased the middle-class observers.

Many Catholics deplored the change in village life introduced by commuting. They complained that the once joyful rural villages where customs and rituals defined the rhythms of daily life had disappeared. "Everyone rose before dawn and went to the fields, returning to the sound de l'Angelus to leave again together in the afternoon. In the evening, the fires went out at the same time in all the houses," Demain remembered.[10] Before the trains, everyone had shared political and religious beliefs; they had all lived alike, moral Catholic peasants. But the villages no longer seemed to be an extension into the public of the traditional family to Demain. Now, commuters lived close to the train stations, their new houses lining the roads, all with blue stone lintels, colored bricks, and individual vegetable gardens.

Demain championed the traditional peasantry who, "in jealously conserving the cult of the foyer, in maintaining an attachment to traditions, by its peaceful and simple customs, . . . is the safeguard of order and public prosperity as well as of the stability of institutions." Demain feared that the male commuters who traveled back and forth to the cities were bringing back urban ways and corrupting their wives and children in the country. "The

9. Prosper Thuysbaert, *Het land van waes: Bijdrage tot de Geschiedenis der landelijke Bevolking in de 19e Eeuw* (Kortrijk: J. Vermaul, 1913), 80.
10. Demain, *Les migrations*, 132.

beautiful pure stream that flows by the mouth of the factory is contaminated as it continues along its course," Demain commented, describing the erosion of the traditions of the countryside.[11] Before the trains ran with their cars full of workers, the laborers had all been good Catholics, but now Demain was not so sure; the commuters read Socialist papers on the trains. Selfish individualism also seemed to be creeping in, replacing the collective family spirit and conjugal love this Catholic writer idealized in rural life. Young women who ventured into the unfamiliar city were rumored to have turned to prostitution to support themselves. Those women who eventually married had not been home long enough to learn from their mother how to keep house. Their young husbands often abandoned their homes, at first in search of a meal, and then of other pleasures.

Mahaim agreed with Demain that traveling awakened ideas among the commuting workers, but he cited that as a benefit. The trains educated "the peasant of La Bruyère, a man with a primitive, rudimentary language and without culture, close to brute animals," by exposing him to modern life.[12] Where Demain complained about the lack of discipline and respect, Mahaim recognized the worker's desire to see new things, have new friends, and experience different places. Workers in their train compartments sang and played cards; they did not moan about their long hours away from their village.

Belgian Socialist Emile Vandervelde followed an eighteen-year-old joiner who worked in Brussels and lived fifteen kilometers away in La Hulpe. The laborer walked two kilometers to the station and then spent two and a half hours on the train. He preferred his better-paid work to that of his father who labored outside year round for a large landowner. Although tired out by the commuting, the joiner did not want to live in the city. In the countryside his family could rent a four-room house and garden for 150 francs a year. The air was better, and they had land to grow wheat and potatoes and to keep chickens, a pig, a cow, and a calf. Vandervelde worried, not about the commuters who knew city life, but about their wives and children who remained rustic. Despite their work in the city, Vandervelde complained, the laborers did not experience the beauty, science, or social solidarity of the modern city because they left the city right after work, as soon as their trains arrived.[13]

Another worker described by Vandervelde, a forty-nine-year-old metallurgist from Hal, calculated that even with his monthly rent of 12 francs 50 and his daily train ticket that cost 1 franc 35, he still saved. It would have cost twenty francs a month to rent in Brussels.[14] Although the sum was not

11. Demain, *Les migrations,* 205 and 3.
12. Mahaim, *Les abonnements,* 199.
13. Vandervelde, *L'exode rural,* 223.
14. Ibid., 147.

substantial, in the countryside he and his wife had a whole house of four rooms with cellar and attic for their six unmarried children. They did not have to go up and down four flights of stairs for water as they would have in the city. His family had tried living in Brussels, he explained, but moved back to Hal for the convenience. One of their married sons living down the street also commuted, preferring the air of Hal and relishing the freedom that his children enjoyed to play in the streets without having to be watched. Vandervelde noted that metallurgists worked relatively short days, which made commuting easier. Similarly, workers in the building trades had a dead season that necessitated finding other work, an easier task in the countryside. Other than the masters who tended to move to Brussels to supervise their workshops more closely, Vandervelde explained, most skilled labor in the building trades lodged in their ancestral villages.

Another Socialist, Auguste De Winne, also rode the worker trains and conversed with the commuters, many of whom he found asleep on the hard wooden benches. He interviewed workers who left their homes at 4 a.m. to catch trains at 6 a.m., and who did not return until nine or ten in the evening.[15] They ate their morsel of bread for breakfast in the train before falling back to sleep, and ate their dinner on the platform between trains. Many commuters, including twelve girls who worked in the mills in Tourcoing and Roubaix, lived in villages one and a half hours walk from the nearest train stations.

In the brief moments when the Belgian parliament discussed the workmen's trains, very few critics mentioned the daily hardship of the commuting workers. The Mons industrialist Louis Hardenpont, after observing firsthand the demoralizing effects of the long journeys by workmen's trains on his laborers, volunteered that employers should build more worker housing close to work sites.[16]

The Liberal Count Goblet d'Alviella described the sordid existence of the commuters who left their homes at four in the morning to trudge in darkness to the station where they piled into the trains for the mine or the factory, not returning until late in the evening.[17] They had so little time at home that after devouring their soup, they did not bother to change their clothes before going to bed; few hours remained before they had to begin the walk to the train. What, he wondered had happened to their family life? On the other hand, looking at the overcrowding of British cities, the count did not advocate halting the train service. That would leave the laborers no alternative but to abandon their rural villages in search of work as members

15. Auguste De Winne, *A Travers les Flandres* (Ghent: Volksdrukkerij, 1902), 81–84.
16. Louis Hardenpont, 26 July 1899, *Annales parlementaires: Sénat (1898–1899)*, 524.
17. Comte Goblet d'Alviella, 22 January 1903, *Annales parlementaires: Sénat (1902–1903)*, 130. Goblet d'Alviella's answer was to develop the mines in Limbourg so that the workers did not have to commute to Liège and Charleroi.

of an industrial army in the cities. At least with their workmen's trains, he conceded, the Belgians had avoided the disastrous overcrowding that the British were struggling to alleviate.

This Belgian discussion had no British counterpart. London reformers could not imagine that life in the greenery beyond the rookeries could be worse than what they had observed within the urban hovels. In contrast to Belgian trains that transported peasants back to their villages where they had always lived, British trains carried formerly urban-dwelling workers to the developing suburbs.

The prominent British reformer Benjamin Seebohm Rowntree traveled to Belgium in 1911 to see the changes across the Channel for himself. Rowntree focused his attention on what he described as typically Belgian, "large suburban tracts in which industrial workmen live a life halfway between that of town and country." Most Belgian workmen and their families lived in these villages, half urban, half rural, Rowntree explained, where "the life is healthier for his wife and children. He gets a larger house, probably for less rent, and he has the advantage of a plot of land where, besides growing vegetables, he can keep a pig, a goat, and a few hens." Rowntree held up the Belgian experience of rural living made possible by the workmen's trains for emulation by the British; the agricultural population per square mile of cultivated land in Belgium was at least three times that of Britain. "If there are certain things which Belgium may learn from Britain, there are many which she may teach her, for Belgium is in advance of Britain in many directions," Rowntree argued in his *Land and Labour: Lessons from Belgium,* published in 1911.[18]

Rowntree believed the cheap and convenient workmen's trains were solving the problem of urban overcrowding created by industrialization in Belgium. The Belgian railways equalized the wages in town and country, although Belgian workers earned lower wages than their British counterparts. More women and children, therefore, worked in Belgium than in Britain and for much longer hours. Unlike a British worker who struggled to pay rent, however, a commuting Belgian laborer could retire as "a small [land] holder," Rowntree reported. In part that was because the subdivision of land made it possible for more Belgian workers to own their own plots. But it was also the result of the 1889 Belgian housing legislation that did not interfere with the private market as did the London County Council housing estates. Rowntree concluded: "If we follow the lead of Belgium in these matters, and in various others which are dealt with in this volume, we may expect to see the rural districts of Britain repeopled and her agriculture once more prospering."[19]

---

18. B. Seebohm Rowntree, *Land and Labour: Lessons from Belgium* (London: MacMillan, 1911), 593.
19. Ibid., 434, 292, and 544.

Vandervelde, traveling in Britain at the same time that Rowntree was investigating Belgium, observed similar differences in settlement patterns between the industrial neighbors. "Nothing is more striking for the visitor who goes from London to Brussels than the contrast between the deserted pastures of Kent and the animated fields bordering our major cities," he wrote.[20] Unlike Britain, the Belgian landscape was still covered with little villages of red-roofed white houses. During the day, they were populated only by old people, women, and children, but at night, after the long trains had disgorged their "human cargo," the Belgian villages came to life.

"Human Cargo": Commuting Working Men and Women

The chairman of the Great Eastern Railway, Lord Claud John Hamilton, would have preferred to carry fewer workers in and out of London on his trains. He complained about the unsavory habits of the commuters who traveled at cheaper fares as "workmen." "The passengers by the twopenny trains are not to be commended as models either in language or attire; in fact, they form no inconsiderable proportion of London's vast army of unskilled labourers."[21] But, most of the workmen who commuted on workmen's trains into London, limited by the railway to manual laborers earning less than thirty shillings a week, were skilled laborers. That was not true in Belgium, where marginally employed agricultural workers seeking employment took the trains to unskilled jobs in mines and industry. This difference in early ridership between Belgium and Britain passed unnoticed by contemporaries comparing the two systems.

The Belgian and British used similar terms to define passengers eligible to travel on workmen's trains. *Workmen,* according to the London County Council in 1893, included "mechanics, artizans, labourers and others working for wages, hawkers, costermongers, persons not working for wages but working at some trade or handicraft without employing others, except the members of their own families and persons, other than domestic servants, whose income does not exceed an average of thirty-nine shillings a week and their families."[22] The British parliament subsequently agreed to define the working class in the Standing Orders, the official written rules of parliament, as mechanics, laborers, and persons working for wages whose income did not exceed thirty shillings a week. Belgian legislation defined the

20. Vandervelde, *L'exode rural,* 138.
21. Lord Claud John Hamilton, quoted in *The Railway Magazine* (December 1898), as cited by C. E. Lee, *Passenger Class Distinctions* (London: London Railway Gazeteer, 1946), 55.
22. Workmen's Trains, CL/HSG/1/78, London Metropolitan Archives.

category of workers eligible to ride the trains as manual laborers paid by the day or by the piece. Laborers whose work had an artistic character, artisans, and domestic workers were excluded, after some debate in Parliament.

The National Association for the Extension of Workmen's Trains applauded the few British railway companies that, unlike the Great Eastern, permitted travelers who claimed working-class status and showed up for the early trains to purchase tickets.[23] Anyone who was willing to ride a crowded train at 5 a.m. deserved a workman's ticket, they figured. Most of the railways, however, required documentation that sometimes proved difficult to obtain.

In Belgium, the station masters assumed responsibility for checking the credentials of all those commuters who applied for a subscription to the workmen's trains. The worker arrived with two certificates, one signed by either the mayor or the police commissioner attesting to their place of residence and the other from their employer. Only after investigating fully—sending a staff member to interview the employer—were the tickets delivered to the worker.

Mahaim worried initially about fraud. Were intellectual workers claiming to be manual laborers? Were employers asking their workers to purchase tickets for them to ride at a lower fare? His interviews with the station masters revealed the occupations of the workers. Thirty percent (293,922) of the commuters on the workmen's trains to Brussels were factory workers, 16 percent (152,261) manual laborers, 15 percent (145,825) construction workers, 10 percent (97,612) miners, 10 percent (101,189) government workers, and 19 percent (185,645) belonged to other categories.[24] Industrial census data revealed that of the 9,233 commuters coming to Brussels in 1896, some, but not all of whom arrived by train, 41 percent (4,073) worked in construction, 12 percent (1,143) worked in the furniture trades or with wood, 8 percent (744) were metalworkers, 7 percent (652) manufactured clothing, 7 percent (633) worked in food industries, 5 percent (494) worked in chemicals, 5 percent (445) worked in ceramics, 4 percent (395) worked in textiles, 3 percent (311) in tanning, and 8 percent in other industries.[25] Mapping the census of 1913 shows the dispersion of Brussels workers each evening throughout the country. Salaried employees traveled longer distances than manual workers; men commuted longer distances than women.

Construction workers rode workmen's trains to both Brussels and London. Their places of employment shifted so often that they could not move

23. Minutes of Conference with the Board of Trade, 28 June 1893, RAIL 410 367, National Archives.
24. Mahaim, *Les abonnements,* 103. Although it is possible to count the commuters' professions locally by the station from which they departed based on Mahaim's data, it is not possible to determine the occupation of the commuters traveling to Brussels.
25. Mahaim, *Les abonnements,* 78.

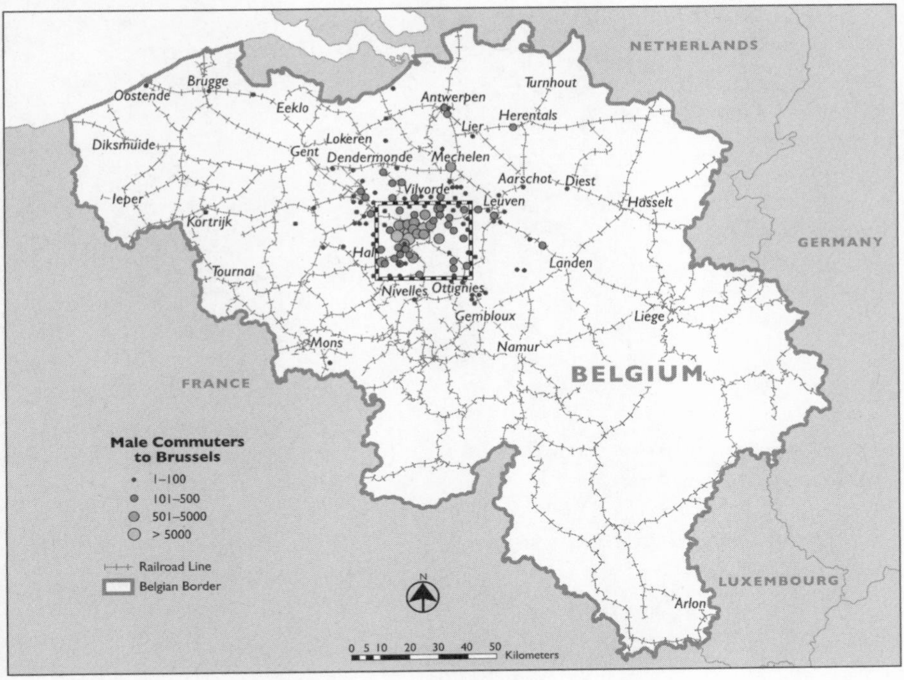

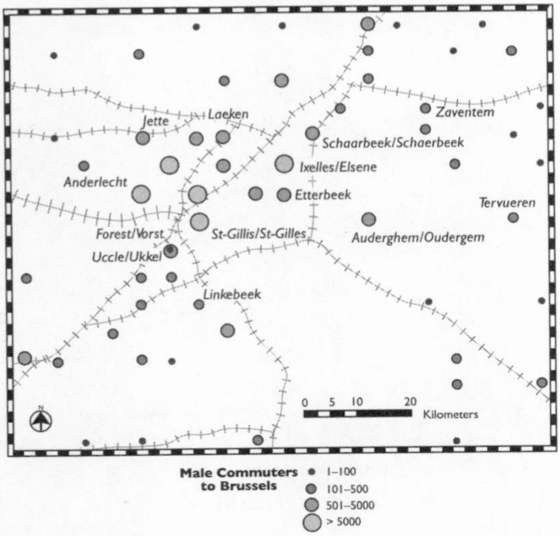

Male commuters to Brussels, 1910. Data from *Recensement de l'industrie et du commerce de 1910*. Vols. 7 and 8. (Brussels: Office de publicité, 1913).

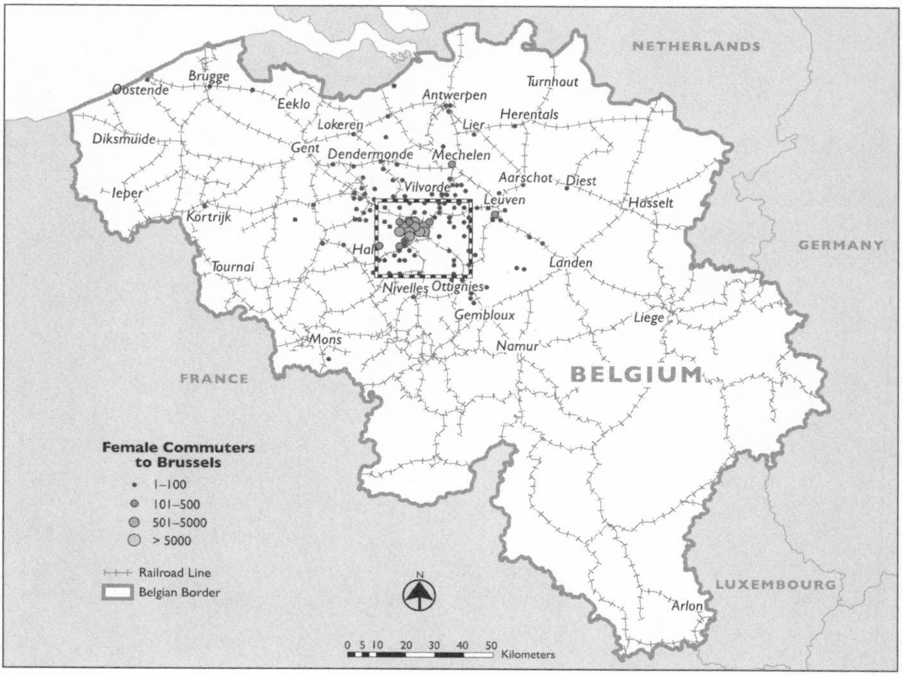

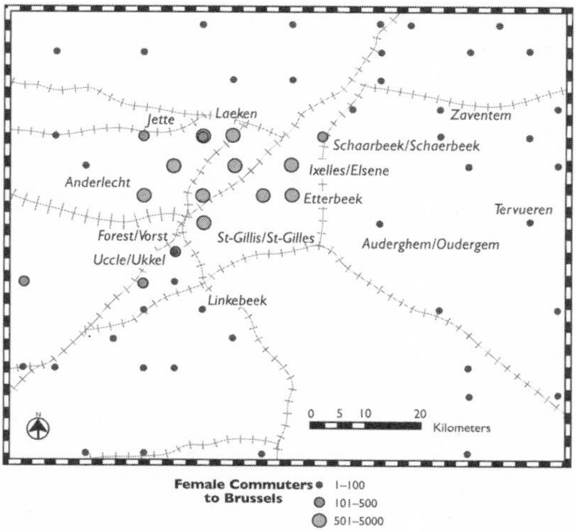

Female commuters to Brussels. Data from *Recensement de l'industrie et du commerce de 1910*. Vols. 7 and 8. (Brussels: Office de publicité, 1913).

with their jobs. Otherwise, the commuting populations differed from one side of the Channel to the other. The Royal Commission on London Traffic and Select Committees on Workmens Trains in Britain found that most of the commuters on workmen's trains to London were shoe and boot makers, bookbinders, bakers, and printers.[26]

The London County Council categorized the riders of the workmen's trains from each station by occupation. In 1897, the South Eastern Railway carried 3,250 bookbinders, curriers, hatters, skinners, boilermakers, plasterers, laborers, and employees of the engineering trades and of the building trades from Spa Road, Deptford, New Cross, Greenwich and Blackheath and 750 arsenal employees, military head dress makers, and employees in the engineering and building trades from Blackheath, Charlton, Woolwich, Plumsted, Abbey-wood, Erith, Dartford, and Belvedere to the terminus at London Bridge. Riding the London, Chatham and Dover Railway were 15,724 carpenters and joiners, bookbinders, bricklayers, laborers, iron founders, postmen, correctors for the press, masons, sorters, brass workers, shoemakers, polishers, bakers and confectioners, pattern makers, furriers, glass painters, zinc workers, telegraph operators, bill posters, wheelwrights and smiths, stonemasons, hammer men, and coopers. These figures held for the London and South Western, and London, Brighton and South Coast railways.[27] To the north, carpenters and joiners, house painters, printers' warehousemen, plumbers and fitters, gas workers, general laborers, porters, carpenters, cabinet makers, engineers, and printers rode the workmen's trains from Willesden Junction and Broad Street. On the Great Eastern Line, there were bricklayers, carmen, laborers, warehousemen, employees in the furniture trades, mechanics, clerks, employees in the clothing trade, and boot makers.[28] Housing was segregated by income level along the railway line, with the more elite workers living farther from London.

The unskilled could not afford to move beyond the city center. Marginally employed workers were stranded in the deteriorating neighborhoods in the center of the capitals because they could not afford to commute. The reformer H. D. Davies had praised plans to remove "many of the labouring classes every night to more wholesome habitations and a purer air," yet he noted "that many families are fixed to particular spots." These workers could not move because they "need to live near their jobs, . . . many have

26. Royal Commission on London Traffic, Report of the Royal Commission appointed to inquire into and report upon the means of locomotion and transport in London (London, 1905–1906); Report of the Statistical Officer on the inadequacy of Workmen's Train Services of the South London Railways, 24 March 1897, CL/HSG/1/78, London Metropolitan Archives.
27. Report of the Statistical Officer on the inadequacy of Workmen's Train Services of the South London Railways, 24 March 1897, CL/HSG/1/78, London Metropolitan Archives.
28. Evidence prepared by Statistical Officer, London County Council, 23 December 1898. CL/HSG/1/78, London Metropolitan Archives.

wives who work as charwomen or washerwomen, and . . . the boys and girls obtain little odd jobs whereby they eke out the week's income."[29] Unskilled laborers displaced by the demolitions in London tended to migrate to other neighborhoods close to labor markets. Skilled laborers were less likely to depend on the labor of other family members or on access to casual labor markets.

Ernest Mahaim was convinced that in Belgium, young men were the ones who commuted to work. That was the assumption behind the organization of workmen's trains on both sides of the Channel. Fathers would leave their families and commute when they had young children at home to help their mother with agricultural work. Mahaim and the organizers of the trains expected the roles would then be reversed as parents aged and children matured. Then the older children would commute, while husband and wife worked the fields side by side. Demain, however, discovered in his study of two Belgian towns that it was not the young men who were riding the rails, returning in the evening to their wives and children. Of the 3,003 women workers living in Leuven, 16 miles to the northeast of Brussels, he found that 504 (17 percent) commuted; 1,586 of the 3,552 (45 percent) women workers from Nivelles, 16 miles to the south, commuted. Most of these commuting women were between the ages of twelve and twenty-five and worked in textiles and clothing manufacturing. Women worked not only outside the home but also outside their Belgian village. Demain suspected that most commuting women looked for local work after marriage.[30]

Trackside observers for the London County Council estimated that 10 percent of the commuters on the workmen's trains coming into London in 1899 were women. Emma Inman, a fifteen-year-old stationery folder took the 6:15 a.m. train daily to London. The 6:21 was always full, she added, so she took the earlier train, even though she did not begin work until 8. Asked what she did between 6:50 and 8, she answered that she went to a coffee shop, had her breakfast, and then passed time in a neighboring church. Another commuter, Helen Taylor, testified that she had finally stopped taking the workmen's trains because she had caught a bad cold waiting around in the London station. She now paid the considerably higher regular fare to take the 7:19 train.[31]

The 1910 industrial census of Belgium revealed that of the 99,304 commuters coming into Brussels to work each day, 18,956 (19 percent) were

29. H. D. Davies, *The Way Out: A Letter Addressed (by permission) to the Earl of Derby, K.G. in which the Evils of the Overcrowded Town Hovel and the Advantages of the Suburban Cottage are Contrasted* (London: Longman, Green, Longman, & Roberts, 1861), 16–17.

30. Demain, *Les migrations,* 68.

31. CL/HSC/1/79, Workmen's Trains, Misc. Printed Papers 1898–1902, London Reform Union and Great Eastern Railway Col, London Metropolitan Archives.

women.[32] This reflects the pattern of Belgian employment in the decade before the First World War; 56.45 percent of Belgian men and 23.88 percent of women worked in commerce or industry. Women made up 96,507 (57 percent) of the 169,493 workers in textiles.[33] In 1885, one carpenter complained to an official that before the workmen's trains, women had not worked in their industry. But now they traveled to their jobs, performing tasks for a salary that no men from the city would ever accept.[34] Although the railways were willing to include women within their definition of "workmen," they refused to adjust their schedules to meet the women's later morning starting hours.[35]

British surveyors usually did not report the age of the commuters. They seem to have assumed that all commuters would be middle-aged men supporting a family. Observers in the East London neighborhood of Shoreditch reported that workers emigrated outward to the suburbs until the number of laboring family children reached the point that it was too expensive to pay train or tram fares and dinners away from home. Then the families would move back to the city to reduce commuting costs.[36] Belgian observers believed that young workers often met and married in the city but later moved to the countryside to raise their children.[37] Migration to the suburbs promised upward mobility on both sides of the Channel.

The British also assumed that commuting workers traveled daily year round. Mahaim was not so sure. He asked the station master in Louvain to keep track of the commuters and discovered that of the 2,008 workers who commuted to Brussels, 495 (25 percent) traveled for only one week at a time, 249 (12 percent) for two weeks. Only 173 (9 percent) of the 2,008 workers seem to have traveled more than forty weeks a year.[38] The station master explained that many ticket holders on workmen's trains commuted in search of work. He grumbled that these commuters were workers easily dissatisfied with their employers, so they frequently changed jobs. Other workers were

32. *Recensement de l'industrie et du commerce de 1910,* vols. 7 and 8 (Brussels: Office de publicité, 1913).

33. Stephan Bauer, ed. *Le travail de nuit des femmes dans l'industrie: rapports sur son importance et sa réglementation légale* (Brussels: Iena G. Fischer. Office International du Travail, 1903).

34. *Recueil des rapports des ouvriers délégués par la ville de Bruxelles: Exposition universelle d'Anvers 1885* (Brussels: Imprimerie Ve Baertsoen, 1885), 11.

35. Andrew Bonar Law, Harry Samuel, Thomas Lough, and Colonel Bowles, Select Committee on Workmen's Trains, British Parliamentary Papers (1903) (29 July 1903), 7–8; CL/HSC/1/79, Workmen's Trains, Misc. Printed Papers 1898–1902, London Reform Union and Great Eastern Railway Co., London Metropolitan Archives.

36. Helen Bosanquet, "Housing Conditions in London," *Economic Journal* 27, no. 107 (September 1917): 343.

37. *Moniteur des Comités de patronage et des sociétés d'habitations ouvrières* 13, no. 265 (25 January 1905).

38. Mahaim, *Les abonnements,* 46.

sent on jobs by their employers for short durations. Mahaim concluded, in contrast to the planners' original assumptions, that few workers regularly commuted year-round.

Mahaim's study also showed that while Brussels drew commuters from a national labor market, most of the workers came from closer stations. Not surprisingly, weekly commuters in Belgium traveled farther, an average of 62.32 kilometers (38.72 miles) each way as compared with the daily commuters who traveled only 17.74 kilometers (11.02 miles).[39] Most of these weekly commuters were one stage removed from relocating. The daily commuters who traveled the longest distances were the most skilled laborers; for example, a hat maker and a seamstress from Longlier. Agricultural workers recruited seasonally for public works and construction projects in Brussels commuted the shortest distances. Only 2 percent of Brussels commuters in October 1896 traveled less than 5 kilometers, while 37 percent traveled 6 to 9 kilometers, 36 percent 10 to 20 kilometers, and 24 percent more than 20 kilometers.[40] The dense railway network made the longer commutes possible.

British workers traveled shorter distances from the suburbs to the capital than did the Belgians from their rural villages to jobs dispersed throughout their much smaller country. Ninety-seven percent traveled less than 5 kilometers and 3 percent traveled 6 to 9 kilometers in October 1907.[41] British railways limited the distance over which workers could travel with a workman's ticket. Workmen's trains ran from 270 stations to London. The most distant stations from London were Enfield, 10.75 miles to the north, South Croyden, 11.25 miles south, Dartford 17 miles east, and to the west, Weybridge, 19 miles out of London.[42] Around London, most passengers with workmen's tickets traveled between 6 and 8 miles. In this region, 40 percent of all tickets issued were for workmen. Farther out, between 8 and 10 miles, 35 percent of the total tickets were for workmen. Still farther, in a 12- to 15-mile radius, only 20 percent of tickets were for workmen.[43]

The differences in ridership between Belgium and Britain reflected the divergent housing reform strategies of the two nations. The Belgians were trying to root workers in the countryside, while the British were transplanting them from the city to the suburbs. Too, Britain was not a national labor market like Belgium. The displaced or marginally employed Belgian rural laborer rode the rails from their villages in search of work; in Britain the

39. Ibid., 52 and 80.
40. Ibid., 79.
41. Report of the London Traffic Branch of the Board of Trade, 1907. London Metropolitan Archives.
42. London County Council Report on Workmen's Trains, *London Statistics* 2 (1891–1892): 325.
43. Harold J. Dyos, "Workmen's Fares in South London, 1860–1914," *Journal of Transport History* 1 (1953): 16.

skilled worker who could afford a house in the suburbs was transplanted and so commuted to London.

"The Perpetual Coming and Going": The Capital and the Countryside

The advent of commuting on a mass scale created conditions that few reformers in these two industrialized societies could have foreseen. The authors of a 1908 report on the housing problem in London, looking back, mused that housing reform had involved far more than just securing better housing for the poor, its original aim.[44] With locomotion, the reformers redefined not only the lives of the poor tenants, but land use and housing patterns for the society as a whole. In the years before the First World War, the British and Belgian reformers believed that they had set off in a bold new direction. And they were right.

In 1884, the British economist Alfred Marshall observed: "The population of London is already migratory in a great measure."[45] That was just the beginning. The number of commuters using railways, tramways, and bus companies to get to London rose from 269,662,649 in 1881 to 847,212,335 in 1901—a 68 percentage increase in twenty years.[46] By 1907, one of every five Belgian workers (20 percent) was commuting by train. Forty-three percent of all travelers on the Belgian national railway used worker tickets.[47] Better transit had indeed resulted in increased mobility, at least for the regularly employed. The Fabian Socialist Sidney Webb counted the provision of workmen's trains to affordable suburban housing as "among the [London County] Council's greatest triumphs."[48] By 1913, at least 820,000 London workers a day were traveling into the city from the suburbs, 520,000 of them by workmen's train.[49]

Although Demain decried "this perpetual coming and going from the countryside into the cities and from the cities back to the countryside," which, he said, "has slowly, coldly accomplished its demoralizing work" of destabilizing peasant life, the workmen's trains in Belgium accomplished

44. Mansion House Council on the Dwellings of the Poor, "The Present Position of the Housing Problem in and Around London," (1908).
45. Alfred Marshall, "The Housing of the London Poor," *Contemporary Review* 45 (1884): 228.
46. William Ashworth, *The Genesis of Modern Town Planning* (London: Routledge & Kegan Paul, 1954), 151.
47. Mahaim, *Les abonnements,* 38.
48. Sidney Webb, *The Work of the London County Council* (London: London Reform Union, 1895).
49. Anthony S. Wohl, "The Housing of the Working Classes in London, 1815–1914," in Stanley D. Chapman, *The History of Working Class Housing* (Newton Abbot: David and Charles, 1971), 33.

most of the reformers' goals.[50] The trains that had allowed middle-class professionals to commute from their new villas in the suburbs now permitted laborers to remain in their native villages while they too worked in the city. Despite declining employment in agriculture, the population of the countryside remained stable in Belgium through the First World War. That meant that unemployed workers did not pose as great a threat in Belgium as elsewhere in Europe. During the sporadic periods of economic crisis, workers returned to their small parcel of land, cultivating instead of striking. Meanwhile, employers could draw from a veritable army of peasants as well as workers for the labor force.

The development of working-class housing estates around London also accomplished the goals of British planners. They promoted the segregation of neighborhoods by social class. The reforms removed the skilled workers, who the reformers believed were capable of improvement, to the suburbs. There, they would be far away from the nefarious influence of casual laborers tempting them to follow them in profligacy and drink.

In contrast to the builders of the London estates, Brussels housing developers consciously chose not to segregate residents by social class. The 1889 housing law encouraged smaller, more dispersed semi-private efforts rather than the geographic concentration by social class of the developments that ringed London. Other than a few isolated projects such as Godin's Familistère or the Brussels Council's Cité Hellemans, social mixing prevailed throughout the prewar period in and around Brussels.

In Belgium, as in Britain, instead of fostering social integration, the workmen's trains intensified social division. But in Belgium, commuting reinforced geographic rather than class divisions. It rooted workers and their families firmly in a locality and a region, whether Wallonia or Flanders. The transportation and housing schemes did not, as Mahaim had expected, create a national citizenry.

The commuting of Flemish agricultural workers to the French-speaking Walloon mining districts of the south raised particular questions in Belgium. Walloon mine owners had promoted the expansion of workmen's trains as a solution to the agricultural crisis in Flanders. They employed otherwise underemployed rural laborers from the Flemish-speaking North to do the most menial, least well-paid work in their mines.[51] These Flemish laborers left no trace behind when they caught their trains in the evening from around Mons and Charleroi, the director of administration of one of the mines testified.[52] That was in contrast to Flemish workers who had started

50. Demain, *Les migrations ouvrières,* 3.

51. Yves Quairiaux, "Abonnements ouvriers et problème de main-oeuvre," in *Le centre mémoire du rail, 1839–1989* (La Louvière: Ecomusée régional du Centre, 1989), 64.

52. H. Gravez, "L'ouvrier mineur du centre," *Revue sociale et politique* (1893): 481–504.

as seasonal commuters and migrated to Wallonia permanently, often marrying local girls and raising children who learned French in school.[53] Unlike these weekly or seasonal commuters, the daily commuters rarely relocated, continuing to speak Flemish and to identify themselves as residents of their ancestors' villages.

The commuting Belgian laborers traveled nationally, but they resided locally, rooted firmly in their ancestral village. Even when they worked in Brussels, they identified themselves as residents of their native village where their family lived and their land lay. In London, with a few exceptions, migrating workers lost the ties that had bound them so closely together in their old London neighborhoods with their strong sense of place. There are few suggestions that they developed an alternative sense of belonging outside of the city, surrounded by other commuters. At the time, neither the Belgian nor the British reformers saw the residential identification of the Belgian commuters or its loss around London as a troubling issue.

Emile Vandervelde, writing in his villa in the suburban village of La Hulpe, 15 kilometers south of Brussels, far from the turmoil of Parliament, sang the praises of the quiet countryside that restored the urban laborer. He expected that the reversal of the "rural exodus" would eventually lead to the urbanization of the countryside and the greening of the city. Drawing inspiration from William Morris's utopian vision of a rural London, described in *News from Nowhere,* where laborers abandoned the polluted industrial cities to live in the countryside amidst the hay and clean air, the Belgian Socialist foresaw cities in the twentieth century that would no longer be residential.

Charles Didier, the Belgian editor of *Le Cottage,* shared Morris's dream: Saint Paul's Cathedral would dissolve in ruins, the Houses of Parliament would be converted into a hayloft, and Trafalgar Square would be a big meadow. Didier predicted that the redesigned city would guide the transformation of society. The countryside would be covered by quaint thatched cottages. Didier consequently defined the twentieth century as the century of transportation. Thanks to the railways, cities would cease to be residential centers; they would be transformed into meeting and work centers.[54] As he dreamed of this new century of transportation, Didier proudly asserted that the past had nothing to teach the reformers. The British and Belgian reformers were forging a new path from the industrial revolution to the future. Urban laborers and their families would reside in the greenery of the suburbs and the countryside, transported back and forth from their urban workplace on the rails.

53. *Mémoires d'une région: Le Centre (1830–1914)* (Mariemont: Musée royal de Mariemont, 1984), 193; Quairiaux, "Abonnements ouvriers et problème de main-oeuvre," 64.
54. Charles Didier, *L'évolution de l'habitation urbaine* (Brussels: P. Weissenbruch, 1902).

7 *"To Live Like Everyone Else"*

Commuting Labor, 1918–2010

> The social Utopia of the garden districts encouraged this drift from the cities and strengthened the ideal of the farm-style house with its own patch of ground in the middle of the "potato fields." ... Today everyone agrees that the city must be given priority.
>
> —Alain Malherbe, *Round Table Discussion: "Brussels, The Return of Social Housing,"* 83

The French writer and former minister of agriculture Jules Méline was not convinced in 1905 that the workmen's trains daily plying the tracks between the industrial capitals and the countryside littered with laborers' cottages would reform the working class. His description of the threat of rural exodus had contributed to the anxiety that triggered the nineteenth-century housing and transportation reforms in London and Brussels. He did not, however, share the British and Belgian reformers' conviction that their housing and transportation schemes would cause their industrial nations to evolve "towards a semi-industrial, semi-agricultural society."[1] He was skeptical that the urban capitals could be reclaimed from the slums into which they had degenerated during his lifetime and doubted that living like the middle class in the suburbs from ten at night until five the next morning would mold workers into model citizens. The few hours in the greenery with family was not worth the exhausting daily commute, he grumbled.

1. Jules Méline, *Le retour à la terre et la surproduction industrielle* (Paris: Librairie Hachette, 1905), 225, 226, 238.

Few other Belgian or British reformers doubted the social benefits of the pioneering housing and transportation reforms. They did not share Méline's pessimism about the future of their urban centers in the twentieth century or the laborers and their families. Rather than fomenting disorder from the shadows of the rookeries and impasses of the central cities, respectable workers, removed to the suburbs and the countryside, increasingly resembled the stable, law-abiding middle class. Geographic mobility had opened the path to social mobility, encouraging regularly employed workers to garden, to save, and to educate their children. The *New Survey of London Life and Labour,* an updating of Charles Booth's nineteenth-century study, reported in 1931 that by commuting together on the trains to the suburbs, "the whole demeanour of the different social classes has tended towards a closer approximation in the past generation."[2] Workers were even dressing like the middle-class commuters. Transplanted by the reformers, these commuting workers seemed to be as deeply rooted in the suburbs and the countryside of the twentieth century as the middle class. The laborers who had propelled their societies into industrial prosperity in the nineteenth century had been transformed into law abiding, property respecting citizens who would responsibly cast votes in the twentieth century.

These seemingly successful reforms had significant and unforeseen consequences for the commuters and, ultimately, for the social fabric of their society. In Belgium, Ernest Mahaim and other Belgian reformers expected the introduction of workmen's trains and housing legislation that encouraged ownership in the countryside to build national unity. Instead, they reinforced the laborers' local and regional identity. Commuters identified themselves with their ancestral villages, continuing to speak and to educate their children in their forefathers' language, whether French or Dutch. The reforms contributed to the splintering rather than the unification of the small country.

Working-class housing estates around London encouraged residential segregation, too. As the reformers separated home from work, they divided the Londoners by social class. Even though policy makers abandoned the class-based categories that had previously determined eligibility for subsidized housing and transportation, in 2007, the estates built by the London County Council a century earlier were even more segregated than the slums they replaced in 1907. Over the twentieth century in Britain, the schemes designed to integrate workers and their families into the middle-class society as citizens exacerbated existing divisions.

The devastation of two world wars presented unprecedented opportunities for reconstructing the built environment of the cities that earlier

2. London School of Economic and Political Science, *New Survey of London Life and Labour* (London: P. S. King & Son, 1930–1935), 1:192.

reformers denigrated as uncivilized and barbaric. In February 1915, planners from across Europe gathered at London's Guild Hall to draw up plans for rebuilding the extensively bombed and burned cities as soon as hostilities ceased. They chose Belgium to "be the first country where the prototype of the modern city will be realized."[3] Dotted with monuments and civic buildings constructed at the end of the nineteenth century, Brussels promised to rise anew from the ashes of the First World War, a symbol of a progressive, civil-minded postwar society.

At the same time, the British garden city architect Raymond Unwin and his team of planners designed residential estates for the economically self-sufficient and socially stable workers' families around the periphery of the Belgian capital.[4] Following a similar vision, the British Ministry of Reconstruction's housing panel, including reformers Benjamin Seebohm Rowntree and Beatrice Webb, proposed equally comprehensive schemes to meet their housing shortage, projected to be five hundred thousand units on the other side of the Channel. In contrast to the original nineteenth-century housing reforms, these schemes were not intended exclusively for the working class, but were designed for the "heroes" of the Great War.

The Tudor Walters Report of 1918 called on the British government to provide affordable, quality housing for families left without shelter by the war. The British Homes for Heroes Act was intended to bring "light and beauty into the lives of the people," middle class and working class alike.[5] The Belgian government pulled from a drawer the prewar plans of Socialist Hector Denis for a Société nationale des habitations à bon marché (National Society for Low-Cost Housing).[6] As in Britain, the National Society melded workers into this more inclusive category of heroic but homeless citizens.

Architectural forms for the new Belgian housing varied from clusters of ivy-covered, half-timbered English-style cottages, such as Logis-Floréal in the Brussels suburb of Boitsfort/Bosvoorde to the modernist blocks designed by Victor Bourgeois in 1922 for the Cité Moderne in the suburb of Berchem. Architects purposefully disguised differences in the size and price of individual units so that the residents of the heterogeneous community might mix together more readily, unencumbered by class. Many of the estates operated

---

3. *La Cité* 1 (July 1919): 6, as cited by Marcel Smets, *L'avènement de la cité-jardin en Belgique. Histoire de l'habitat social en Belgique de 1830 à 1930* (Brussels: Pierre Mardaga, 1976), 98.

4. Jan Maes, "De Tuinwijk-experimenten in het Kader van de Belgische Wederopbouw na 1918," in *Resurgam: Belgische Wederopbouw,* ed. Marcel Smets (Brussels: Gemeentekredit, 1985), 38.

5. Lloyd George, quoted in Alison Ravetz, *Council Housing and Culture: The History of a Social Experiment* (New York: Routledge, 2001), 77; Mark Swenarton, *Homes Fit for Heroes* (London: Heinemann Educational Books, 1981), 109.

6. H. Denis, Commission pour l'étude des réformes à préconiser en matière d'habitations à bon marché, *Questions diverses: Procès-verbaux des séances. Rapport* (Brussels: P. Wittembercq, 1913), 26–27.

"Le Logis" housing in the suburbs of Brussels. Watermael-Boitsfort/ Watermaal-Bosvoorde (November 1998). Photo by author.

as cooperatives with a flourishing communal life. In the Brussels suburb of Anderlecht, the garden city of Moortebeek was built by former Belgian prisoners of war with subsidies from labor unions and the National Society.[7] Ieder zijn Huis (to each his house) in the suburb of Evère interspersed individual houses amid blocks of flats to promote social mixing, just as the Belgians had done in the nineteenth century when they built small clusters of working-class housing in well-established suburban neighborhoods. Public transport linked the new estates to the center of Brussels.

The London County Council acquired three thousand acres north of London at Becontree in Essex on which they planned to site 24,000 houses. "The largest municipal housing estate in the world," Becontree appeared to critical observers to stretch on and on in a vast homogeneous plot of working-class dwellings.[8] Undeterred by charges of segregating citizens by social class, the Council then planned five thousand additional cottages for its estates at White Hart Lane and Old Norbury and two new estates, Roehampton in the Southwest and Bellingham at the edge of the county bordering Kent, in the Southeast.

7. "Décider son logement: L'habitat coopératif à Bruxelles," *Les Cahiers de la Fonderie* (September 1993): 20.

8. Ken Young and Patricia Garside, *Metropolitan London* (London: Edward Arnold, 1982), 154–155.

Changing economic conditions in the years after the First World War doomed the innovative programs on both sides of the Channel. Critics attacked government-subsidized municipal housing schemes as extravagant in a time of budgetary crisis. The demand for immediate, affordable shelter for the 550,000 Belgians whose housing had been destroyed and the 789,000 Londoners residing in inadequate housing quietly but firmly pushed aside utopian visions of social reform. Plans for "model houses with parlours and palace-like amenities in picturesque surroundings" were replaced by sketches of wooden barracks lined up in makeshift camps.[9] Built as temporary shelters, they housed their inhabitants through the next war.

The Second World War flattened whole neighborhoods and once again forced planners to abandon their costly designs for cottage clusters. British and Belgian architects alike turned to high-density urban housing. Vertical towers were oriented to receive sunlight and standardized within to promote social mixing. In the housing complex Cité Modèle, inspired by the Swiss-French architect Le Corbusier, two great towers formed a Y in the center of a vast green space in the Brussels suburb of Ganshoren. Le Corbusier's ideas also guided the development of blocks at the Acton West Estate in London. By the end of the 1960s, similar high-rise blocks, many rising to fifteen stories, made up at least half of the housing stock of many inner London boroughs.

In 1968, a gas explosion at the Ronan Point Estate in North London toppled one side of a high-rise Council block, killing five people and condemning all tower blocks in the eyes of Council tenants. That explosion seemed to call into question council housing in general. Council housing in cottage estates had been designed for the elite sector of the working class, but most of the tenants of the newer high-rise blocks were either marginally employed or unemployed. As housing of the last resort, subsidized municipal housing in London served a very different purpose from the original reforms designed to uplift the respectable poor, and it frightened the middle class.

Margaret Thatcher's Conservative government, believing that owning was better than renting and assuming that unionized workers had disposable income to invest, offered council tenants a chance to purchase their homes in 1980—a program so popular that the Labour party adopted it in 1985. By 1986, local British governments gained the right to empty entire estates and sell them; in 1989, Conservatives proposed a "rent to mortgage scheme" for the poorest tenants.[10] In Belgium, a less ambitious "Promise to Purchase" program allowed 160,000 tenants of social housing to buy their homes. Rates of home ownership in London increased from 37 percent in 1961 to

---

9. Ibid., 161.

10. As a result, by 1991, 10 percent of all mortgages were in arrears of more than two months, and 250,000 new home owners owed more than six months' rent. Still, the policy was pursued. Anne Power, *Hovels to High Rise* (London: Routledge, 1993), 232.

56 percent in 2001, while the rates in Brussels grew from 22 percent in 1961 to 41 percent in 1998.[11] In the nineteenth century, it had been the Belgians, not the British, who believed everyone should aspire to owning their own home. British Conservatives now consciously promoted home ownership to reestablish the private market as an effective tool of social reform. Their rhetoric matched that of the nineteenth-century Belgians.

By 1998, fewer than a hundred government-subsidized housing units were being built annually in Britain; only fourteen new units were constructed in Brussels in 2000.[12] The dramatic reduction in municipal housing construction reflected in part the need to finance repairs on the already extensive properties managed by the municipalities, but it also marked a turn away from the class-based subsidies that had been the foundation of the original housing reforms before the First World War. At least in the minds of the policy makers, they had achieved their goal of blending the elite workers into the middle class.

British housing policy adapted throughout the twentieth century to reflect the shifting ideological positions of the political party in power. The British Housing Act of 1949 eliminated all references to social class. When the Conservatives came to power in 1979, social housing in the form of council estates proved to be the most easily dismembered sector of the British welfare state. They cast property not as a social right, like streets and sewers, but as a private commodity, as the cornerstone of individualism.[13] Once again, the argument over public services in London pitted the government against the market as competitors.

In Belgium, the terminology of social housing evolved from the prewar "workers' housing," to "inexpensive housing" between the wars, to "housing" in the postwar period. In contrast to Britain, however, municipal officials in Belgium continued to expect the semi-official housing societies to select sites, contractors, and building plans and to set and subsidize rents and purchase prices, as the central government, through the National Housing Society, enforced statutes and housing regulations and made financing available. Other than terminology, not much changed. The overseers of the Belgian National Housing Society, celebrating their fiftieth anniversary in 1969, asserted that "social housing is so tightly tied with the social and

---

11. A. H. Halsey, *British Social Trends since 1900* (London: Macmillan Press, 1988).
12. Jill Matheson and Gwyneth Edwards, *Focus on London 2000* (London: The Stationery Office, 2000); Société du Logement de la Région Bruxelloise, *Rapport annuel: Exercice 2001* (Brussels: SLRB, 2002), 54. Brussels and London planners struggled in the 1980s and 1990s to keep subsidized housing from turning into ghettos. In 1988, 60 percent of Council housing tenants in London were "economically inactive" and 50 percent were classified as "very poor." Much of the housing constructed over the course of the twentieth century stands vacant.
13. Ian Cole and Robert Furbey, *The Eclipse of Council Housing* (New York: Routledge, 1994), 1.

economic evolution of our society" that it would be impossible to conceive of one without the other.[14] Article 23 of the Belgian Constitution declared housing to be a fundamental right.

In 1980, social housing in Belgium was made the responsibility of the regional not the national government, and in 1985, La Société du Logement de la Région de Bruxelles-Capitale/Brusselse Gewestelijke Huisvesting-Smaatschappij (SLRB/BGH; Housing Society for the Region of Brussels) was established to promote social housing through thirty-three housing societies. Responsibility for financing, building, and renovating the social housing stock in the Belgian capital fell to the SLRB/BGH, while municipal communes maintained and administered the housing. Although the regions of Flanders to the north and Wallonia to the south continued in the spirit of the law of 1889 to subsidize home ownership, in Brussels, with its significant impoverished population, the SLRB/BGH subsidized rental housing. To promote social mixing and to prevent the creation of ghettos—both priorities for the SLRB/BGH—Brussels permitted residents whose incomes rose above the set maximum to remain in municipal housing as models for the other tenants, even though that resulted in longer waiting lists for subsidized housing. Belgian reformers continued to assume both that the government and the private sector should cooperate and that social housing would reform its tenants.

The world wars caused both Belgian and British reformers to reconsider the government's responsibility for transporting workers from home to work. The nationalization of the British railways during the First World War reopened debate over the relationship of private railways to society and of the state to the railways. Critics who wanted to nationalize the railways accused the private British railways of having pandered to the corporate interests from the beginning. Meanwhile, Belgian critics who opposed government control of the railway questioned the efficiency of the national railway, proposing to reorganize the railway along corporate lines to energize a national postwar economic recovery. After 1918, even more than before, reformers on both sides of the Channel cited the experience of the other's railway in arguments for change at home.

The first British minister of transport, Sir Eric Geddes, previously general manager of the North Eastern Railway, proposed the nationalization of British railways in 1919, but Parliament decided that it was not the time for dramatic change. Instead, Parliament aligned the 120 competing main-line railways into "the Big Four companies." The Belgian parliament also decided to stay the course. For them that meant not abdicating what they defined as their public responsibility: to run the railways in the national

14. *Nationale Maatschappij voor de Huisvesting: 1919–1969* (Brussels: Van Muysewinkel, 1969), 17.

interest. In 1926, the Belgians established the Société Nationale des Chemins de Fer Belge/Nationale Maatschappij der Belgische Spoorwegen (National Belgian Railways, SNCB/NMBS), a public enterprise to be run in the interest of the state, but by industrialists adopting the management principles of private enterprises.

Belgian opponents of privatization focused on potential disruption to workmen's fares, which were seen as serving the national economic interest. Although the SNCB/NMBS raised general passenger fares by 25 percent in 1926, it limited the increase in special fares for workers, then 50 percent of the traffic on the railway, and of students and season ticket holders, to 12.5 percent.[15] By 1939, 82 percent of all passengers on the Belgian railways rode with special fares, including workmen's tickets.[16] British railway fares, which increased by 100 percent in 1920, cost workers more than four times the price of Belgian tickets in 1926. As in the nineteenth century, British railways looked to the more profitable long-haul journeys, rather than commuters, to fill their trains.

At midnight on 31 December 1947, drivers of night trains throughout Britain blew their whistles to signal the end of one hundred years of private ownership of the British railways and the consolidation of the Big Four railways, the minor railways, and the London Passenger Transport Board under public ownership. Labour's overwhelming victory after the Second World War had led the British public to expect nationalization of the railways, but perhaps not so precipitously.

Throughout the twentieth century, both national railways struggled to curb deficits caused by rising labor costs and by increasing competition from private automobiles. The British responded by raising fares, the Belgian government by shifting half the financial burden for subsidizing workers' fares to employers. In 1962, the Belgians fused workers' fares with other reduced-price tickets to create "social season tickets for workers and employees," and in 1991, the government replaced "social season tickets" with kilometer-based tickets, the "trajet-treinkaart."[17] In Britain, the national railway also phased out workmen's fares for the general non–class-based category of "early morning fares."

---

15. Georges De Leener, *Les Chemins de fer en Belgique. Leur passé. La nouvelle Société nationale des chemins de fer belges. Ses perspectives d'avenir* (Brussels: Maurice Lamertin, 1927), 143; Edgar Milhaud, "L'idée de la gestion publique des chemins de fer traverse-t-elle une crise?" *Les Annales de l'économie collective* 20 (September–December 1928): 331.

16. Guy Vanthemsche, "L'entre-deux-guerres, période charnière de l'histoire des chemins de fer belges 1919–1939," in *Sporen in België. 175 Jaar Spoorwegen. 75 Jaar NMBS,* ed. Bart Van der Herten, Michelangelo Van Meerten, and Greta Verbeurgt (Louvain: Universitaire Pers Leuven, 2001), 170. The low fares were protected because passenger fares constituted only 23 percent of the rail revenues, the rest being made up by freight. Low passenger fares clearly appealed to voters.

17. Société nationale des chemins de fer belges, *Rapport annuel* (1967).

Although both railways eliminated subsidies based on social class, the fundamental difference has endured between a Belgian railway that uses fares as an instrument for effecting social policy and a British railway that operates as a commercial enterprise. In its 2000 annual report, the SNCB/NMBS reported that it took in 13,321,000,000 francs in total ticket receipts, while providing 264,000,000 francs in subsidies for students, the elderly, and children, and an additional 208,000,000 francs to meet what it identified as "its social mission."[18] Only 13 percent of domestic passengers on Belgian rail paid full fare for regular tickets; 42 percent rode to work as "employees." At the same time, British Rail, the rebranded British Railway, proudly proclaimed that, as a result of cost savings, it led all the principal European railways in productivity, while receiving the lowest level of government funding. The Conservative politician and shadow minister of transport, Norman Fowler, summed up his party's view of the relationship of government to the railways: "Conservatives reject the idea that transport ought to be regarded primarily as a social service to which the taxpayer must be forced to contribute huge and continuing subsidies in order to secure social and political objectives selected by government."[19]

The European Union, in 1992, acknowledged the "historical, legal and cultural disparities . . . between Member States concerning the concept and organisation of pubic services in rail transport." In a White Paper, it advocated a mixed system of state and public service contracts for railways, giving "priority in its policy and legislative proposals to market-based approaches that provide price incentives, whenever these are likely to achieve social and environmental objectives in a flexible and cost-effective way."[20] Although the Belgians remained the outliers in a European Union where privatized railways had become the norm, none of the member states looked to the British as a model of successful privatization.

The Conservative government privatized British Rail in 1994, breaking it up into one hundred separate companies. In 2001, after Railtrack, the privatized owner of the track, signaling, and stations, declared bankruptcy, the Ministry of Transport guaranteed its deficits and reorganized Railtrack as Network Rail, a private company run by members rather than share holders. The recurring deficits incurred by the Belgian railway between 1956

18. Société nationale des chemins de fer belges/Nationale Maatschappij de Belgische Spoorwegen (SNCB/NMBS), *Rapport annuel* (2000), 40.
19. Norman Fowler, "A Paper on Conservative Transport Policy," in *The Right Track* (Conservative Political Center, 1978), quoted in Jon Shaw, "Designing a Method of Rail Privatisation," in *All Change: British Railway Privatisation,* ed. Roger Freeman and Jon Shaw (London: McGraw-Hill Companies, 2000), 3.
20. Commission of the European Community, White Paper COM(96)421, July 1996. http://europa.eu.int/eur-lex/en/com/cnc/2001_0244en01.pdf.

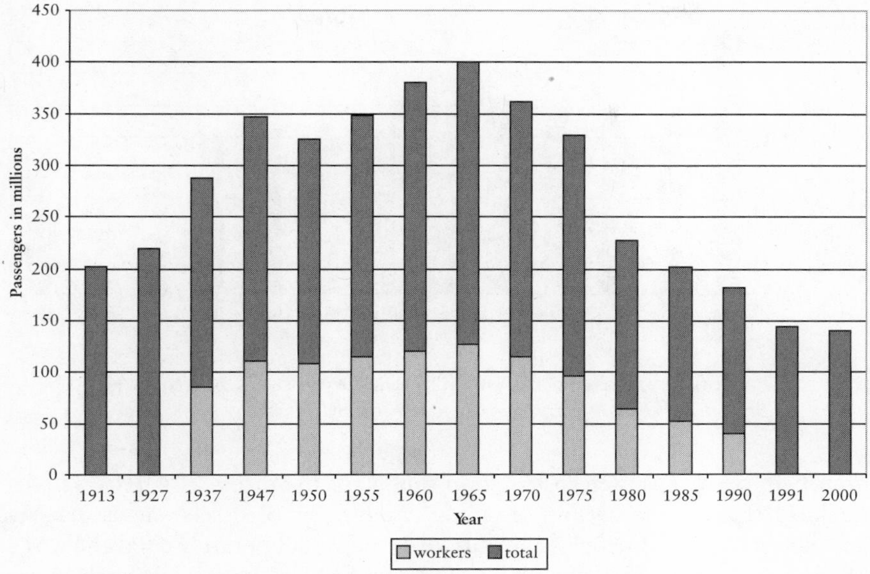

Belgian rail passengers in millions. Data from Société nationale des chemins de fer belge/Nationale Maatschappij der Belgische Spoorwegen (SNCB/NMBS), *Rapport annuel* (1913–2000).

and 1995 forced Belgian politicians to reexamine the relationship between the railways and the government. The Belgian Parliament defended its traditional model of a semi-autonomous national railway until 2005, when it, too, turned the management of the rail infrastructure over to a private enterprise, Infrabel.

Despite the marked trend toward privatization engineered by conservative national governments at the end of the twentieth century, few policy makers in Europe denied the responsibility of national, regional, or municipal governments, or of the European Union, to oversee social housing and public transportation. Faced with severe constraints on public spending, national governments throughout Europe continued to allocate funds to house the inadequately sheltered and to subsidize transportation for commuters, children, the elderly, and other socially defined categories.

The environmental crisis forced planners at the turn of the twenty-first century to recognize what the pioneering nineteenth-century reformers knew, that the land use/housing policies and transportation questions were inextricably intertwined. Urban planners throughout Europe acknowledged, as the European Conference of Ministers of Transport declared in 2001, that "sustainability requires that policy-making for urban travel be viewed in a holistic sense; that planning for transport, land use and the environment

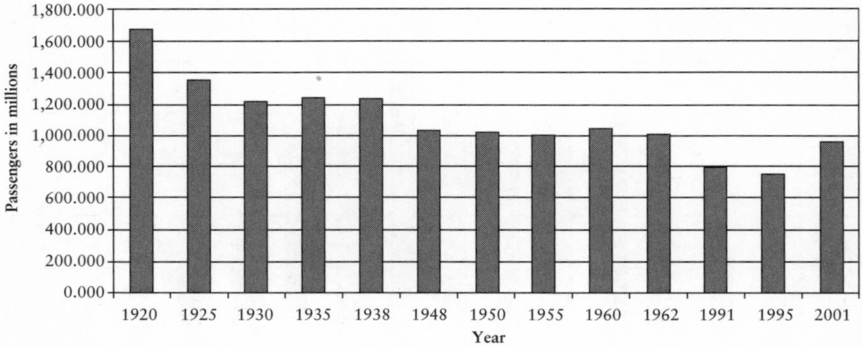

British rail passengers in millions. Data from Derek Aldcroft, *British Railways in Transition* (New York: St. Martin's, 1968), 151.

no longer be undertaken in isolation one from the other."[21] That was particularly true in the second (London) and third (Brussels) most densely populated cities of Europe. The City of London deliberately sited the 2012 Olympics to develop brown fields in the East End of London where the most notorious nineteenth-century slums were located. The regional government of Brussels responded to outcry over the "unbuilding" of Brussels to accommodate the burgeoning institutions of the European Union with plans for residential development and new rail lines in the "ghetto d'Eurocrats."[22] Both cities have questioned the sustainability over the long-term of commuting by their burgeoning workforce.

A century after the introduction of the interlinked housing and rail schemes, citizens of all social classes throughout Europe had come to assume personal mobility as a basic right. The nineteenth-century reformers' dream of commuting home to the suburbs or the countryside from work in the city had become a reality by the end of the twentieth century, for workers as for the middle class. More and more of those commuters journeyed to work in their own cars, rather than on public transport. The number of private automobiles on European roads tripled in the last three decades of the twentieth century in Europe.[23] Even if "everyone realizes that the car is no longer the best

---

21. European Conference of Ministers of Transport, "Implementing Sustainable Urban Travel Policies" (2001), quoted in Harry Geerlings and Dominic Stead, "The Integration of Land Use Planning, Transport and Environment in European Policy and Research," in *Transport Policy* 10 (2003): 187.
22. Nicolas Bernard, "Les mutations du logement en région bruxelloise," *Courrier hebdomadaire* 1993 (2008): 16.
23. *European Transport Policy for 2010: Time to Decide,* White Paper of the Commission of the European Communities, Brussels (12 November 2001), http://europa.eu.int/eur-lex/en/com/cnc/2001_0244en01.pdf.

means of travelling to and around the city," planners for the Brussels Capital Region acknowledged, "it is difficult to let go of it, as the protective 'cocoon' it represents has become essential to many people."[24] In 2001, the European Commission diagnosed "transport congestion…approaching gridlock."[25]

The solutions envisioned by nineteenth-century reformers in Brussels and London to reduce the overcrowding in their industrial capitals evolved into problems demanding solutions from the European Union. More commuters traveled from ever greater distances each year as workers moved outward to less densely populated rural and suburban areas. Increasingly, commuters worked on the periphery of the capitals, traveling from home in one suburb to work in another. These journeys were not well-served by public transit that was designed to bring commuters into the capitals from the suburbs. The number of commuters into central London increased by 50,000 every decade. In 1991, 32 percent of the workers employed in central London lived in outer London suburbs.[26] In 2001, 722,539 (19%) of 3,805,655 workers commuted from beyond London.[27] The number of commuters in Brussels grew even more rapidly, so that by 1991, more than half of the workers in the Brussels Capital Region commuted, coming from almost every Belgian commune. In 2008, of the 686,500 Brussels workers, 129,000 (19%) commuted from Wallonia and 228,000 (33%) from Flanders.[28] Increasingly, these commuters traveled by car more than by train, bus, or subway.

In response to what it urgently defined as an environmental crisis, the European Commission called for a return to more environmentally friendly modes of transport, especially rail.[29] In 2006, transport accounted for 21 percent of London's total carbon dioxide emissions.[30] London responded by

24. Brussels Capital Region, "Mobility in Brussels," http://www.bruxelles.irisnet.be/en/citoyens/home/mobilite_a_bruxelles.shtml.
25. *European Transport Policy for 2010: Time to Decide.*
26. R. Mols, "La mobilité bruxelloise," *Bulletin de la Société belge d'études géographiques* 35, no. 1 (1966): 50; B. Merenne-Schoumaker, H. Van der Haegen, and E. Van Hecke, *Recensement général de la population et des logements au 1er mars 1991* (Brussels: Institut National de Statitisque, 1991), 87; *London Facts and Figures, 1995 ed.* (London: HMSO, 1995), 33.
27. Gareth Piggot, "Commuting in London. DMAG Briefing 2007-03." (London: Greater London Authority, 2007), 10.
28. The nineteen communes of Brussels were designated one of three regions in the federal state of Belgium in 1989. The Brussels Capital Region replaced the Brussels Agglomeration, the municipal authority that was created in 1971 and vested with powers in urban planning, housing, transportation, public safety, public health, and economic development. "Brussels Capital Region IRIS-plan. Een geweestelijk Vervoersplan voor Brussels Hoofstedelijk Gewest," Brussels, 1997. "Minibru 2009" (Brussels: Ministry of the Brussels Capital Region, Brussels Institute for Statistics and Analysis, 22009), 18–19, http://www.bruxelles.irisnet.be/cmsmedia/en/mini_bru_2009.pdf?uri=ff808181260b034c01260d0f369d0014.
29. Ibid.
30. Greater London Authority, "Delivering London's Energy Future. The Mayor's Draft Climate Change and Energy Mitigation Strategy for Consultations with the London Assembly and Functional Bodies" (February 2010), http://legacy.london.gov.uk.

planning new underground and rail lines, including the cross-London link and electric bus networks on the periphery of the metropolis, "to encourage smart travel—helping people choose public transport, cycling and walking instead of cars as a convenient and cheap way of getting around London." Congestion charges for drivers entering the city of London helped them meet their goal of shifting 9 percent of the commuters away from private automobiles.[31] The first Belgian government of the twenty-first century, a coalition of Liberals, the Green Party, and the Socialists advocated "reequilibrating" the balance in the transport sector by "écoligisant" (greening) the tax structure and increasing government subsidies to the railway.[32] Their plan, "Mobility on the Horizon 2020," introduced by the Green minister of transport Isabelle Durant actively encouraged the use of public transport and discouraged automobile use, especially in urban areas. Planning documents for the Brussels Capital Region called for a turn away from the car to "'gentler' travel for all Bruxellois," through significant infrastructure investments and a prioritization of walking and biking on urban thoroughfares.

Commuting produced, in the words of the European Commission, "sprawling suburbs, and concentrations of acute poverty and social exclusion."[33] A century of transportation subsidies and housing reforms encouraging residential development outside of city centers made Brussels and London vibrant centers of activity by day, as nineteenth-century reformers had envisioned, but rendered the capitals, "hostile deserts" at night.[34] A Belgian architect complained that "the social Utopia of the garden districts encouraged this drift from the cities and strengthened the ideal of the farm-style house with its own patch of ground in the middle of the 'potato fields'." He concluded, "what was a good solution in its time is no longer adequate in its present form. Today everyone agrees that the town must be given priority."[35] That meant the repopulation of the central city, the return of workers' families to Brussels and London.

In their planning document for the first quarter of the twenty-first century, *Transport 2025—Transport Vision for a Growing World City,* London planners projected that London would grow from 7.5 million people in 2005 to 8.3 million in 2025. To meet the anticipated housing demand, London planners envisioned new town centers of high-density, low-rise housing built

31. Greater London Authority, *Draft London Plan* (London: Greater London Authority, 2002); Nicky Gavron, Interview, 30 April 2003, City Hall, London. The election of Boris Johnson redirected efforts at climate change mitigation through transportation.
32. Philippe de Boeck, *Le Soir* (28 September 2000).
33. Commission of the European Communities, Communication from the Commission, "A Sustainable Europe for a Better World: A European Strategy for Sustainable Development," http://europa.eu.int/eur-lex/en/com/cnc/2001_0244en01.pdf.
34. Pierre Muelle, Directeur Général du Germinal, "Midi du Logement Social au Musée," 5 May 2003, Brussels.
35. Alain Malherbe, Round Table Discussion: Brussels, 83.

around transportation hubs. They set targets for the provision of affordable housing in all of its boroughs—50 percent of housing was to be affordable; 70 percent of that affordable housing was to be social housing—to promote "mixed and balanced communities" within London.[36] Reversing the mid-twentieth-century Abercrombie plan for London that was designed to reduce the population of central London by moving residents to peripheral New Towns, the Greater London Council called for an urban renaissance to recentralize an ecologically friendly residential London around public transport, especially rail.[37]

The Brussels regional government launched construction projects in the first decade of the twentieth century to add lower-income residents to areas "of some standing" in the center of the capital.[38] In these mixed-use projects, "socially stimulating conditions" would allow urban tenants of modest means "to live like everyone else," rather than being isolated in immigrant and low-income ghettoes.[39] In 2003, Brussels allocated 150 million euros to restore 17,000 of its 38,000 social housing units. In 2006, François Dupuis, secretary of state for housing, committed the regional Brussels government to finance five thousand new housing units in Brussels, with 1,500 units for middle-income renters at market value and 3,500 units of social housing; debates over high versus low rise and density of development delayed construction.[40] In the first decade of the twenty-first century, in Brussels, as in London, housing was identified as a critical piece of "a sustainable urban agenda."[41]

Forty thousand people were employed by the European Union in Brussels in 2000.[42] In the so-called European Quarter in the heart of Brussels, bulldozers razed centuries-old townhouses located in the path of new institutional structures of the European Union. These towering structures shut their doors every evening, spilling their multilingual staffs into private automobiles to begin their commutes home to the outer suburbs. To counter the trend, planners in Brussels proposed schemes for "social and functional

---

36. Greater London Authority, *The London Plan,* http://www.london.gov.uk/thelondonplan/working/.
37. Nicky Gavron Interview, 30 April 2003, City Hall, London.
38. Alain Hutchinson, Round Table Discussion: Brussels, "The Return of Social Housing," *A+. Architecture + Urbanism + Design + Art* 181 (April–May 2003): 85.
39. Pierre Vanderstraeten, Round Table Discussion: Brussels, "The Return of Social Housing," *A+. Architecture + Urbanism + Design + Art* 181 (April–May, 2003): 90.
40. Ville de Bruxelles, *Programme de politique générale* (Brussels, 2006).
41. The European Liaison Committee for Social Housing, "Social Housing and the 2020 EU Strategy," http://www.cecodhas.org/content/view/875/70. The Belgian expectation of government involvement in housing, funded at a national level and implemented at a national, regional, or municipal level persisted, virtually unchallenged.
42. Eric Corijn, Christian Vandermotten, Jean-Michel Decroly, and Erik Swyngedouw, "Brussels as an International City," *Brussels Studies,* http://loftus.blog.activ.eu/files/2009/03/brussels-internationalcity.pdf.

mixed use" in the Quarter with plans for new tram and subway access to the major rail hubs. The minister-president of the Brussels region, Charles Picqué, looked forward optimistically in 2008 to the revitalization of his city as the European capital: "The city's goal is to move from the status of a national capital (the head of a small, bicultural European country with limited visibility) to the status of an international metropolis (the head of a large, multicultural body with global visibility)."[43]

Robert Skinner, executive director of the Transportation Research Board of the National Academy of Sciences, acknowledged in 1996 that in the United States, as in Europe, "the timeless debate about the interaction between transportation and land use continues today, but increasingly that debate is less about transportation or land use per se and more about how the combination of the two affects environmental quality, economic growth, and social equity."[44] That interaction involved more than the siting of housing projects near railway stations and the extension of rail lines to centers of residential development, crucial questions for the nineteenth-century reformers.

The twenty-first-century discussions of land use and transportation, societal control, and social mobility resonated with questions posed by reformers at the end of the nineteenth century.[45] The urban commuters asked by planners in the first decade of the twenty-first century to move back into the city were the descendants of workers set in motion by nineteenth-century reformers, but no one in Brussels or London worried about a workers' revolution. These new urban residents bore little resemblance to the masses inhabiting the urban rookeries spawned by the industrial revolution. Rooted, voting property owners, the commuting laborers had become responsible citizens supporting law and order, far from the residuum. The dreams shared by the Belgian and the British reformers confronting the crisis of industrialization in the nineteenth century had become a reality a century later, but a reality that brought with it a new cycle of challenges.

---

43. Charles Picqué, "Europe in Brussels: A Great Asset and a Great Responsibility," In *Brussels: Perspectives on a European Capital,* ed. Pierre Laconte and Carola Hein (Brussels: The Foundation for the European Environment, 2008), 6.

44. Robert E. Skinner Jr., "The Transportation-Land Use Interaction," *TR News* 187 (November–December 1996): 6.

45. See Organisation of Economic Co-operation and Development and the European Conference of Ministers of Transport, *Urban Travel and Sustainable Development* (Paris, 1995), 149; *Development in Practice: Sustainable Transport, Priorities for Policy Reform* (Washington, D.C., 1996); Anthony Downs, *Stuck in Traffic: Coping with Peak-Hour Traffic Congestion* (Washington, D.C., 1992).

Bibliography

Archives

Archives de la Ville de Bruxelles/Stadsarchief Brussel.

Fonds "Maisons Ouvrieres." Boîte 2. Procès verbaux du Comité officiel de Patronage des Habitations à Bon Marché et des Institutions de Prévoyance; Boîte 10. Bulletins de renseignement sur les ménages participant au concours et correspondance divers. 1892–1900; Boîte 11. Bulletins de renseignement sur les ménages participant au concours et correspondance divers; Boîte 12. Concours d'ordre et de propreté; Boîte 22. Carnets de ménage.

Fonds Charles Buls, III 20 A-D; Habitations ouvrières et à bon marché. 1887–1914.

Book of Clippings 1. 1906–1908.

Varia I à VI.

Leicester University Library

London County Council. Third Class Season Tickets. May 1902. Box III.

London Metropolitan Archives

Housing Committee. 1904–1906.

Locomotion in London. LCC\MIN\7342 E 56; LCC\MIN\7352.

London County Council and others v. The Great Eastern Railway and others. Minutes of Proceedings and Judgement, 1911.

London County Council. Housing Development and Workmen's Fares. Report by the Valuer to the Housing of the Working Classes Committee. London: London County Council, 1933.

London County Council Report on the Inadequacy of workmen's train services on the South London Railways.

London County Council Report of the Public Health and Housing Committee on Workmen's Trains for Districts South of the Thames (1892) and (1893).

London County Council. Workmen's Trains and Trams, with Particulars of the Council's Dwellings for Workmen. 2 February 1914 and 1 May 1914 LCC\CL\HSG\1\78–81.

Minutes. Displacement of housing by railroads. LCC\MIN\7371\50; Proceedings of the Housing of the Working Classes Committee. LCC\MIN\7257, LCC\MIN\7258, LCC\MIN\7259; Public Health and Housing Committee—Presented Papers, 1889–1892. LCC\MIN\7330 E 16, 1893–94. LCC\MIN\7336 E 16 LCC\MIN\7343\E56, 1896–1897. LCC\MIN \7359\38.

Published reports on workmen's trains. LCC\HSG\GEN\2\4.

Railways and Canal Traffic Cases, X, 293.

Signed Minutes. LCC\MIN\7254–7271.

Workmen's trains. General. CL/HSG/1/78. Reports on workmen's trains from London County Council, Committee on workmen's trains; Misc. printed papers re: the individual railways 1898–1902. CL/HSC/1/79; 1898–1900. LCC\MIN\7368; 1901–1902. LCC\Min\7378 38; 1903–04. LCC\MIN\7387 38; Workmen's trains 1905–6. LCC\MIN\7397 38.

London Transport Museum

Book of Clippings, 1900–1908.

Muséé Royale de Mariemont

Rayon 25 Merbes le Chateau—Habitations ouvrières. Farde No 7.

The National Archives, Kew

RAIL: Artizans, Labourers and General Dwellings Companys' application for reduced fares to Hornsey and Wood Green (Noel Park Estate Houses). Workmen's Trains and Fares, 1884. RAIL 236 353 6; Cheap Trains Act. RAIL 1053 210, RAIL 1053 211; Committee on Workmen's Fares 1904–1905. RAIL 1124 157; Great Eastern Railway Record Book 1896–1897. RAIL 227 24; Great Northern Railway. RAIL 236 373 14; Great Northern Railway. RAIL 236 724 9; Great Northern. Workmen's Trains 1899. RAIL 236 384; Great Northern Railway. Workingmens' Trains. RAIL 236 338 15; Memorial Workmen of Barnet, 1908. RAIL 7249; Minutes of Board of Directors, Great Eastern Railway. RAIL 227 25, RAIL 227 26; Minutes of Land & Construction and Rates & Taxes Committee, Great Eastern Railway, RAIL 227 149, RAIL 227 150; North London Railway. Workmen's Early Trains Inquiry Before Colonel Yorke, R.E. Board of Trade Inspector. November and December 1901. RAIL 529 103; Report of the Board of Trade Railway Conference, 1909. RAIL 1053 274; South Eastern & Chatham Railway Companies Parliamentary Sub Committee Index to Minutes. RAIL 633 104, RAIL 633 103; Workmen's Fares 1888 to 1910. Index to Statements re Workmen's Fares. RAIL 410 367; Workmen's Ticket Arrangements. RAIL 527 1311.

Parliamentary Papers

Annales parlementaires [de Belgique]: Chambre des représentants [Chambre]. Belgische Kamer van Volksvertegenwoordigers Handelingen, 1869–1875, 1888–1904.

Annales parlementaires [de Belgique]: Sénat. 1903–1904.
Royal Commission on London Traffic. *Report of the Royal Commission appointed to inquire into and report upon the means of locomotion and transport in London*. London: HMSO, 1905.
Select Committee on Artizan's and Labourers' Dwellings Improvements. British Parliamentary Papers, vol. 7. 1881–1882.
Select Committee on Workmen's Trains. British Parliamentary Papers. 1903–1905.

Primary Sources

"Abonnements aux Chemins de Fer." *Pandectes belges*. Vol. 49. Brussels: Larcier, 1894.
Baertsoen, M. *Gentsche Maatschappij der Werkmanswoningen. Historisch overzicht*. Ghent: Hoste, 1913.
Barnes, Harry. *The Slum: Its Story and Solution*. London: P. S. King & Son, 1931.
Bertrand, Louis. *Le logement de l'ouvrier et des pauvres en Belgique*. Brussels: Chez l'auteur, 1888.
Booth, Charles. *Life and Labour of the People in London. 1889*. Reprint, New York: Augustus M. Kelley, 1969.
Booth, M. *Charles Booth: A Memoir*. London: Macmillan, 1918.
Bosanquet, C. B. P., E. Chadwick, Professor Fawcett, G. Godwin, C. Wren Hoskyns, E. Lankester, J. S. Mill, Lord Shaftesbury, Sir J. Kay-Shuttleworth, Alderman Waterlow. "Report: Committee on Dwellings for the Labouring Classes," *Journal of the Society of Arts* (May 12, 1865): 13, 651 (1864–1865): 427–431.
Brodsky, A. *La politique municipale de l'habitation. Union des villes et des communes belges*. Brussels: Union des Villes et Communes belges, 1919.
Buls, Charles. *Esthétique des villes*. 1894. Brussels: Sint-Lukasdossier, 1981.
Collet, Collet D. "Repeal of the Tax on Locomotion. Syllabus of Lecture to be read by Mr. C. D. Collet, at the Society of Arts." (26 February 1877).
Compte rendu des opérations de chemins de fer. Brussels: Goemaere, 1894–1912.
Dauby, Joseph. *Des grèves ouvrières: Aperçu sur l'état économique et social actuel des classes ouvrières en Belgique*. Brussels: Imprimerie Delfosse, 1879.
——. *La question ouvrière en Belgique: Causes de nos crises ouvrières; remèdes possibles*. Brussels: Librairie de A.-N. Lebègue, 1871.
Davies, Albert Emil. *The London County Council, 1887–1937*. London: Fabian Society, 1937.
De Leener, Georges. *Les Chemins de fer en Belgique. Leur Passé. La nouvelle société nationale des chemins de fer belges. Ses perspectives d'avenir*. Brussels: Maurice Lamertin, 1927.
——. *Chemins de fer et canaux en Belgique*. Brussels: Maurice Lamertin, 1928.
——. *La politique des transports en Belgique*. Brussels: Misch & Thron, 1913.
——. "La question des tarifs de chemins de fer en Belgique," *Annales des travaux publics de Belgique* 3 (June 1912): 449–494.
De Litwinski, Léon. *La question de la situation financière des chemins de fer de l'état belge*. Brussels: Goemaere, 1911.
Gissing, George. *The Nether World*. 1889. Reprint, London: Dent, 1973.
Gosseries, Fernand. *L'habitation à bon marché en Belgique*. Brussels: A. Dewit, 1926.

——. *L'oeuvre du logement populaire urbain et rural en Belgique*. Brussels: l'Association des Patrons et Ingénieurs Catholiques de Belgique, nd.

"Habitations ouvrières." *Pandectes belges*. Vol 49. Brussels: Larcier, 1894.

"Les habitations ouvrières." *Vers l'Avenir.* Brussels: Société anonyme belge d'imprimérie, 1912.

Hellemans, Emile. *Enquete sur les habitations ouvrières en 1903, 1904, 1905*. Brussels: Imprimerie des institutions de prévoyance, 1905.

Jacquart, Camille. "Migrations de la population belge (1888—1897)." *Revue sociale catholique* (1899): 358–366 and (1900): 11–21.

——. *Mouvement de l'état civil et de la population*. Brussels: Hayez, 1906.

Laverty, Kevin. *Annual Abstract of Statistics*. London: TSO, 2003.

Lawson, W. R. *British Railways: A Financial and Commercial Survey.* London: Constable., 1913.

London County Council. "Houses Adapted as Tenement Houses." London: P. S. King & Son, 1904.

——. *Housing of the Working Classes in London*. London: Oldhams, 1913.

——. *The Housing Question in London*. London: Truscott, 1900.

London County Council Report on Workmen's Trains, *London Statistics* 2 (1891–1892): 299–317.

Mahaim, Ernest. *Les abonnements d'ouvriers sur les lignes de chemins de fer belges et leurs effets sociaux*. Brussels: Misch & Thron, 1910.

Mearns, Andrew. *The Bitter Cry of Outcast London: An Inquiry into the Condition of the Abject Poor.* London: James Clarke, 1883.

Méline, Jules. *Le retour à la terre et la surproduction industrielle*. Paris: Librairie Hachette, 1905.

Merenne-Schoumaker, B., H. Van der Haegen, and E. Van Hecke. *Recensement général de la population et des logements au 1er mars 1991*. Brussels: Institut National de Statitisque, 1991.

Meuriot, Paul. *Des agglomérations urbaines dans l'Europe contemporaine*. Paris: Belin Frères, 1898.

Nève, Eugène, and Hippolyte de Royer de Dour. *Plans types d'habitations ouvrières: Notices et devis*. Brussels: Librairie Scientifique, Industrielle et Agricole, 1892.

Nicolai, Edmond. *La dépopulation des campagnes*. Brussels: P. Weissenbruch, 1903.

——. *Les chemins de fer de l'état en Belgique, 1834–1884*. Brussels: Félix Callewaert Pére, 1885.

Nizet, F. *Notes bibliographiques sur les habitations ouvrières et sur le Grisou.* Brussels: Vanbuggenhoudt, 1889.

Office of Population Censuses and Surveys. *1991 Census. Workplace and Transport to Work. Great Britain*. London: Government Statistical Service, Her Majesty's Stationery Office (HMSO).

L'ouvrier mineur. 1904–1906.

L'ouvrier propriétaire de son habitation. Maaseyck: Vanderdonck-Robyns, 1899.

Passelecq, Fernand. *Socialisme communal en Belgique*. Brussels: Société belge de librairie, 1903.

Pastur, Paul. *Ce que nous pouvons faire pour les jeunes filles de la classe ouvrière.* Ghent: Volksdrukkerij, 1908.

Paterson, Alexander. *Across the Bridges, or Life by the South London Riverside.* 1911. Reprint, New York: Garland, 1980.
Perrot, Frank D. *Overcrowded London.* Smethwick: Smethwick Telephone Co., 1900.
Picard, Alfred. *Les chemins de fer français.* 4 vols. Paris: J. Rothschild, 1884.
Pierrard, Alfred. *Les chemins de fer, vicinaux et les voies navigables.* Antwerp: M. Weissenbruch, 1913.
Pourbaix, Gustave. *Les sociétés d'habitations ouvrières: Guide pratique.* Brussels: Société belge de librairie, 1897.
Pratt, Edwin A. *Railways and Nationalisation.* London: The Railway Gazette, 1911.
——. *Railways and Their Rates.* London: John Murray, 1906.
——. *State Railways: Object Lessons from Other Lands.* London: P. S. King & Son, 1907.
Proost, Alphonse. *L'éducation de la femme selon la science.* Brussels: Société belge de librairie, 1896.
Purdom, Charles B. *The Building of Satellite Towns.* London: J. M. Dent, 1925.
——. *The Garden City.* London: J. M. Dent, 1913.
Putzeys, Félix. *L'hygiène dans la construction des habitations privées.* Paris: Michelet, 1885.
——. *Note sur les habitations ouvrières.* Extrait de la *Revue universelle des Mines* 15 (1884).
——. *La réforme hygiénique des habitations ouvrières.* Liège: J. Pierre, 1900.
Raffalovich, Arthur. "Le Congrès National des Habitations Ouvrières en Belgique." *Bulletin des Sociétés: Français des habitations à bon marché* (1894): 318.
——. *Le logement de l'ouvrier et du pauvre, Etats Unis, Grande Bretagne, France, Allemagne, Belgique.* Paris: Librarie Guillaumin, 1887.
Railway News. (21 June 1890), 1229–1230.
Ranwez, Maurice, "Les sociétés d'habitations ouvrières en Belgique." *Revue catholique du droit* (December 1898): 308–317; (January and February 1899): 325–334; 353–384.
Rapport sur l'exploitation pendant le quatrième exercice. Année 1930. Brussels: Societé nationale des chemins de fer belges, 1930.
Rapport sur la question des habitations ouvrières, présenté à l'assemblée générale de la fédération des sociétés ouvrières catholiques belges tenue les 3 et 4 decembre 1878.
Rawlinson, Sir Robert. *The Social and National Influence of the Domiciliary Condition of the People.* London: P. S. King & Son, 1883.
Recensement de l'industrie et du commerce de 1910. Vols. 7 and 8. Brussels: Office de publicité, 1913.
Les Recensements de 1910. Brussels: E. Guyot, 1912.
Recueil administratif des lois arrêtés et decisions concernant le service des chemins de fer. Ghent: La Nouvelle Imprimerie, 1903.
Recueil des rapports des ouvriers délégués par la ville de Bruxelles. Exposition universelle d'Anvers 1885. Brussels: Imprimerie Ve Baertsoen, 1885.
Reeves, Maud S. *Round about a Pound a Week.* 1913. Reprint, London: Virago Press, 1979.
Renkin, J. "Les chemins de fer belge." *Revue Economique International* (1904).

Revue de l'Association pour l'amélioration des logements ouvriers. Brussels: Stanislas Feron, 1909.
Rivington, Francis. *A New Proposal for Providing Improved Dwellings for the Poor upon an Adequate Scale in the Metropolis and Other Populous Places*. London: W. Skeffington and Son, 1880.
Robbins, M. "Railway Passenger Duty." *Journal of the Railway & Canal Society* 6, no. 3: 43–45.
Roberts, Henry. *De la condition physiaque des classes ouvrières résultant de l'état de leurs habitations et des heureux effets des améliorations sanitaires récemment adoptées en Angleterre*. Paris: Imprimerie centrale de Napoleon chaix, 1855.
——. *The Dwellings of the Labouring Classes*. 4th ed. London: Society for Improving the Condition of the Labouring Classes, 1867.
——. *Efforts on the Continent for Improving the Dwellings of the Labouring Classes*. Florence: Claudian Press, 1874.
——. *Improvement of the Dwellings of the Labouring Classes*. London: J. Ridgway, 1859.
Ronse, Edmond. *L'émigration saisonnière belge*. Ghent: Het Volk, 1913.
——. "Les ouvriers émigrants de la Belgique." *Revue social catholique* 17 (1912–1913): 267–279.
Rowntree, B. Seebohm. *Land and Labour: Lessons from Belgium*. London: Macmillan, 1911.
——. *The Destitute of Norwich and How They Live*. London: Jarrold & Sons, 1912.
Rowntree, B. Seebohm, and A. C. Pigou. *Lectures on Housing*. Manchester: University Press, 1914.
Rutten, Adolf. *Het Samenwonen in Steden: Een maatschappelijk Vraagstuk*. Ghent: A. Siffer, 1902.
Salisbury, Robert. "Labourers' and Artisans' Dwellings." *National Review* 9 (November 1883): 301–316.
Sart, R. du. *Instructions pour les sous-comités de propagande*. Tournai: Decallonne-Liagre, 1893.
Saunders, William. *History of the First London County Council, 1889-1890-1891*. London: National Press Agency, 1892.
Sherwell, Arthur. *Life in West London: A Study and a Contrast*. London: Methuen & Co., 1897.
Sinzheimer, Ludwig. *Der Londoner Grafschafstrat*. Stuttgart: J. G. Cotta'sche buchhandlung Nachfolger, 1900.
Slosse, A., and E. Waxweiler. *Enquête sur l'alimentation de 1065 ouvriers belges*. Brussels: Misch & Thron, 1910.
Smith, Alfred. *The Housing Question*. London: Swan Sonnenschein, 1900.
Smith, Hubert L. *New Survey of London Life & Labour*. London: P. S. King & Son, 1930.
Société Coopérative d'Ixelles. *Rapports de la Société coopérative d'Ixelles pour la construction de maisons à bon marché*. Brussels: L. Narcisse, 1894.
Société française des habitations à bon marché. *Bulletin*. Paris: Secrétariat de la Société, 1901.
Le Société du Logement de la Région de Bruxelles Capitale. *Le Logement social bruxellois, 1989–2005*. Brussels: SLRB, 2007.

Société du Logement de la Région bruxelloise [SLRB]. *Rapport annuel.* Brussels: SLRB, 2002.

Soenens, Albert. *Les habitations ouvrières en Belgique: Extrait des Pandectes Belges.* Brussels: Veuve Ferdinand Larcier, 1894.

——. *Inspection des habitations ouvrières: Rapport présenté par M. Albert Soenens.* Brussels, 1913.

——. *Règlement du Concours entre ouvriers propriétaires de leur habitation et du Concours-Exposition de mobiliers ouvriers modèles a l'occasion de la célébration du XXVe anniversaire de la loi du 9 août 1889.* Brussels: Schaumans, 1914.

Souchon, A. *La crise de la main-d'oeuvre en France.* Paris: Librairie Arthur Rousseau, 1914.

Statistique de la Belgique. *Recensement général des industries et des métiers (31 octobre 1896).* Vol. 18. Brussels: Ministere de l'industrie et du Travail, 1902.

Statistique de Belgique. *Recensement de l'Industrie et du Commerce (31 décembre 1910).* Brussels, 1911–21.

Statistisch Jaarboek. Brussels: Nationale Maatschappij der Belgische Spoorwegen, 1998.

Streuvels, Stijn, *De Werkman.* 1913. Reprint, Amsterdam: L. J. Veen, 1965.

Terwagne-Delloye, Gustave. *Comment l'ouvrier deviendra propriétaire de sa maison.* Huy: Colin-Houbeau, 1900.

Thompson, William. *The Housing Handbook.* London: National Housing Reform Council, 1903.

Thuysbaert, Prosper. *Het and van Waes: Bijdrage tot de Geschiedenis der landelijke Bevolking in de 19e Eeuw.* Kortrijk: J. Vermaul, 1913.

Transport Statistics Report. *National Travel Survey.* London: HMSO, 1993–1995.

Le travail chrétien: Revue mensuelle. Seraing, 1896–1902.

Turot, Henri. *Le surpeuplement et les habitations populaires.* Paris: F. Alcan, 1907.

Turquan, Victor. *Le mouvement de la population en France pendant l'année 1889.* Paris: Berger-Levrault, 1891.

Ulrich, Franz. *Traité général des tarifs de chemins de fer.* Paris: Librairie Polytechnique, Baudry, 1890.

Unwin, Raymond. *L'étude pratique des plans de villes.* Paris: Librairie centrale des Beaux-Arts, n.d.

——. *Town Planning in Practice: An Introduction to the Art of Designing Cities and Suburbs.* London, 1909.

Valpy, Robert A., ed. *An Inquiry into the Condition and Occupations of the People in Central London.* London: Edward Stanford, 1889.

Van der Linden, Edouard. *Etude sur l'amélioration des habitations ouvriéres et sur l'organisation du domicile de secours.* Brussels: Librairie Polytechnique Decq & Duhent, 1875.

Van der Moere, A. *Habitations ouvrières.* Roulers-Brussels, n.d.

Vandervelde, Emile. *L'exode rural et le retour aux champs.* Brussels: A. Vromant, 1901.

Van Leempoel, (Vicomte). *Les habitations d'ouvriers.* Brussels: H. Thiry-Van Buggenhoudt, 1867.

Van Nerom, P. *Les lois ouvrières et sociales en Belgique. Epargne, alcoolisme, salaires, conseils de l'industrie, maisons ouvrières.* Brussels: Emile Bruylant, 1890.

Velghe, Oscar. *Recueil des Lois arrêtés et instructions concernant les habitations ouvrières annoté par O. Velghe.* Brussels: E. Daem, 1911.

Vergote, A. *Amélioration des logements d'ouvriers, Rapport fait à M. le Ministre de l'Intérieur.* Brussels: l'Imprimerie de Deltombe, 1866.
Verhaegen, Arthur. *A propos du programme ouvrier des catholiques*. Brussels: J. Goemaere, 1900.
——. *Vingt-cinq années d'action sociale*. Brussels: Dewit, 1911.
Vermeersch, Arthur. *Manuel social: la législation et les oeuvres en Belgique*. Louvain: Uystpruyst, 1904.
Verslag over de exploitatie gedurende het vijf en twintigste boek. Brussels: NMBS, 1951.
Ville de Bruxelles. *Les recensements de 1910*. Brussels: F. Guyot, 1912.
Ville de Gand. *Proposition du Collège concernant la construction d'habitations pour les ouvriers*. Ghent: Annoot-Braeckman, 1868.
Villermé, Louis R. *Sur les cités ouvrières*. Paris: Libraire de l'Académie Nationale de Médecine, 1850.
Vliebergh, Emile. *De Boeren en de maatschappelijke Zaak*. Eernegem: Laga- van de Casteele, 1894.
——. *Une causette avec nos amis les paysans*. Brussels: J. Goemaere, 1900.
——. *Etudes d'économie rural*. Louvain: Bibliothèque Choisie, 1911.
——. *De Kempen in de 19e en in 't begin der 20e eeuw*. Ypres: Callewaert-De Meulenaere, 1908.
——. *Het Landbouwsocialisme*. Ghent: Het Volk, 1912.
——. *De landelijke Bevolking der Kempen gedurende de 19e Eeuw*. Brussels: Hayez, 1906.
Vliebergh, Emile, and Robert Ulens. *La population agricole de la Hesbaye au XIXe Siècle*. Brussels: Hayez, 1909.
Waucquez, Victor, *Les travaux publics depuis quinze ans*. Brussels: J. Goemaere, 1900.
Webb, Sidney, and Beatrice Webb. *The Prevention of Destitution*. London: Longmans, Green, 1911.
Webb, Sidney. *The Work of the London County Council*. London: London Reform Union, 1895.
Weber, Adna Ferrin. *The Growth of Cities in the Nineteenth Century. A Study in Statistics*. Ithaca, New York: Cornell University Press, 1965 (1899).
Woeste, Charles. "Les Catholiques belges et les intérêts ouvriers," *Revue générale* 65 (April 1897): 481–501.
Woods, Robert A., et al. *The Poor in Great Cities: Their Problems and What Is Being Done to Solve Them*. London: Kegan Paul, Trench, 1896.
Wright, Thomas. *The Great Unwashed*. London: Tinsley Brothers, 1868.
——. *Some Habits and Customs of the Working Classes*. London: Tinsley Brothers, 1867.
X. *Simple discussion à propos de la construction de cités ouvrières*. Brussels: A. N. M. Lebègue, 1867.

Secondary Sources

Articles

A+. Architecture + Urbanisme + Design + Art 181 (April–May 2003).
Aalen, Frederick H. "English Origins." In *The Garden City: Past, Present and Future,* ed. Stephen Ward. London: E. F. Spon, 1992.

Aldcroft, Derek. "The Efficiency and Enterprise of British Railways, 1870–1914." *Explorations in Entrepreneurial History* 5, no. 2 (1968): 158–174.
Allan, C. M., "The Genesis of British Urban Redevelopment," *Economic History Review* 28 (1965): 598–613.
Anderson, Michael. "Sociological History and the Working-Class Family: Smelser Revisited." *Social History* 6 (1976): 317–334.
Andre, R. "Géographie des mouvements migratoires intérieurs en Belgique (de 1964 à 1968)." *Revue de l'Institut de Sociologie* 43 (1970): 383–402.
André, R., J. Reybroeck-Quenon, and E. Ruelens. "Les migrations dans la banlieue bruxelloise." *Revue de l'Institut de Sociologie* 43 (1970): 781–790.
Andries, Bernard. "Les Chemins de fer à Bruxelles." *Revue belge de géographie* 100, no. 2–3 (1976): 183–219.
Avakian, Léon. "Le rythme du développement des voies ferées en Belgique de 1835–1935." *Bulletin de l'institut des sciences economiques* (1935–1936): 449–497.
Bagwell, Philip S. "The Railway Interest: Its Organisation and Influence, 1839–1914." *Journal of Transport History* 7 (1965–1966): 65–86.
Barker, Theo C. "Passenger Transport in 19th Century London." *Journal of Transport History* 6 (1963–64): 166–174.
Barral, Pierre. "Note historique sur l'emploi du terme 'paysan,'" *Etudes rurales* 21 (April–June, 1966): 72–80.
Baudet, H. "Over de Verhouding van Literatuur en Sociale Geschiedenis." *Tijdschrift voor Geschiedenis* 72, no. 1 (1959): 44–56.
Bernard, Nicolas. "Les mutations du logement en région bruxelloise." *Courrier hebdomadaire* 1993 (2008): 7–49.
Bloch, Marc. "Pour une histoire comparée des sociétés européennes." *Mélanges historiques* 1 (Paris: EHESS, 1983): 16–40.
Bolleey, F., and K. Hartmann. "A Patriarchal Utopia: The Garden City and Housing Reform in Germany at the Turn of the Century." In *The Rise of Modern Urban Planning,* ed. Anthony Sutcliffe, 135–164. New York: St. Martin's Press, 1980.
Bond, Maurice. "Materials for Transport History among the Records of Parliament." *Journal of Transport History* 4 (1959–1960): 37–52.
Bousset, Gunter, and Marie-Thérèse Delmer. "La Société de Saint-Vincent de Paul à Bruxelles (1842–1992)." In *De Vincentianen in Belgie 1842–1992,* ed. Jan De Maeyer and Paul Wynants. Louvain: Universitaire pers Leuven, 1992.
Broster, E. J. "Railway Passenger Receipts and Fares Policy." *Economic Journal* 47 (1937): 451–464.
Bruneel, C., F. Daelemans, M. Dorban, and C. Vandenbroeke. "Population et subsistance dans l'espace belge." In *Evolution agraire et croissance démographique,* ed. A. Fauve Chamoux, 293–324. Liège: Ordina Editions, 1977.
Bruwier, Marinette, Anne Merant, and Christiane Pierard. "Les ateliers et la cité du Grand-Hornu." *Industrie* (January 1968): 39–56.
Capillon, Macheline. "Une ligne d'autobus parisien le '84,'" *Vie Urbaine* 59 (January–March 1951): 25–46.
Cannadine, David. "Victorian Cities: How Different." *Social History* 4 (1977): 457–487.
Carter, H., and S. Wheatley. "Residential Segregation in Nineteenth-Century Cities." *Area* 12 (1980), 57–62.

Carton de Wiart, Xavier. "Le problème des grandes agglomérations." *La revue générale* 70 (15 December 1937): 702–719.
Cassiers, Isabelle. "La création et la gestion des chemins de fer (1850–1914): Une fonction importante de l'Etat libéral." *Contradictions* 23–24 (1980): 153–164.
Cassiers, Myriam, Michel De Beule, Alain Forti, and Jacqueline Miller. "Bruxelles, 150 ans de logements." *Les Dossiers Bruxellois* 7–8 (December 1989).
Caulier-Mathy, N. "La composition d'un prolétariat industriel, Le cas de l'entreprise Cockerill." *Revue d'histoire de la sidérurgie* 4 (1963): 207–222.
Chapelle-Dulliere, Jacqueline. "Septembre 1893 au charbonnage de bois du Luc: Une grève au féminin." *Belgisch Tijdschrift voor Nieuwste Geschiedenis/Revue belge d'histoire contemporaine.* 9, no. 1–2 (1988): 247–265.
Chatelain, Abel. "Les Usines-internats et migrations féminines dans la région lyonnaise." *Revue d'Histoire Economique et Sociale* 48, no. 3 (1970), 373–394.
Chauvet, J. "La ligne de Sceaux et le développement d'une banlieue parisienne." *Vie Urbaine* 58 (1950): 250–282.
Colle-Michel, Marcella. "Le Chemin de Fer en Wallonie au XIXe Siècle en relation avec l'essor de l'aciérie." In *La sidérurgie aux XVIIIe et XIXe siècles: Aspects technologiques, économiques et sociaux*. La Louvière: Centre hennuyer d'histoire et d'archéologie industrielles, 1985.
Collini, S. "Hobhouse, Bosanquet and the State: Philosophical Idealism and Political Argument in England, 1880–1918." *Past and Present* 72 (1976): 86–111.
Content, André-Claude. "L'Habitat ouvrier à Bruxelles au XIXe siècle." *Belgische Tijdschrift voor nieuwste Geschiedenis/Revue belge d'histoire contemporaine* 3–4 (1977): 501–517.
Cottereau, Alain. "Problèmes de conceptualisation comparative de l'industrialisation: l'exemple des ouvrières de la chaussure en France et en Grande Bretagne." In *Villes ouvrières 1900–1950,* ed. Susanna Magri and Christian Topalov, 41–83. Paris: L'Harmattan, 1989.
Daniel, Philip L. "The Nation's Shame: Three Decades in the Fight for Housing." *East London Papers* 13, no. 2 (1970–1971): 106–112.
Daunton, Martin. "The Building Cycle and the Urban Fringe." *Journal of Historical Geography* 4 (1978): 175–191.
——. "Miners' Houses: South Wales and the Great Northern Coalfield, 1880–1914." *International Review of Social History* 25 (1980): 143–175.
——. "Trusting Leviathan: British Fiscal Administration from the Napoleonic Wars to the Second World War." In *Trust and Governance,* ed. Valerie Braithwaite and Margaret Levi. New York: Russell Sage, 1998.
Davis, John. "The Progressive Council, 1889–1907." In *Politics and the People of London. The London County Council,* ed. Andrew Saint. London: Hambledon Press, 1989.
Day, Michael G. "The Contribution of Sir Raymond Unwin (1863–1940) and R. Barry Parker (1867–1947) to the Development of Site Planning Theory and Practice, c. 1890–1918." In *British Town Planning: The Formative Years,* ed. Anthony Sutcliffe. Leicester: Leicester University Press, 1981.
De Beule, "Du droit au logement au droit de cité," *La Fondérie* 3 (November 1987): 43–46.
Decroos, Frans, and Jef Deneut. "Het woningvraagstuuk in Belgie. De Huisvesting der Arbeidende Klasse: drager van de maatschappelijke Tegenstellingen." 1972. Katholieke Universiteit Leuven.

De Meulder, Bruno. "'A bas les taudis!' Taudisards et logements sociaux à Bruxelles (1920–1960)." *Les Cahiers de la Fonderie* 6 (June 1989): 2–12.
——. "De 'Cité Hellemans,' 1906–1915," *Wonen TABK* (November 1985): 27–36.
——. "Gallerijwoningen te Brussel." Eind verhandeling voorgedragen voor het behalen van de graad van burgeerlijk ingenieur architect door Bruno De Meulder. Katholieke Universiteit Leuven, 1982–1983.
De Meulder, Bruno, Jan Schreurs, Annabel Cock, and Bruno Notteboom. "Sleutelen aan het Belgische stadslandschap." *Tijdscrift voor architectuur* 52:88.
De Meyer, Ronald, and Marcel Smets. "De recente stedebouwkundige geschiedeschrijving in Belgie omtrent negeniende en begin twinigste eeuw." *Belgische Tijdschrift voor Nieuwste Geschiedenis* 13, no. 2–3 (1982): 465–517.
Dennis, R. "The Geography of Victorian Values: Philanthropic Housing in London 1840–1900." *Journal of Historical Geography* 15 (1984): 40–54.
——. "Hard to Let' in Edwardian London." *Urban Studies* 26 (1989).
——. "Intercensal Mobility in a Victorian City." *Transactions of the Institute of British Geographers* 2, no. 3 (1977): 349–363.
——. "The Victorian City." *Transactions of the Institute of British Geographers* 4, no. 2 (1979): 125–128.
Dennis, R. J., and S. Daniel. "Community and the Social Geography of Victorian Cities." *Urban History Yearbook*. 1987.
Detry, P. "Les Transports en Commun à Bruxelles." *Annales de Sciences Economiques Appliquées* 26, no. 1 (1968): 23–77 and 157–199.
Doutrelepont, René. "Le logement dans la province de Liège vu à travers les statistiques." *Revue belge d'histoire contemporaine/Belgische Tijdschrift voor nieuwste geschiedenis* 8, no. 3–4 (1977): 519–538.
Dumont, Maurice E. "Les migrations ouvrières du point de vie de la délimitation des zones d'influence urbain et la notion de zone d'influence prédominante. Application à l'agglomération gantoise." *Bulletin de la société belge d'études géographiques* 19, no. 1 (1950): 21–35.
Dussart, F. "Quelques réflexions sur l'urbanisation des campagnes et ses répercussions sur l'habitat rural de la Belgique." In *Mélanges Tulippe*. Brussels: Duculot, 1967.
Dyos, Harold J. "Greater and Greater London: Notes on Metropolis and Provinces in the Nineteenth and Twentieth Centuries." In *Britain and the Netherlands*, vol. 4, ed. J. S. Bromley and E. H. Kossmann. The Hague: Martinus Nijhoff, 1971.
——. "Railways and Housing in Victorian London." *Journal of Transport History* 2, no. 1 (1955): 11–21, and 2, no. 2 (1955): 90–100.
——. "Slums and Suburbs." In *The Victorian City: Images and Realities*, ed. H. J. Dyos and Michael Wolff. London: Routledge & Kegan Paul, 1973.
——. "The Slums of Victorian London." *Victorian Studies* 11, no. 1 (September 1967): 5–40.
——. "Workmen's Fares in South London, 1860–1914." *Journal of Transport History* 1 (1953): 3–19.
Faure, Alain. "A l'aube des transports de Masse: L'exemple des 'trains-ouvriers' de la banlieu de Paris (1883–1914)." *Revue d'histoire moderne et contemporaine* (April–June 1993), 218–255.
——. "Nous travaillons 10 heures par jour, plus le chemin," Les déplacements de travail chez les ouvriers parisiens, 1800–1914." In *Villes ouvrières, 1900–1950*, ed. Susanna Magri and Christian Topalov, 93–108. Paris: Editions L'Harmattan, 1989.

Fido, Judith. "The Charity Organisation Society and Social Casework in London 1869–1900." In *Social Control in 19th Century Britain*, ed. A. D. Donajgrodzki. London: Croom Helm, 1977.
Fontanon, Claudine. "Mobilité citadine et transports en commun," Paris, 1855–1914." *Annales de la recherche urbaine* 14 (1982): 100–117.
Fournier, Georges, and Martine Antoine. "Les habitations ouvrières à Binche." *De l'habitation ouvrière au logement social. de 1850 à nos jours*. La Louvière: Ecomusée régional du centre, 1900.
Fredrickson, George M. "From Exceptionalism to Variability: Recent Developments in Cross-National Comparative History." *Journal of American History* 82, no. 2 (1995): 587–604.
Gachon, Lucien. "Géographie des rapports villes-campagnes." *Bulletin de la Société royale belge de géographes* 26, no. 1 (1957): 19–70.
Gaskell, S. Martin. "A Landscape of Small Houses: The Failure of the Workers' Flat in Lancashire and Yorkshire in the Nineteenth Century." In *Multi-Storey Living: the British Working-Class Housing*, ed. Anthony Sutcliffe, 88–121. London: Croom Helm, 1974.
——. "The Suburb Salubrious': Town Planning in Practice." In *British Town Planning: The Formative Years*, ed. Anthony Sutcliffe. Leicester: Leicester University Press, 1981.
Gourou, Pierre. "L'Agglomération Bruxelloise: Eléments d'une géographie urbaine." *Bulletin de la Société Royale belge de Géographie* 82, no. 1 (1958): 3–84.
Green, Nancy. "L'histoire comparative et le champ des études migratoires." *Annales: Economies, Sociétés, Civilisations* 45, no. 6 (1990): 1335–1350.
Grimmeau, Jean Pierre. "Les mouvements de la main-d'oeuvre et la dimension des communes en Belgique." *Bulletin de la Société belge d'études géographiques/ Tijdschrift van de Belgische Vereniging voor aardrijkskundige Studies* 42 (1973): 289–312.
Gubin, Eliane. "Les enquêtes sur le travail en Belgique au Canada à la fin du 19e siècle." In *La question sociale en Belgique et au Canada*, ed. Ginette Kurgan-van Hentenryk. Brussels: Presses de l'Université libre de Bruxelles, 1988.
Henderyckx-Rigo, E., and René Leboutte. "Une solution originale au logement des houilleurs: l'Hôtel Louise à Micherous (1872)." *Revue belge d'histoire contemporaine/Belgische Tijdschrift voor nieuwste geschiedenis* 8 (1977): 569–578.
Hennock, E. P. "Poverty and Social Theory in England: The Experience of the 1880s." *Social History* 1 (1976): 67–91.
Hobsbawm, E. J. "19th Century London Labour Market." In *London: Aspects of Change*, ed. Ruth Glass et al., 3–28. London: Centre of Urban Studies, 1964.
Hoyse, Susan. "The First Battle for London: The Royal Commission on Metropolitan Termini, 1846." *London Journal* 7 (1982): 140–155.
Hugueney, Jeanne. "Le problème de l'habitation en Belgique et la société nationale des habitations et logements à bon marché." *Vie urbaine* 59 (January–March 1951): 47–60.
Jacquemyns, Guillaume. "Le problème de la 'Cuve' de Bruxelles de 1795 à 1854." *Revue de l'université de Bruxelles* (1932): 347–375.
——. "Rôle de l'administration dans le développement de l'agglomération bruxelloise." *Revue de l'université de Bruxelles* (1931): 52–66.

Jahn, Michael. "Suburban Development in Outer West London, 1850–1900." In *The Rise of Suburbia,* ed. F. M. L. Thompson. London: Leicester University Press, 1982.

Karush, G. E. "Industrialisation et changements de la population active en Belgique de 1846 à 1910." *Populations et Familles* 40 (1977): 37–76.

Kellett, John R. "Writing on Victorian Railways: An Essay in Nostalgia." *Victorian Studies* (September 1969): 90–96.

Koven, Seth, and Sonya Michel. "Womanly Duties: Maternalist Politics and the Origins of Welfare States in France, Germany, Great Britain and the United States, 1880–1929." *American History Review* 95 (1990): 1076–1108.

Laffut, Michel. "Belgium." In *Railways and the Economic Development of Western Europe,* ed. Patrick O'Brien, 203–226. London: Macmillan Press, 1983.

——. "Les chemins de fer belges et l'industrialisation." In *L'industrie en Belgique: Deux siècles d'evolution 1780–1980.* Brussels: Credit Communal, 1981.

Leboutte, René. *Le livret d'ouvrier dans la province de Liège.* Liège: Editions de la musée de la vie Wallonne, 1988.

Lawrence, R. J. "Domestic Space and Society: A Cross-Cultural Study." *Comparative Studies in Society and History* 24 (1982): 104–130.

Lawton, R. "The Journey to Work in England and Wales: Forty Years of Change." *Tijdschrift voor economische en sociale geografie* 44 (1963): 61–69.

Leblicq, Yvon. "L'urbanisation de Bruxelles." *Villes en mutation XIX et XX siècles.* Brussels: Credit Communal, 1982.

Lee, Charles E. "Passenger Class Distinctions—The Workmen's Fares," *Journal of the Institute of Transport* 21 (May 1944): 756–760.

Lis, Catharina. "Krotten en Getto's: Exponenten van Verpaupering en Polarisering." *Tijdschrift voor Geschiedenis* 88 (1975): 626–636.

——. "Proletarisch Wonen in west-Europese Steden in de 19de Eeuw: van Wildgroei naar sociale Controle." *Revue belge d'histoire contemporaine/Belgische Tijdschrift voor nieuwste Geschiedenis* 7, no. 3–4 (1977): 325–366.

Malherbe, Alain. Round Table Discussion: Brussels, "The Return of Social Housing," *A+. Architecture + Urbanism + Design + Art* 181 (April–May 2003): 83.

McKibbin, R. "Social Class and Social Observation in Edwardian England." *Transactions of the Royal Historical Society* 5th series, 28 (1978): 175–199.

Merenne, Emile. "The Geography of Transportation." *Revue belge de géographie* 112 (1988): 45–48.

Milhaud, Edgard. "L'idée de la gestion publique des chemins de fer traverse-t-elle une crise?" *Les Annales de l'économie collective* 20 (September–December 1928): 318–333.

Miller, J., M. Cassiers, and A. Forti. "De l'habitation ouvrière au logement social. De 1898 à nos jours." *De l'habitation ouvrière au logement social. De 1850 à nos jours.* La Louvière: Ecomusée régional du centre, 1900.

Mitchell, B. R. "The Coming of the Railway and United Kingdom Economic Growth." *Journal Economic History* 24 (1964): 315–336.

Mols, R. "La mobilité bruxelloise." *Bulletin de la Société belge d'Etudes Géographiques* 34, no. 2 (1965): 301–334; 35, no. 1 (1966): 35–66.

Morris, Susannah. "Organizational Innovation in Victorian Social Housing." *Nonprofit and Voluntary Sector Quarterly* 31, no. 2 (June 2002): 186–206.

——. "Market Solutions for Social Problems: Working Class Housing in Nineteenth-Century London." *Economic History Review* 54, no. 3 (2001): 525–545.

Morton, Jane. "Cheaper than Peabody." In *Local Authority Housing from 1789 to 1919*. London: Joseph Rowntree, 1991.

Mottequin, G., and J. Vanhese. "Les sociétés agrées par la caisse générale d'épargne et de retraite." *De l'habitation ouvrière au logement social. de 1850 à nos jours.* La Louvière: Ecomusée régional du centre, 1900.

Nandrin, Jean-Pierre. "La laborieuse genèse du droit social belge: Un utopie récupérée?" In *La question sociale en Belgique et au Canada,* ed. Ginette Kurgan-van Hentenryk, 123–138. Brussels: Presses de l'Université libre de Bruxelles, 1988.

Neele, George P. *Railway Reminiscences.* London: McCorquodale, 1904.

Neukermans, Gaston, "Nos villages au XIXème siècle. Impact du chemin de fer périphérique et d'une première industrialisation de nos vallées sur la vie des gens," *Entre Senne et Soignes* 62 (1989), 4–27.

O'Brien, Patrick. "Transport & Economic Development in Europe 1789–1914." In *Railways and the Economic Development of Western Europe 1830–1914,* 1–27. London: Macmillan, 1983.

Olsen, Donald. "Victorian London. Specialization, Segregation, and Privacy." *Victorian Studies* 17, no. 3 (March 1974), 265–278.

Ost, L. "Sinds 1867 rijden er Treinen door Zuid-Pajottenland." *Oude Land van Edingen en Omliggende* 8, no. 3 (1980): 137–142.

Pasleau, Suzy. "Les migrations alternantes." *Revue belge de philologie et d'histoire* 66, no. 4 (1988): 829–852.

——. "Une population ouvrière au XIXe siècle: Les metallurgistes de Grivegnée." In *La sidérurgie aux XVIIIe et XIX e siècles: aspects technologiques, économiques et sociaux.* La Louvière: Centre hennuyer d'histoire et d'archéologie industrielles, 1985.

Pennybacker, Susan. "The Millennium by Return of Post: Reconsidering London Progressivism, 1889–1907." In *Metropolis London: Histories and Representations since 1800,* ed. David Feldman and Gareth Stedman Jones. London: Routledge, 1989.

Pierard, Christine. "Les logements sociaux à la fin du 19e siècle et la cité hoyaux à Mons." *Revue belge d'histoire contemporaine/Belgische Tijdschrift voor nieuwste Geschiedenis* 3–4 (1977): 539–567.

Pirenne, Henri. "De la méthode comparative en histoire." *Ve Congrès international des sciences historiques,* ed. G. Des Marez and F. L. Ganshof, 19–23. Brussels: Weissenbruch, 1923.

Pollins, H. "Transport Lines and Social Divisions." In *London, Aspects of Change,* ed. R. Glass et al. London: MacGibbon & Kee, 1964.

Pooley, Colin G., "England and Wales." In *Housing Strategies in Europe, 1880–1930,* ed. Colin G. Pooley, 73–104. London: Leicester University Press, 1992.

——. "Residential Mobility in the Victorian City." *Transactions of the Institute of British Geographers* 4, no. 2 (1979): 258–275.

Poulain, M., and M. Foulon. "L'immigration flamande enWallonie: évaluation à l'aide d'un indicateur anthroponymique." *Revue belge d'histoire contemporaine* 12 (1981): 205–244.

Puissant, Adlophe. "Housing and Reconstructing." *Annals of American Academy of Political and Social Sciences* 247 (1946): 103–106.

Puissant, Jean. "Les Belges et la brique dans le ventre." *Les cahiers de la Fonderie: Le Logement ouvrier dans l'impasse* 6 (June 1989).
——. "Bertrand, Louis Philippe." In *Dictionnaire biographique des militants du mouvement ouvrier en Belgique*. Brussels: Evo, n.d.
——. "La brique dans le ventre des Belges: une construction politique efficace." In *Les logements sociaux. Les cahiers des sciences administratives,* ed. Geoffroy Generet. 13 (2007): 9–22.
——. "La politique municipaliste socialiste des trois communes de l'agglomération bruxelloise (Bruxelles, Molenbeek, Schaerbeek) 1884–1895." In *Contributions à l'histoire économique et sociale,* 93–112. Bruxelles: Institut de sociologie, 1966–1967.
Quairiaux, Yves. "Abonnements ouvriers et problème de main-oeuvre." In *Le centre mémoire du rail, 1839–1989*. La Louvière: Ecomusée régional du Centre, 1989.
——. "Le stéréotype du flamand en Wallonie. Explications économiques et sociales (1880–1940)." In *Stéréotypes nationaux et préjugés raciaux aux... UCL, Recueil de travaux d'histoire et de philologie,* ed. J. Pirotte, 138–154. Louvain la Neuve: Editions Nauwelaerts, 1982.
Reeder, D. A. "A Theatre of Suburbs: Some Patterns of Development in West London, 1801–1911." In *The Study of Urban history,* ed. H. J. Dyos. London: Edward Arnold, 1966.
"Human Geography in Belgium." *Revue Belge de Geographie* 112, no. 1–2 (1988).
Roelants Du Vivier, F. "Bois du Luc. Une cité industrielle." *La maison d'hier et d'aujourd'hui* 20 (December 1973).
Rogier, M. C. G. "Bijdragen tot de Geschiedenis van de Belgische Spoorwegen te Mechelen." Mechelen, 1979.
Ross, Ellen. "Fierce Questions and Taunts': Married Life in Working-Class London, 1870–1914," *Feminist Studies* 8 (Fall 1982): 575–603.
——. "'Not the Sort That Would Sit on The Doorstep': Respectability in Pre-World War I London Neighborhoods." *International Labor and Working Class History* 27 (1985): 39–59.
——. "Survival Networks: Women's Neighbourhood Sharing in London before World War One." *History Workshop Journal* 15 (1983), 4–27.
Saint Moulin, Léon. "Wonen in Seraing sinds 1829." *Spiegel Historiael* 3, no. 2 (1968): 108–114.
Schaevers, M. "Veel meer dan huizen bouwen: Belgische arbeidershuisvesting en politiek gezien vanuit M. Foucault." *Heibel* 15, no. 3 (1981): 2–46.
Scholliers, E. "De Kinderarbeid, de Leerplicht en de Burgerij (1843–1871)." In *Onderwijs, opvoeding en maatschappij in de 19de en 20ste eeuw. Liber Amoricum Prof. Dr. Maurits de Vroede M. De Paepe en M. d'Hoker,* 175–184. Leuven-Amersfoort: ACCO, 1987.
Schreurs, A. "Ouvriers flamands immigrés en Wallonie. Etude comparative de groupes de personnel de la gare de Haine-Saint-Pierre." *Travaux du Séminaire de Sociologie de la Faculté de Droit de Liège* 11 (1951): 53–89.
Skocpol, Theda, and Margaret Somers. "The Uses of Comparative History in Macrosocial Inquiry." *Comparative Studies in Society and History* 22 (April 1980): 174–197.

See, Henri, "Remarques sur l'application." *Revue de synthèse historique* 36 (1923): 37–46.
Sellier, Henri. "Essai sur les évolutions comparées du logement & de la population dans le département de la Seine de 1896 à 1911." *Vie urbane* 3 (1921), 5–46.
——. "Le Mouvement de la population et l'habitation à Londres." *Vie urbane* (15 August 1922): 285–294.
Servais, Paul. "Van de consolidering van het netwerk tot de nieuwe Europese uitdagingen." In *Sporen in België. 175 Jaar Spoorwegen. 75 Jaar NMBS,* ed. Bart Van der Herten, Michelangelo Van Meerten, and Greta Verbeurgt, 200–232. Louvain: Universitaire Pers Leuven, 2001.
Sewell, William, Jr. "Marc Bloch and the Logic of Comparative History." *History and Theory* 6, no. 2 (1967): 208–218.
Shannon, Herbert. "Migration and the Growth of London." *Economic History Review* 5 (1935): 79–86.
Shapiro, Ann-Louise. "Paris." In *Housing the Workers: A Comparative History, 1850–1914,* ed. M. J. Daunton, 33–66. London: Leicester University Press, 1990.
Simmons, Jack. "Suburban Traffic at King's Cross, 1852–1914." *Journal of Transport History* (1985): 71–78.
——. "The Power of the Railway." In *The Victorian City: Images and Realities,* ed. H. J. Dyos and M. Wolff. Boston: Routledge & Kegan Paul, 1973.
Simpson, M. "Urban Transport and the Development of Glasgow's West End, 1803–1914," *Journal of Transport History* 1 (1972): 146–160.
Het Spoor (February 1977): 6–9.
Steensels, Willy. "De Tussenkomst van de Overheid in de Arbeidershuisvesting: Gent, 1850–1914." *Belgisch Tijdschrift voor Nieuwste Geschiedenis/Revue belge d'histoire contemporaine* 3–4 (1977): 447–499.
Steffel, Richard Vladimir. "Housing for the Working Classes in the East End of London 1890–1907." PhD diss., Ohio State University, 1969.
——. "The Slum Question." *Albion* 5, no. 4 (1973): 314–325.
——. "The Boundary Street Estate: An Example of Urban Redevelopment by the London County Council, 1889–1914." *Town Planning Review* 47 (1976): 161–173.
——. "The Evolution of a Slum Control Policy in the East End, 1889–1907." *East London Papers* 13 (1970): 25–35.
Stélandre, Annick. "Contribution à l'histoire des habitations ouvrières 1889–1919." Mémoire présenté en vue de l'obtention du grade de licenciée en philosophie et lettres group histoire, 1982–1983. Université libre de Bruxelles.
——. "Les habitations ouvrières dans la région bruxelloise: l'application de la loi de 1889." *Bulletin Trimestriel: Le Crédit Communal* (1991): 71–96.
Stengers, Jean. *Emigration et immigration en Belgique.* Brussels: Académie royale des sciences d'outre mer, 1978.
——. "Léopold Ier et le Chemin de fer d'Anvers au Rhin." In *Mélanges offerts à G. Jacquemyns.* Brussels: Université libre de Bruxelles, 1968.
——. "Les mouvements migratoires en Belgique aux XIX et XXe siècles." In *Les migrations internationales de la fin du XVIII siècle à nos jours.* Paris: CNRS, 1980.
Sutcliffe, Anthony, "Architecture and Civic Design in Nineteenth Century Paris." In *Growth and Transformation of the Modern City,* 89–100. Stockholm: Swedish Council for Building Research, 1979.

——. "A Century of Flats in Birmingham 1875–1973." In *Multi-Storey Living: the British Working-Class Housing,* ed. A. Sutcliffe. London: Croom Helm, 1974.

——. "Environmental Control and Planning in European Capitals 1850–1914: London, Paris, and Berlin." In *Growth and Transformation of the Modern City, 71–88.* Stockholm: Swedish Council for Building Research, 1979.

——. "The Growth of Public Interventions in the British Urban Environment during the Nineteenth Century: A Structural Approach." In *The Structure of Nineteenth-Century Cities,* ed. J. H. Johnson and C. G. Pooley, 107–124. London: Croom Helm, 1982.

——. "Working Class Housing in Nineteenth Century Britain: A Review of Recent Research." *Bulletin. Society for the Study of Labour History* 24 (Spring 1972), 24–25, 40–51.

Swenarton, Mark. "The Scale and Nature of Growth of Owner Occupation between the Wars." *Economic History Review* 38 (1985): 373–392.

Sykes, John. "The Results of State, Municipal and Organized Private Action on the Housing of the Working Classes in London and in Other Large Cities in the United Kingdom." *Journal of the Royal Statistical Society* 64 (June 1901): 189–253.

Tarn, John Nelson. "French Flats for the English in Nineteenth-Century London." In *Multi-Storey Living: The British Working-Class Housing,* ed. Anthony Sutcliffe, 19–40. London: Croom Helm, 1974.

——. "Housing Reform and the Emergence of Town Planning in Britain before 1914." In *The Rise of Modern Urban Planning. 1800–1914,* ed. Anthony Sutcliffe. New York: St. Martin's Press, 1980.

Thorne, Robert. "The White Hart Lane Estate: An LCC Venture in Suburban Development." *London Journal* 12 (1986), 80–88.

Thrupp, Sylvia. "Editorial." *Comparative Studies in Society and History* 1, no. 1 (1958): 1–4.

Topalov, Christian. "From the 'Social Question' to 'Urban Problems': Reformers and the Working Classes at the Turn of the Twentieth Century." *ISSI* (1990): 319–335.

Tulippe, Omer. "Changement d'équilibre entre les villes et les villages." *Bulletin de la Société Royale Belge de Géographie* 85 (1961): 79–87.

Vanbellingen, Paul. "Naissance et evolution du chemin de fer dans la region du centre." *Le Centre Memoire du Rail, 1839–1989.* La Louvière: Ecomusée regional du Centre, 1989.

Vance, James E. "Housing the Worker: Determinative and Contingent Ties in Nineteenth Century Birmingham." *Economic Geography* 43 (1967): 95–127.

Van den Eerenbeemt, H. F. J. M. "Woontoestanden van de volksklasse in de 19de eeuw." *Spiegel Historiael* 9 (1976): 494–501.

——. "Wat leidde tot de woningwet 1901." *Spiegel Historiael* 9 (1976): 516–525.

Van den Eeckhout, Patricia. "Belgium." In *Housing Strategies in Europe, 1880–1930,* ed. Colin G. Pooley. London: Leicester University Press, 1992.

——. "Brussels." In *Housing the Workers: A Comparative Study, 1850–1914,* ed. Martin Dauntin, 67–106. London: Leicester University Press, 1990.

——. "Enquête sur l'habitat ouvrier à Bruxelles au début du 20e siècle." *Les Cahiers de la Fonderie,* 26–33.

Vandenheede, Liliane. "Aspecten van de Spoorweggeschiedenis van België." *Tijdschrift voor Geschiedenis van Techniek en Industriele Cultuur* 2 (1983): 8–20.

Vanden Herrewegen, Herman. "Gesprekken met mijnwerkers uit zuid-oost vlaanderen en zuid Brabant." *AMSAB Tijdlingen* 4, no. 2 (1985–1986): 45–53.

Van der Haegen, H. "De actuele Toestand van de binnenlandse Pendel in België en meer in het bijzonder deze naar Brussel." *Bulletin de la Société Belge d'études géographiques.* 34, no. 1 (1965): 171–216; 35, no. 1 (1966): 79–100.

——. "De Brusselse banlieu." *Bulletin de la Société belge d'étude géographiques* 31, no. 2 (1962): 269–303.

Van der Haegen, H. "Honderd jaar pendel naar Brussel. Evolutie en Evaluatie." *De Aardrijkskunde* 2 (1982): 119–128.

Van der Haegen, H., M. Pattyn, and C. Cardyn. "The Belgian Settlement System." *Acta Geographica Lovaniensia* 22: 251–315. Louvain: Instituut voor sociale en economische Geografie, 1982.

Vanderrijdt, H. "Recent Belgian Railway Development." *Railway Gazette* (21 April 1911).

Van Isacker, K. "De sociale mentaliteit van de katholieke burgerij in de XIXe eeuw." *Economisch en sociaal Tijdschrift.* 8, no. 3 (1954): 143–153.

Vanthemsche, Guy. "L'entre-deux-guerres, période charnière de l'histoire des chemins de fer belges 1919–1939." In *Sporen in België. 175 Jaar Spoorwegen. 75 Jaar NMBS,* ed. Bart Van der Herten, Michelangelo Van Meerten, and Greta Verbeurgt. Louvain: Universitaire Pers Leuven, 2001.

Verniers, Louis. "La déconcentration urbaine de la ville de Bruxelles," *Extrait du 1er congrès international de Géographie Historique* 2 (1931).

——. "Démographie et Expansion territoriale de l'Agglomération Bruxelloise depuis le début du XIXe siècle," *Bulletin de la Société royale belge d'etudes géographiques* 5, no. 1 (1935): 79–123.

——. "Les Impasses Bruxelloises," *Le Folklore Brabançon* 14 (August 1934): 30–109.

Ward, D. "A Comparative Historical Geography of Streetcar Suburbs in Boston, Mass and Leeds: 1850–1920." *Annals of the Association of American Geographers* 54 (1964): 477–489.

Wardle, D. B. "Sources for the History of Railways at the Public Record Office." *Journal of Transport History* 2 (1955–1956): 214–234.

Wattez, Omer. "De Vlamingen in het Walenland." *Germania* (1903): 14–26.

Williams, Peter. "Constituting Class and Gender: A Social History of the Home, 1700–1901." In *Class and Space,* ed. Nigel Thrift and Peter Williams. London: Routledge & Kegan Paul, 1987.

Williams, P. M. "Public Opinion and the Railway Rates Question in 1886." *English Historical Review* 67 (1952): 37–73.

Wohl, A. S. "The Housing of the Working Classes in London, 1815–1914." In *The History of Working Class Housing,* ed. S. D. Chapman. Newton Abbot: David and Charles, 1971.

Books

Agulhon, Maurice, et al. *Apogée et crise de la civilisation paysanne de 1789 à 1914.* Paris: Seuil, 1976.

Alborn, Timothy. *Conceiving Companies: Joint-stock Politics in Victorian England.* London: Routledge, 1998.

Aldcroft, Derek. *British Railways in Transition.* New York: St. Martin's, 1968.

——. *Studies in British Transport History 1870–1970.* Newton Abbot: David & Charles, 1971.

Aldcroft, Derek H., and Michael J. Freeman. *Transport in the Industrial Revolution.* Manchester: Manchester Union Press, 1983.

Alderman, Geoffrey. *The Railway Interest.* Leicester: Leicester University Press, 1973.

Allen, Cecil J. *Great Eastern Railway.* London: Ian Allan, 1955.

Ashworth, W. *The Genesis of Modern Town Planning.* London: Routledge & Kegan Paul, 1954.

Aspecten van een dagelijkse Realiteit: 150 Jaar Spoorwegen in Belgie. Brussels: Paleis voor Schone Kunsten Brussel, 1985.

Association ferroviaire des Cheminots de Charleroi. *150 Ans de rail à Charleroi.* Brussels: Edition PFT, 1983.

Baldwin, Peter. *Contagion and the State in Europe, 1830–1930.* Cambridge: Cambridge University Press, 1999.

——. *The Politics of Social Solidarity: Class Bases of the European Welfare State, 1875–1975.* Cambridge: Cambridge University Press, 1990.

Balfour, Arthur, cited by Charles Booth. *Improved Means of Locomotion as a First Step towards the Cure of Housing Difficulties of London.* London: Macmillan, 1901, 2.

Ball, Michael, Michael Harloe, and Maartje Martens. *Housing and Social Change in Europe and the USA.* New York: Routledge, 1988.

Barker, Theodore C., and Michael Robbins. *A History of London Transport. Passenger Travel and the Development of the Metropolis.* London: George Allen & Unwin, 1963.

Barker, Theodore C., and C. I. Savage. *An Economic History of Transport in Britain.* London: Hutchinson, 1959.

Barral, Pierre. *Les Agrariens français de Méline à Pisani.* Paris: Librairie Armand Colin, 1968.

Barret-Ducrocq, Françoise. *Pauvreté, charité et morale à Londres au XIXe siècle.* Paris: Presses Universitaires de France, 1991.

Beattie, Susan. *A Revolution in Housing: LCC Housing Architects and Their Work, 1893–1914.* London: The Architectural Press, 1980.

Berg, Christian, Pierre Halen, and Christian Angelet. *Littératures belges de langue française (1830–2000): histoire et perspectives.* Brussels: Le Cri, 2000.

Biernacki, Richard. *The Fabrication of Labor: Germany and Britain, 1640–1914.* Berkeley: University of California Press, 1995.

Bogaert-Damin, Anne-Marie, and Maréchal, L. *Bruxelles: Développement de l'ensemble urbain 1846–1961.* Namur: Presses Universitaires de Namur, 1978.

Bonavia, Michael R. *The Nationalisation of British Transport: The Early History of the British Transport Commission 1948–53.* London: Macmillan Press, 1987.

Boydston, Jeanne. *Home & Work: Housework, Wages, and the Ideology of Labor in the Early Republic.* New York: Oxford University Press, 1990.

Briggs, Asa. *Social Thought and Social Action: A Study of the Work of Seebohm Rowntree. 1871–1954.* London: Longmans, 1961.

——. *Victorian Cities.* Berkeley: University of California Press, 1963.

Broeckaert, P. F. *Predikatie en Arbeidersprobleem.* Mechelen: Sint-Franciscus-Uitgeverij, 1963.

Brusselse Haarden: 75–Jaar Bestaan. Brussels: Les Dossiers de la Fonderie, 1997.

Bruwier, Marinette, Nicole Caulier-Mathy, Claude Desama, and Paul Gérin, eds. *1886. La Wallonie née de la grève? Colloque organisé à l'Université de Liège.* Brussels: Editions Labor, 1990.

Bullock, Nicholas, and James Read. *The Movement for Housing Reform in Germany and France, 1840–1914*. Cambridge: Cambridge University Press, 1985.

Bulmer, Martin, Kevin Bales, and Kathryn Kish Sklar. *The Social Survey in Historical Perspective, 1880–1914*. Cambridge: Cambridge University Press, 1991.

Burnett, John. *A Social History of Housing 1815–1970*. London: David & Charles, 1978.

Butler, R., and P. Noisette. *De la cité ouvrière au grand ensemble. La politique capitaliste du logement social, 1815–1975*. Paris: Maspero, 1977.

Caron, François. *Histoire de l'exploitation d'un grand réseau. La Compagnie du chemin de fer du nord 1846–1937*. Paris: Mouton, 1973.

Channon, Geoffrey. *Railways in Britain and the United States, 1830–1940: Studies in Economic and Business History*. Aldershot: Ashgate, 2001.

Chapman, Stanley D. *The History of Working Class Housing*. Newton Abbot: David and Charles, 1971.

Les charbonnages du Bois-du-Luc et d'Havré 1685–1935. Bois du Luc, 1935.

Chatelain, Abel. *Les migrants temporaires en France de 1800 à 1914*. Lille: l'Université de Lille III, 1977.

Cherry, Gordon E. *Cities and Plans: The Shaping of Urban Britain in the Nineteenth and Twentieth Centuries*. London: Edward Arnold, 1988.

Chew, Kenneth, and Anthony Wilson. *Victorian Science and Engineering Portrayed in the Illustrated London News*. London: Alan Sutton Publishing, 1993.

Clark, John Joseph. *The Housing Problem: Its History, Growth, Legislation and Procedure*. London: Sir I. Putnam & Sons, 1920.

Cleveland-Stevens, E. *English Railways, Their Development and Their Relation to the State*. London: Routledge, 1915.

Colard, Jean. *La coordination des transports en Belgique. Etude de politique économique*. Louvain: Nouvelles Publications Universitaires, 1945.

Cole, Ian, and Robert Furbey. *The Eclipse of Council Housing*. New York: Routledge, 1994.

Coleman, Alice. *Utopia on Trial: Vision and Reality in Planned Housing*. London: Hilary Shipman, 1985.

Coleman, Bruce I. *The Idea of the City in Nineteenth Century Britain*. London: Routledge, Kegan, Paul, 1973.

Coles, C. R. L. *Railways through London*. London: Allan, 1983.

Colls, Robert, and Philip Dodd, eds. *Englishness: Politics and Culture, 1880–1920*. London, 1988.

Corr, Helen, and Lynn Jamieson. *The Politics of Everyday Life: Continuity and Change in Work, Labour and the Family*. New York: St. Martin's Press, 1990.

Course, Edwin. *London Railways*. London: B. T. Batsford, 1962.

Creese, Walter. *The Search for Environment: The Garden City: Before and After*. New Haven, Conn.: Yale University Press, 1966.

Cross, Gary. *Worktime and Industrialization: An International History*. Philadelphia: Temple University Press, 1988.

Culot, Maurice, et al. *100 ans de débat sur la ville*. Brussels: Editions des Archives d'architecture moderne Bruxelles, 1984.

Dalling, Graham. *All Stations to Enfield Town: The Great Eastern Railway in Enfield*. Enfield: Enfield Public Libraries, 1986.

Damer, Sean. *State, Class and Housing: Glasgow 1885–1919, Housing, Social Policy and the State*. London: Croom Helm, 1980.
Daunton, Martin J. *House and Home in the Victorian City: Working Class Housing 1850–1914*. London: Edward Arnold, 1983.
——, ed. *Housing the Workers. A Comparative Study, 1850–1914*. London: Leicester University Press, 1990.
——. *A Property-Owning Democracy*? London: Faber and Faber, 1978.
——. *Trusting Leviathan: The Politics of Taxation in Britain, 1799–1914*. Cambridge: Cambridge University Press, 2001.
Davies, Ernest. *The National Enterprise: The Development of the Public Corporation*. London: Victor Gollancz, 1946.
Davin, Anna. *Growing Up Poor: Home, School and Street in London 1870–1914*. London: Rivers Oram Press, 1996.
De Groe, R. *Vijftig jaar syndicale Werking 1911–1961*. Louvain: Christelijke centrale voor arbeiders van voedingsbedrijven, 1961.
De Laveleye, A. *Histoire des vingt-cinq premières années des chemins de fer en Belgique*. Ghent: VVIA, 1985.
Delfosse, Pascale. *La politique agricole de l'état belge en période de crise au XIXème siècle: les rapports de force dans une société en transition ver le capitalisme industriel*. Louvain la Neuve, Crehides, 1983.
Delmelle, Joseph. *Histoire des chemins de fer belges*. Brussels: Paul le Grain, n.d.
——. *Historie des tramways et vicinaux belges*. Brussels: Paul le Grain, n.d.
De Maeyer, Jan, and Paul Wynants, eds. *De Vincentianen in Belgie 1842–1992*. Louvain: Universitaire pers Leuven, 1992.
Dennis, Richard. *English Industrial Cities of the 19th Century*. Cambridge: Cambridge University Press, 1984.
De Pillecijn, Philip. *Sociaal Probleem en verhalend Proza, 1830–1886*. Antwerp: De Standaard, 1967.
Dessouroux, Christian. *Espaces partagés, espaces disputés. Bruxelles, une capitale et ses habitants*. Brussels: CIRHIBRU, Université libre de Bruxelles, 2008.
Dhaene, Leon. *Boeren en Burgers. Sociale Geschiedenis van het Negentiende Eeuwse Plaatland. Zingem 1796–1900*. Zingem: Gemeentebestuur Zingem, 1986.
Dickens, Peter, Simon Duncan, Mark Goodwin, and Fred Gray. *Housing, States and Localities*. London: Methuen, 1985.
Divall, Colin, and Winstan Bond. *Suburbanizing the Masses: Public Transport and Urban Development in Historical Perspective*. Hants, England: Aldershot, 2003.
Dow, George. *Grand Central*. London: Locomotive Publishing, 1962.
Downs, Laura Lee. *Manufacturing Inequality: Gender Division in the French and British Metalworking Industries, 1914–1939*. Ithaca, N.Y.: Cornell University Press, 1995.
Dyos, H. J. *Exploring the Urban Past: Essays in Urban History*, ed. David Cannandine and David Reeder. Cambridge: Cambridge University Press, 1982.
——. *Victorian Suburbs: A Study of the Growth of Camberwell*. Leicester: Leicester University Press, 1961.
Dyos, H. J., and D. H. Aldcroft. *British Transport*. London: Leicester University Press, 1969.

Edwards, Arthur. *The Design of Suburbia.* London: Pembridge Press, 1981.
Englander, David. *Landlords and Tenant in Urban Britain 1838–1918.* Oxford: Clarendon Press, 1983.
Everaet, H. *De Landbouwersvrouw in Heden en Verleden. Een sociologische verkenning van haar deelneming aan de Arbeid op het Bedrijf.* Brussels: Landbouw-economisch Instituut, 1972.
Fainstein, Susan S., Ian Gordon, and Michael Harloe. *Divided Cities: New York and London in the Contemporary World.* Oxford: Blackwell, 1992.
Faure, Alain. *Les premiers banlieusards: Aux origines des banlieus de Paris 1860–1940.* Paris: Editions creaphis, 1991.
Fishman, Robert. *Urban Utopias in the Twentieth Century.* New York: Basic Books, 1977.
Fishman, William Jack. *East End, 1888: A Year in a London Borough among the Labouring Poor.* London: Duckworth, 1988.
Fontanon, Claudine, and Dominique Larroque. *Analyse historique de l'évolution des transports en commun dans la région parisienne de 1855 à 1939.* Paris: Ecole des Hautes Etudes en Sciences Sociales, 1977.
Fourcaut, Annie. *Un siècle de banlieue Parisienne (1859–1964).* Paris: L'Harmattan, 1988.
Fourastie, Jean. *Migrations professionnelles: Données statistiques sur leur évolution en divers pays de 1900 à 1955.* Paris: Institut National d'Etudes Démographiques, 1957.
Fraser, Derek. *The Evolution of the British Welfare State.* London: Macmillan, 1984.
Freeden, Michael. *The New Liberalism: An Ideology of Social Reform.* Oxford: Oxford University Press, 1978.
Freeman, Michael. *Railways and the Victorian Imagination.* New Haven, Conn.: Yale University Press, 1999.
Freeman, Roger, and Jon Shaw, eds. *All Change: British Railway Privatisation.* London: McGraw-Hill, 2000.
Freeman, Thomas W. *The Conurbations of Great Britain.* Manchester: Manchester University Press, 1959.
Garnier, H. *La législation et la réglementation anglaise en matière de salubrité de l'habitation.* Paris: Giard et Brière, 1902.
Gaskell, Martin. *Slums.* Leicester: Leicester University Press, 1990.
Gaskell, S. M. *Model Housing from the Great Exhibition to the Festival of Britain.* London: Mansell, 1986.
Gauldie, Enid. *Cruel Habitations: A History of Working-Class Housing 1780–1915.* London: George Allen & Unwin, 1974.
Generet, Geoffroy. *Les logements sociaux: Les cahiers des sciences administratives* 13 (2007).
Gérard, Emmanuel, and Paul Wynants. *Histoire du mouvement ouvrier chrétien en Belgique.* Louvain: Leuven University Press, 1994.
Gibbon, Gwilym, and R. Bell. *History of the London County Council.* London: Macmillan, 1939.
Gilissen-Valschaerts, S., L. Martin, E. Hanotiau-Venken, S. Petit. *Une Commune de l'agglomération bruxelloise: Uccle.* Brussels: Université libre de Bruxelles, 1962.
Gomme, Sir George Laurence. *The London County Council: Its Duties and Powers According to the Local Government Act of 1888.* London: Nutt, 1888.

Goossens, L. "Het sociaal Huisvestingsbeleid in België. Een historisch-sociologische analyse van de maatschappelijke Probleem behandeling op het Gebied van Wonen." Doctoraat, KUL Faculteit Sociale Wetenschappen, 1982.
Gourvish, Terry. *British Rail 1974–1997: From Integration to Privatisation.* Oxford: Oxford University Press, 2002.
Gray, B. Kirkham. *Philanthropy and the State.* London: King & Son, 1908, 265.
Gregory, S. *Railways and Life in Britain.* London: Ginn, 1969.
Grigg, David. *English Agriculture: An Historical Perspective.* London: Basil Blackwell, 1989.
Gros, Brigitte. *Quatre heures de transport par jour.* Paris: Denoel, 1970.
Groux, Guy, and Catherine Levy. *La possession ouvrière: De taudis à la propriété.* Paris: Les Editions Ouvrières, 1993.
Guerrand, Roger-Henri. *Une Europe en construction: Deux siècles d'habitat social en Europe.* Paris: Editions La Découverte, 1992.
——. *Le logement populaire en France: sources documentaires et bibliographie.* Paris: Ecole nationale supérieur des beaux-arts, 1985.
——. *Les origines du logement social en France.* Paris: Les Editions Ouvrières, 1967.
——. *Propriétaires & locataires: Les origines du logement social en France (1850–1914).* Paris: Quintette, 1987.
Gwilliam, Kenneth M. *Transport and Public Policy: London.* London: George Allen & Unwin, 1964.
Hardy, Dennis. *From Garden Cities to New Towns: Campaigning for Town and Country Planning, 1899–1946.* London: E & F Spon, 1991.
Harsin, Paul, Fernand Dehousse, and Jean Rey. *Le centenaire de la naissance du Professeur Ernest Mahaim.* Liège: Association des amis de l'université de Liège, 1965.
Harvey, David. *Social Justice and the City.* London: Edward Arnold, 1973.
——. *The Urbanization of Capital.* Baltimore: Johns Hopkins University Press, 1985.
Hauben, Rein. *Een band tussen de Vlamingen in Wallonië.* Namur: Rein Hauben, 1987.
Havelange, Carl, Etienne Helin, and René Leboutte. *Vivre et survivre: Témoignages sur la condition populaire au pays de Liège XII–XX siècles.* Liège: Editions de la Musée de la Vie Wallonne, 1994.
Hebbert, Michael, and Tony Travers. *The London Government Handbook.* London: Cassell, 1988.
Herbert, David T., and David M. Smith. *Social Problems and the City: New Perspectives.* New York: Oxford University Press, 1989.
Hoekstra, J. S. C. M., and A. A. Reitsma. *De Zorg voor het Wonen: Volksvesting en Verzoringsstaat in Nederland en België.* Delft: Delft University Press, 2002.
Hopkins, Eric. *Childhood Transformed: Working Class Children in Nineteenth-Century England.* New York: Manchester University Press, 1994.
Howkins, Alun. *Reshaping Rural England: A Social History.* New York: Routledge, 1991.
Jackson, Alan A. *London's Local Railways.* London: David & Charles, 1978.
——. *London's Metropolitan Railway.* London: David & Charles, 1986.
——. *Semi-Detached London.* London: George Allen & Unwin, 1977.

Jackson, Alan A., and Desmond F. Croome. *Rails Through the Clay.* Middlesex: Capital Transport Publishing, 1962.
Jackson, James H., Jr. *Migration and Urbanization in the Ruhr Valley, 1821–1914.* New Jersey: Humanities Press, 1997.
Jackson, W. Eric. *Achievement: A Short History of the London County Council.* London: Longmans, 1965.
Jacquemyns, G. *Histoire de la crise économique des Flandres.* Brussels: Lamertin, 1928.
——. *Histoire contemporaine du grand-Bruxelles.* Brussels: Vanderlinden, 1936.
——. *La maison heureuse: Préférences des Belges en matière et de rapports de voisinage.* Brussels: Parc Léopold, 1949.
Jansen, G. R. M. *Commuting in Europe: Homes, Sprawl, Jobs Sprawl, Traffic Problems Grow.* Delft: TNO report, Traffic and Transportation Unit, 1992.
Johnson, Paul. *Saving and Spending: The Working-Class Economy in Britain 1870–1939.* Oxford: Oxford University Press, 1985.
Jonas, Raymond A. *Industry and Politics in Rural France: Peasants of the Isère, 1870–1914.* Ithaca, N.Y.: Cornell University Press, 1994.
Jones, Gareth Stedman. *Outcast London.* Oxford: Clarendon Press, 1971.
Kaufman, Moritz. *The Housing of the Working Classes and of the Poor.* East Ardsley: EP Publishing, 1975.
Kellett, John R. *The Impact of Railways on Victorian Cities.* London: Routledge & Kegan Paul, 1969.
Kern, Stephen. *The Culture of Time and Space, 1880–1913.* Cambridge, Mass.: Harvard University Press, 1983.
Kleinman, Mark. *Housing, Welfare, and the State in Europe: A Comparative Analysis of Britain, France, and Germany.* Cheltenham: Edward Elgar, 1996.
Klep, Paul M. *Bevolking en Arbeid in Transformatie.* Nijmegen: Socialistische Uitgeverij Nijmegen, 1981.
Kostal, Rande W. *Law and English Railway Capitalism, 1825–1875.* Oxford: Clarendon Press, 1994.
Kurgan, Van Hentenryk, Ginette. *Rail, finance et politique: les entreprises Philippart (1865–1890).* Brussels: Editions de l'Université de Bruxelles, 1982.
Laconte, Pierre, and Caola Hein, eds. *Brussels: Perspectives on a European Capital.* Brussels: Foundation for the Urban Environment, 2008.
Laffut, Michel. *Les chemins de fer belges, 1830–1913.* Genèse du réseau et présentation critique des données statistiques. In *Histoire quantitative et developpement de la Belgique aux XIXe et XX siècles.* Vol. 8. Brussels: Académie Royale de Belgique, 1995.
Lamalle, Ulysse. *Histoire des chemins de fer belge.* Brussels: Office de publicité, 1953.
Larroque, Dominique. *Les transports en commun dans la region parisienne: Enjeux politiques et financiers (1855–1939).* Thèse de 3e cycle. Ecole des Hautes Etudes en Sciences Sociales Paris, 1980.
Lee, C. E. *Passenger Class Distinctions.* London: London Railway Gazeteer, 1946.
Lees, Andrew. *Cities Perceived: Urban Society in European and American Thought, 1820–1940.* Manchester: Manchester University Press, 1985.
Lees, Lynn Hollen. *The Solidarities of Strangers: The English Poor Laws and the People, 1700–1948.* Cambridge: Cambridge University Press, 1998.

Lehning, James. *Peasant and French: Cultural Contact in Rural France During the Nineteenth Century.* Cambridge: Cambridge University Press, 1995.
Lemonnier, Camille. *La fin des bourgeois.* 1892. Brussels: Editions Labor, 1986.
Linters, A. *Spoorwegen in Belgie.* Ghent: VVIA, 1985.
Le logement social au musée? De sociale Huisvesting naar het Museum? Brussels: Editions Luc Pire, 2003.
Lowe, Stuart, and David Hughes. *A New Century of Social Housing.* Leicester: Leicester University Press, 1991.
Magri, Susanna, and Christian Topalov. *Villes ouvrières, 1900–1950.* Paris: Editions L'Harmattan, 1989.
Mais, S. B. P. *Fifty Years of the LCC.* Cambridge: Cambridge University Press, 1939.
Matheson, Jill, and Gwyneth Edwards. *Focus on London 2000.* London: The Stationery Office, 2000.
Mayne, Alan. *The Imagined Slum.* Leicester: Leicester University Press, 1993.
McBriar, A. M. *An Edwardian Mixed Doubles: The Bosanquets versus the Webbs: A Study in British Social Policy, 1890–1929.* Oxford: Clarendon Press, 1987.
McCrone, Gavin, and Mark Stephens. *Housing Policy in Britain and Europe.* London: UCL Press, 1995.
McDonald, Erica, and David J. Smith. *Artizans and Avenues: A History of Queen's Park Estate.* London: City of Westminster Archives Centre, 1990.
McKibbon, R. I. *The Ideologies of Class.* Oxford: Oxford University Press, 1990.
Meacham, Standish. *A Life Apart: The English Working Class, 1890–1914.* Cambridge, Mass.: Harvard University Press, 1977.
——. *Regaining Paradise: Englishness and the Early Garden City Movement.* New Haven, Conn.: Yale University Press, 1999.
——. *Toynbee Hall and Social Reform 1880–1914: The Search for Community.* New Haven, Conn.: Yale University Press, 1987.
Meller, Helen. *Towns, Plans and Society in Modern Britain.* Cambridge: Cambridge University Press, 1997.
Mémoires d'une région: Le Centre (1830–1914). Mariemont: Musée royal de Mariemont, 1984.
Mendras, Henri. *The Vanishing Peasant: Innovation and Change in French Agriculture.* Cambridge, Mass.: MIT Press, 1970.
Merlin, Pierre. *Les transports parisiens.* Paris: Masson, 1967.
Merrett, Stephen. *State Housing in Britain.* London: Routledge & Kegan Paul, 1979.
Miles, Andrew. *Social Mobility in Nineteenth and Early Twentieth Century England.* New York: St. Martin's Press, 1999.
Miller, Mervyn, and A. Stuart Gray. *Hampstead Garden Suburb.* Chichester: Phillimore, 1992.
Milne, Alastair M., and Austen Laing. *The Obligation to Carry.* London: Institute of Transportation, 1956.
Misonne, Octave. *Une Région de la Belgique: Le centre.* Tournai: H. & L. Casterman, 1900.
Mitchell, Allan. *The Divided Path: The German Influence on Social Reform in France after 1870.* Chapel Hill: University of North Carolina Press, 1991.
Mobiliteit en Binnenlandse Migratie. 40th Studie weekend. Lier, 29–30 January 1955.

Mols, Roger. *Bruxelles et les Bruxellois*. Louvain: Editions de la Société d'Etudes Morales, Sociales, et Juridiques, 1961.

Murard, L., and P. Zylberman. *Villes, Habitat et intimaté: Naissance d'un petit travailleur infatigable*. Paris: Recherches, 1976.

Nationale Maatschappij voor de Huisvesting: 1919–1969. Brussels: Van Muysewinkel, 1969.

Neyens, Jos. *De Buurtspoorwegen in de Provincie Brabant 1885–1978*. Lier: Van In, 1982.

Nock, Oswald Stevens. *The Great Northern Railway*. London: Ian Allan, 1958.

——. *The London and North Western Railway*. London: Ian Allan, 1960.

Norman-Butler, Belinda. *Victorian Aspirations: The Life and Labour of Charles and Mary Booth*. London: George Allen & Unwin, 1972.

Nuttgens, Patrick. *The Home Front: Housing the People 1840–1990*. London: BBC Books, 1989.

O'Day, Rosemary, and David Englander. *Mr. Charles Booth's Inquiry*. London: The Humbledon Press, 1993.

Offer, Avner. *Property and Politics, 1870–1914*. Cambridge: Cambridge University Press, 1981.

Olechnowicz, Andrzej. *Working Class Housing in England Between the Wars*. Oxford: Clarendon Press, 1997.

Olsen, Donald J. *The Growth of Victorian London*. London: B. T. Botsford, 1978.

Olyslager, Paul M. *De Localiseering der belgische Nijverheid*. Antwerp: Standaard Boekhandel, 1947.

Orbach, Laurence. *Homes for Heroes: A Study of the Evolution of British Public Housing, 1915–1921*. London: Seeley, Service & Col, 1977.

Ottes, Liesbeth, Erica Poventud, Marijke van Schendelen, and Gertje Segond von Banchet, eds. *Gender and the Built Environment: Emancipation in Planning, Housing and Mobility in Europe*. Assen: Van Gorcum, 1995.

Ottley, George. *A Bibliography of British Railway History*. London: HMSO, 1983.

——. *Railway History—A Guide to 62 Collections in Libraries and Archives in Great Britain*. London: The Library Association, 1973.

Palmer, Alan. *The East End: Four Centuries of London Life*. New Brunswick: Rutgers University Press, 2000.

Parris, Henry. *Government and the Railways in the Nineteenth Century*. London: Routledge & Kegan Paul, 1965.

Pasquet, D. *Londres et les ouvriers de Londres*. Paris: Librairie Armand Colin, 1913.

Pauly, Joseph. *Le chemin de fer et le parlement, 1835–1860*. Brussels: H. Wauthoz-Legrand, 1935.

——. *Etude sur les chemins de fer vicinaux. Leur coordination aux grands réseaux*. Brussels: Editions du Comité Central Industriel de Belgique, 1936.

Pector, Daniel, and Etienne Fourier. *La révolte des damnés de la terre*. Charleroi: ASBL, 1986.

Pedersen, Susan. *Family, Dependence, and the Origins of the Welfare State: Britain and France 1914–1945*. Cambridge: Cambridge University Press, 1993.

Pennybacker, Susan D. *A Vision for London. 1889–1914: Labour, Everyday Life and the LCC Experiment*. London: Routledge, 1996.

Pfautz, Harold W. *Charles Booth. On the City: Physical Pattern and Social Structure. Selected Writings*. Chicago: University of Chicago Press, 1967.

Pierres et rues. Bruxelles: Croissance urbaine 1780–1980. Brussels: Sint Lukasarchief, 1983.
Pitié, Jean. *Exode rural et migrations intérieures en France. L'exemple de la Vienne et du Poitou-Charentes*. Poitiers: Norois, 1971.
Polèse, Mario, and Stren Richard. *The Social Sustainability of Cities: Diversity and the Management of Change*. Toronto: University of Toronto Press, 2000.
Pooley, Colin G. *Housing Strategies in Europe, 1880–1930*. London: Leicester University Press, 1992.
Pooley, Colin, and Jean Turnball. *Migration and Mobility in Britain since the 18th Century*. London: UCL Press, 1998.
Potter, Stephen. *Transport Planning in the Garden Cities*. Open University, New Towns Study Unit, 1981.
Pourbaix, Robert. *La grande histoire d'un petit peuple: Les Charbonniers de bois du Luc*. Mons: Fedération du tourisme de Hainaut, 1983.
Power, Anne. *Hovels to High Rise*. London: Routledge, 1993.
Pritchard, R. M. *Housing and the Spatial Structure of the City: Residential Mobility and Housing Market in an English City since the Industrial Revolution*. Cambridge: Cambridge University Press, 1976.
Prochaska, F. K. *Women and Philanthropy in Nineteenth-Century England*. Oxford: Clarendon Press, 1980.
Przeworski, Adam, and Henry Teune. *Logic of Comparative Social Inquiry*. New York: John Wiley and Sons, 1970.
Puissant, Adolphe. *L'urbanisme et habitation*. Brussels: Office de Publicité, 1945.
Quigley, Hugh, and Ismay Goldie. *Housing and Slum Clearance in London*. London: Methuen, 1934.
Raper, Charles Lee. *Railway Transportation: A History of Its Economics and of Its Relation to the State*. New York: G. P. Putnam's Sons: The Knickerbocker Press, 1912.
Ravetz, Alison. *Council Housing and Culture: The History of a Social Experiment*. New York: Routledge, 2001.
Roberts, Elizabeth. *A Woman's Place: An Oral History of Working-Class Women 1890–1940*. Oxford: Basil Blackwell, 1984.
Robson, William A. *The Government and Misgovernment of London*. London: George Allen & Unwin, 1939.
Rodger, Richard. *Housing in Urban Britain, 1780–1914*. Cambridge: Cambridge University Press, 1989.
——. *The Transformation of Edinburgh. Land, Property and Trust in the Nineteenth Century*. Cambridge: Cambridge University Press, 2001.
Rodgers, Daniel T. *Atlantic Crossings: Social Politics in a Progressive Age*. Cambridge, Mass.: Harvard University Press, 1998.
Rokkan, Stein. *Comparative Research across Cultures*. Paris: Mouton, 1968.
Rose, Sonya O. *Limited Livelihoods: Gender and Class in Nineteenth-Century England*. Berkeley: University of California Press, 1992.
Roth, Ralf, and Marie-Noëlle Polino, eds. *The City and the Railway in Europe*. Aldershot: Ashgate, 2003.
Rubenstein, David. *Victorian Homes*. London: David & Charles, 1974.
Rueschemeyer, Dietrich, and Theda Skocpol. *States, Social Knowledge, and the Origins of Modern Social Policies*. Princeton, N.J.: Princeton University Press, 1996.

Rutten, M., and J. Weisgerber. *Van arm Vlaanderen tot de Voorstad groeit: de Opbloei van de Vlaamse literatuur van Teirlinck-Stijns tot L. P. Boon (1888–1946).* Antwerp: Standaard, 1988.

Saint, Andrew, ed. *London Suburbs.* London: Merrell Holberton, 1999.

——. "Spread the People": The LCC's Dispersal Policy, 1889–1965." In *Politics and the People of London: The London County Council,* ed. Andres Saint. London: The Hambledon Press, 1989.

Saint Moulin, Léon. *La construction et la propriété des maisons. Expressions des structures sociales. Seraing depuis le début du XIXe siècle.* Brussels: Pro Civitate, 1969.

De Schaarbeekse Haard. 100 Jaar. Brussels: Les Dossiers de la Fonderie, 1999.

Schepens, Luc. *Van Vlaskutser tot Franschman. Bijdrage tot de Geschiedenis van de westvlaamse Plattelandsbevolking in de Negentiende Eeuw.* Bruges: Westvlaams Ekonomische Studiebureau Wes, 1973.

Schivelbusch, Wolfgang. *The Railway Journey: The Industrialization of Time and Space in the 19th Century.* Berkeley: University of California Press, 1986.

Scholl, S. H., ed. *150 Jaar Katholieke Arbeidersbeweging in Belgie.* Brussels: S. V. de Arbeiderspers, 1963.

Scholliers, E., and P. Scholliers. *Werktijd en Werktijdverkorting. Acta van het Colloquium te Brussel gehouden op 15 en 16 Oktober 1982.* Brussels: Vrije Universiteit Brussel, 1983.

Schoonbrodt, Rene. *Sociologie de l'habitat social.* Brussels: Editions des Archives d'Architecture Moderne, n.d.

Secrétariat régional du développement urbain, *Bruxelles Change…! 10 ans de politique de la ville en région de Bruxelles-capitale: 1995–2005.* Brussels: Luc Maufroy, 2008.

Sekon, George A. *Locomotion in Victorian London.* London: Oxford University Press, 1938.

Shepherd, John, John Westaway, and Trevor Lee. *A Social Atlas of London.* Oxford: Clarendon Press, 1974.

Simey, Thomas S., and M. B. Simey. *Charles Booth: Social Scientist.* London: Oxford University Press, 1960.

Simmons, Jack. *The Railways in England and Wales, 1830–1914.* Leicester: Leicester University Press, 1978.

——. *The Railways of Britain: An Historical Introduction.* London: Routledge & Kegan Paul, 1961.

——. *The Victorian Railway.* New York: Thames & Hudson, 1980.

Simmons, Jack, and Gordon Biddle. *The Oxford Companion to British Railway History from 1603 to the 1990's.* Oxford: Oxford University Press, 1997.

Sims, George R. *How the Poor Live.* 1883. Reprint, New York: Garland, 1984.

Sint Lukasarchief. *Brussel, Breken en Bouwen: Architectuur en Stadsverfraaing, 1780–1917.* Brussels: St Lukas Archief, 1979.

——. *Straten en Stenen, Brussels: Stadsgroei, 1780–1980.* Brussels: St Lukas Archief, 1982.

——. *Inventaris van de Volkswoningen te Brussel.* Brussels: Sint-Lukaswerkgemeenschap, 1985.

Smelser, Neil J. *Comparative Methods in the Social Sciences.* Englewood Cliffs, N.J.: Prentice Hall, 1976.

Smets, Marcel. *L'avènement de la cité-jardin en Belgique: Histoire de l'habitat social en Belgique de 1830 à 1930*. Brussels: Pierre Mardaga, 1976.
——. *Charles Buls: Les principes de l'art urbain*. Liège: Pierre Mardaga, 1995.
——, ed. *Resurgam: Be Belgische Wederopbouw*. Brussels: Gemeentekredit, 1985.
Smith, David Norman. *The Railway and Its Passengers*. Newton Abbot: David & Charles, 1988.
Smith, Sir Hubert Llewellyn. *The Board of Trade*. London: G. P. Putnam's Sons, 1928.
Smolar-Meynart, Arlette, and Jean Stengers. *La région de Bruxelles*. Brussels: Crédit Communal, 1989.
Snell, K. D. M. *Annals of the Labouring Poor: Social Change and Agrarian England, 1660–1900*. Cambridge: Cambridge University Press, 1992.
Société des Transports Intercommunaux de Bruxelles. *Histoire des transports publics à Bruxelles*. Brussels: Société des Transports Intercommunaux publics á Bruxelles, 1976.
Stieber, Nancy. *Housing Design and Society in Amsterdam: Reconfiguring Urban Order and Identity, 1900–1920*. Chicago: University of Chicago Press, 1998.
Stroobants, A. *150 jaar Spoorwegen te Dendermonde 1837–1987. Tentoonstelling 1987*. Dendermonde: Stadsbestuur Dendermonde, 1987.
Struye, Johan, and Karel van Deuren. *De Reizigers worden verzocht van in te stappen*. Amsterdam: Lannoo, 1980.
Sutcliffe, Anthony. *British Town Planning: The Formative Years*. Leicester: Leicester University Press, 1981.
——, ed. *Multi-Storey Living: The British Working-Class Housing*. London: Croom Helm, 1974.
——. *Paris: An Architectural History*. New Haven, Conn.: Yale University Press, 1993.
——. *The Rise of Modern Urban Planning: 1800–1914*. New York: St. Martin's Press, 1980.
——. *Towards the Planned City: Germany, Britain, the United States and France 1780–1914*. New York: St. Martin's Press, 1981.
Swenarton, Mark. *Homes Fit for Heroes*. London: Heinemann Educational Books, 1981.
Tarn, John Nelson, *Five Per Cent Philanthropy: An Account of Housing in Urban Areas between 1840 and 1914*. Cambridge: Cambridge University Press, 1973.
——. *Working-Class Housing in 19th Century Britain*. Architectural Association Paper Number 7. London, 1971.
Taylor, Nicholas. *The Village in the City*. London: Temple Smith, 1973.
Teirlinck, Herman. *Brussel 1900*. Antwerp: Elsevier, 1981.
Thane, Pat. *Foundations of the Welfare State*. London: Longman, 1982.
Thomas, Brinley. *Migration and Urban Development: A Reappraisal of British and American Long Cycles*. London: Methuem, 1972.
Thomas, David St. John. *The Country Railway*. London: David & Charles, 1976.
Thompson, F. M. L. *The Rise of Suburbia*. London: Leicester University Press, 1982.
Thompson, Paul. *Socialists, Liberals and Labour: The Struggle for London, 1885–1914*. London: Routledge & Kegan Paul, 1967.
Topalov, Christian. *Le logement en France: Histoire d'une marchandise impossible*. Paris: Presses de la fondation nationale des sciences politiques, 1987.

Tulippe, Omer. *Densité de la population en 1846, 1880, 1900 et 1930*. Brussels: Académie Royale de Belgique, 1962.
Ulens, Robert. *Le Condroz: Sa population agricole au XIXe siècle*. Brussels: Albert De Wit, 1920.
Van Billoen, Albert. *Et les Taudis?* Brussels, 1930.
Van Coppenolle, Em. *De Belgische Politiek van de Volkswoning*. Brussels: Standaard Boekhandel, 1932.
Van der Herten, Bart, Michelangelo Van Meerten, and Greta Verbeurgt. *Sporen in België. 175 Jaar Spoorwegen. 75 Jaar NMBS*. Louvain: Universitaire Pers Leuven, 2001.
Van der Schaar, J. *De Huisvestingssituatie in Nederland, 1900–1982*. Delft: Delftse Universitaire Pers, 1986.
Vandervelde, Emile. *L'exode rural et le retour aux champs*. Brussels: A. Vromant & Co., 1901, 317.
Vandevenne, M. "Het Werkvolk op de Landbouwbedrijven in Belgie. 1886–1920." Licentie verhandeling moderne geschiedenis. Leuven, 1992.
Vandormael, Herman. *Wij zijn de Fossemannen, anders niks*. Galmaarden: De Mijnwerker, 1991.
Van Isacker, Karel. *Mijn land in de kering, 1830–1980*. Antwerp: Uitgeverij de Nerderlandsche boekhandel, 1978.
Van Molle, Leen. *Katholiken en Landbouw: Landbouwpolitiek in Belgie, 1884–1914*. Symbolae facultatis literarum et philosophiae lovaniensis, series B/vol. 5. Louvain: Leuven University Press, 1989.
Van Royen, Harry. "De Buurtspoorweg, Hamme-Temse-Antwerpen L.O. 1882–199." Unpublished manuscript.
Vanthemsche, Guy. *Les paradoxes de l'Etat: L'état face à l'économie de marché XIX & XX siècles*. Brussels: Editions Labor, 1997.
Varlez, Louis. *Belgique: Economie sociale. Rapport générale. Exposition universelle internationale de Paris 1900*. Brussels: Vromant, 1901.
Veenendaal, A. J., Jr. *De ijzeren Weg in een Land vol Water: Beknopte Geschiedenis van de Spoorwegen in Nederland, 1834–1958*. Amsterdam: De Bataafsche Leeuw, 1998.
Ver Elst, André. *De Belgische Trein bij Leven en Welzijn*. Zaltbommel, Nederland: Europese Bibliotheek, 1993.
Verhaegen, Benoit. *Contribution à l'histoire économique des Flandres*. Vol. 1, *Analyse de la répartition professionnelle 1846–1910*. Louvain: Editions Nauwelaerts, 1961.
Verniers, Louis. *Bruxelles et son agglomération: De 1830 à nos jours*. Brussels: Les Editions de la Librairie Encyclopédique, 1958.
——. *Esquisse provisoire d'une histoire de la plus-value foncière dans l'agglomération bruxelloise depuis un siècle*. Brussels: Imprimerie Alphonse Ballieu, 1938.
Ville, Simon P. *Transport and the Development of the European Economy, 1750–1918*. New York: St. Martin's Press, 1990.
Vincenne, M. *Du village à la ville: Le système de mobilité des agriculteurs*. Paris: Mouton, 1972.
Vlasschaert, Marcel. "De Spoorweg als 'Public Utility'." Licentieverhandeling, Katholieke Universiteit te Leuven, 1957.

Von Saldern, Adelheid. *Hauserleben. Zur Geschichte stadtischen Arbeiterwohnens vom Kaiserreich bis heute*. Bonn: J.H.W. Dietz Nachfolger, 1995.
Walkowitz, Judith. *Narratives of Sexual Delight in Late Victorian London*. Chicago: University of Chicago Press, 1992.
Waller, Philip J. *Town, City and Nation: England 1850–1914*. Oxford: Oxford University Press, 1983.
Ward, Stephen V. *The Garden City: Past, Present and Future*. London: E & F Spon, 1992.
Weber, Eugen. *Peasants into Frenchmen: The Modernization of Rural France, 1870–1914*. Stanford, Calif.: Stanford University Press, 1976.
White, H. P. *A Regional History of the Railways of Great Britain*. Vol. 3, *Greater London*. Birmingham: David St. John Thomas, 1971.
White, Jerry. *Rothschild Buildings: Life in an East End Tenement Block 1887–1920*. London: Routledge & Kegan Paul, 1980.
Whitehand, J. W. R. *The Changing Face of Cities*. Oxford: Oxford University Press, 1987.
Wiener, Lionel. *Les titres de transport: Billets de voyageurs*. Brussels: Dunod, 1937.
Williams, Guy R. *London in the Country*. London: Hamish Hamilton, 1975.
Williams, Karel. *From Pauperism to Poverty*. Boston: Routledge & Kegan Paul, 1981.
Williams, Raymond. *The Country and the City*. London: Hogarth Press, 1993.
Williams, Robert. *London Rookeries and Collier's Slums: A Plea for More Breathing Room*. London: W. Reeves, 1893.
Woestenborghs, Bert. *Vlaamse Arbeiders in de Vreemde*. Ghent: Bijdragen Museum van de Vlaamse Sociale Strijd, 1993.
Wohl, Anthony S. *Endangered Lives: Public Health in Victorian Britain*. London: Methuen, 1984.
——. *The Eternal Slum: Housing and Social Policy in Victorian London*. Montreal: McGill-Queen's University Press, 1977.
Wright, Gordon. *Rural Revolution in France: The Peasantry in the Twentieth Century*. Stanford, Calif.: Stanford University Press, 1964.
Wrottesley, John. *The Great Northern Railway*. London: Batsford, 1979–1981.
Yelling, James A. *Slums and Slum Clearance in Victorian London*. London: Allen & Unwin, 1986.
Young, Ken, and Patricia Garside. *Metropolitan London*. London: Edward Arnold, 1982.
Young, Ken, and John Kramer. *Strategy and Conflict in Metropolitan Housing*. London: Heinemann 1978.

Index